D1305981

The McQuade

Library

North Andover, Massachusetts

THE WELSH
ECONOMY

THE WELSH ECONOMY

Studies in Expansion

EDITED BY

BRINLEY THOMAS

CARDIFF
UNIVERSITY OF WALES PRESS
1962

© *Department of Economics, University College, Cardiff, 1962*

HC
257
·W3T54

64152

5.25

PREFACE

THE aim of this book is to assess the performance of the Welsh economy since the Second World War, and as background we have outlined its growth and fluctuations over the last century in relation to the international community of which it is a member. In view of the extensive surveys made in the twenties and thirties, there is no need to go over the story of the great depression.

Up to 1913 Wales was developing very fast through unrestricted private enterprise and intense specialization. An influx of labour and capital played a crucial part in the rise of the coal and steel industries, and in the climax in the first decade of this century the momentum of growth was such that Wales was not far behind the United States in the rate at which she was absorbing population from outside. The Principality participated handsomely in the benefits—and the risks— of international division of labour, and when the tide turned in the inter-war period the reaction was unprecedented. Prolonged experience of mass unemployment left a deep mark on the Welsh consciousness: people now tend to see only the bad side of specialization and insist on a high and stable level of employment above all else. A dispassionate view of history, however, shows that the hectic expansion up to 1913 brought permanent gains not least in that it provided an ample outlet within Wales for the rural exodus which was a necessary consequence of economic growth.

The contrast with the experience of Ireland is very marked. The population of Ireland fell from over 8 million in 1845 to 4 million in 1931; there was no industrial sector to absorb the people displaced from agriculture, and the process of mass emigration became self-reinforcing. Between 1851 and 1921 the population of Wales increased by 125 per cent., oversea emigration was negligible, and the rate of expansion in the coalfields attracted immigrants on a large scale. Since the Second World War there has been a substantial volume of capital investment in steel, coal, chemicals, nylon, aluminium, oil-refining, electrical engineering, and a wide range of manufacturing industries. Apart from one interlude of stagnation for two decades between the wars, the century 1860–1960 was one of rapid economic growth in Wales.

The keynote of the resurgence since 1945 is a combination of government-sponsored investment and diversification; there has been a striking technical revolution in steel production and the expansion in manufacturing has been nearly twice the rate in Great Britain as a whole. Wales shared with other regions the benefits of the Distribution of Industry Act, and the strength of her present economy is shown by her negligible loss through migration in contrast with Scotland and Northern Ireland. There should be ample opportunities in future for foreign as well as British investment in the expanding industries, but it will be necessary to ensure that technical education and the supply of skilled labour will develop at the right pace.

In recent years there has been a welcome improvement in the official statistics for Wales, though they are still on the whole inferior to what is provided for Scotland and Northern Ireland. Since 1954 an annual *Digest of Welsh Statistics* has been published; the Censuses of Production and Distribution contain new items about Wales, and the Commissioners of Inland Revenue have been more forthcoming. Nevertheless, analysis of economic trends in Wales is still seriously handicapped by the lack of certain official statistics which are published regularly for Scotland by the Scottish Statistical Office in Edinburgh. For example, we need for Wales a quarterly index of industrial production, detailed statistics of current output in the manufacturing industries to supplement the data from the Census of Production, and annual figures of net receipts from income tax, profits tax, death duties, and stamp duties, as well as total remuneration under P.A.Y.E. and the total tax deducted. And the *Digest of Welsh Statistics* might well appear twice a year.

This book is intended to show what can be done with the sources available, and we have included a wide range of statistical tables which we hope will be of value not only to students, but to administrators and business men. Care has been taken to indicate the limitations of the data. No attempt has been made to cover all aspects of the economic life of Wales. For example, it was not strictly relevant to our purpose to examine changes in trade-union organization and the structure of wages. We have tried to show in Chapter III that a regional analysis of excess demand or supply in the labour market can help towards an understanding of the mechanism of fluctuation in the British economy as a whole.

The contributors to this book are present or past members of the Economics Department, University College, Cardiff. The inquiry was organized in the Department's Economic Research Unit. Without the invaluable work contributed by Mr. J. Parry Lewis, who was Lecturer in Economic Statistics at Cardiff before being appointed to his present post at Manchester University, the project could not have been carried out. Much of the research on the demographic sections of Chapters I and IX was done by Mrs. Margaret Lloyd when she was Research Assistant in the Department. We were fortunate in having the maps and a number of the charts expertly drawn by Dr. Margaret Davies. In the final stages Mr. J. Hamish Richards greatly eased my task as editor; he looked after the statistical material and charts, was responsible for many improvements in presentation, and compiled the Index. The whole manuscript was admirably typed by Mrs. Margaret Rees. To all of these I express my warmest thanks.

Finally, I cannot adequately express what I owe to Dr. Elwyn Davies, Secretary of the University of Wales Press, for his unfailing encouragement and, above all, for his forbearance in the face of all the trouble I gave him at the proof stage.

B. T.

University College
Cathays Park, Cardiff
May 1961

ACKNOWLEDGEMENTS

WE owe a great deal to the generous assistance given by civil servants, officials of local authorities, members of the staffs of nationalized industries, and a number of industrialists, particularly those who so willingly replied to the questionnaire on new factories located in rural Wales; and we wish to record our appreciation. We were fortunate, too, in being given access to unpublished data; in expressing our gratitude we would mention in particular the kindness of Dr. B. Benjamin, General Register Office, Somerset House, London; Mr. R. E. Hills, Statistics Section, South Western Division of the National Coal Board; Mr. L. N. Hopper, Welsh Office of the Board of Trade; Mr. W. Jeffers, Chief Docks Manager, South Wales Docks; Mr. A. G. Liptrott, Divisional Road Engineer, Ministry of Transport, Cardiff; Mr. S. Owen, Statistics Section, Wales Office, Ministry of Labour; and the Statistics Branch of the Ministry of Agriculture, Fisheries, and Food, Guildford, Surrey. None of these persons is in any way responsible for the use made of the data or the conclusions drawn from them.

I am grateful to Professor A. K. Cairncross, Editor of the *Scottish Journal of Political Economy*, and the publishers, Messrs. Oliver & Boyd, Edinburgh, for their kind permission to reproduce in Chapter I of this book my article, 'Wales and the Atlantic Economy', which appeared in the November 1959 issue of that journal. My thanks are also due to Messrs. Oliver & Boyd for allowing their blocks of Figures 1 and 4–8 to be used, and to the Cambridge University Press for permission to use the blocks of Figures 2 and 3 from my book, *Migration and Economic Growth: a Study of Great Britain and the Atlantic Economy* (Cambridge University Press, 1954).

B. T.

CONTENTS

LIST OF TABLES

LIST OF FIGURES

I

WALES AND THE ATLANTIC ECONOMY

By BRINLEY THOMAS

THE major influences which have shaped the growth of the Welsh economy have been international, and in order to gain a sense of perspective we shall attempt a short sketch of its evolution in relation to the Atlantic economy since 1850. The story can be unfolded by concentrating on two fundamental features of economic growth— redistribution of population and fluctuations in the rate of investment.

1. *Some implications of economic growth*

One generation after another has viewed with alarm the flight of people from the country-side and its effect on the life of the nation. This experience, however, is by no means peculiar to Wales. The tragedy of the deserted village has been enacted in the history of most nations; it is unfortunately the price that has to be paid for economic progress. The richest countries are as a rule those which have a small proportion of their occupied population engaged in agriculture. At the top of the scale there are eight countries in the world with an average annual real income per head of 1,700 dollars, and their combined working population is distributed as follows: agriculture 15 per cent., manufacturing, mining, and construction 40 per cent., and services 45 per cent. At the other extreme we find six countries with an average real income per head of 100 dollars, and the distribution of their labour force is as follows: agriculture 80 per cent., manufacturing, mining, and construction 7 per cent., and services 14 per cent.[1] A rising standard of living entails a shift of labour away from agriculture into industrial activity in which productivity is higher. This can be shown in quantitative terms. For example, in the United States, the Union of South Africa, and Sweden, real product per head in the first half of this century grew at the rate of 16 per cent.,

---

[1] S. Kuznets, *Quantitative Aspects of the Economic Growth of Nations, II, Industrial Distribution of National Product and Labor Force*, Research Center in Economic Development and Cultural Change, University of Chicago, July 1957, p. 23. The figures include unpaid family labour.

24 per cent., and 29 per cent. respectively per decade. The movement of labour from agriculture into manufacturing, mining, construction, and services contributed between a quarter and a third of this rise in productivity.[1]

In interpreting these facts one must be careful not to fall into error. One cannot say that a country becomes richer *because* of the relative decline in its agriculture or that a country is poor *because* most of its people earn their living on the land. The causal sequence runs differently. Agriculture occupies a smaller segment of a nation's economy *as a result* of the growth of its real income; where we find 80–90 per cent. of a country's labour engaged in agriculture it is because the general level of productivity in the economy is very low. In the typical underdeveloped country, with the vast majority of its population living on the land, there is usually 'disguised unemployment'; this means that a certain proportion of the workers in agriculture could be taken away without affecting the total volume of output from the land. Such an economy has only a very small amount of capital per head; the mass of its people are unable to save anything, for they must spend the whole of their tiny incomes on bare necessities; agricultural technique remains primitive and yields per acre are low; the birth-rate is very high but the death-rate, particularly among children, is also high, so that much of the country's small supply of capital is spent on the rearing of children who never survive to reach the age when they can contribute to the national product. Such countries are caught in a vicious circle; their peoples give all their time and energies to tilling the soil and they achieve only a bare subsistence level. Contrast with this the advanced countries which have the highest standard of feeding with only about one in every eight of their workers engaged in agriculture.

What are the fundamental reasons for this important characteristic of economic growth? Let us take the case of a closed community. We must first consider the demand side. Beyond a certain minimum level, when real income per head rises, the tendency is for the demand for food to increase at a lower rate; in a cross-section of family budgets at a point of time, the relative importance of food in total expenditure is much smaller in the higher income groups than it is in the lower. On the other hand, as income rises, the demand for manufactured goods tends to rise more than proportionately. Thus, in the course of time, as the community becomes richer, the structure of consumer

---

[1] Kuznets, op. cit., p. 53.

demand changes; relatively more factors of production are used in supplying manufactures and services and relatively less in supplying food.

There is, however, another side to the picture; forces on the supply side must be taken into account. Agriculture comes under the influence of technical progress and the accumulation of capital; a classic case was the transformation of Britain's rural economy during the Industrial Revolution. With more capital per head and better methods of production—mechanization, rotation of crops, and fertilizers—labour in agriculture becomes increasingly effective and the yield per acre rises.

Thus, there are two long-run forces at work—the growth in demand for food as income rises, and the growth in the productivity of agriculture. If the amount of food demanded per head rises less rapidly than agricultural output per head,[1] the proportion of the country's working population needed on the land will decline. The richest countries will have the lowest proportion of their population engaged in producing food. The change in the structure of consumer demand and the change in the distribution of the labour force are two sides of the same coin. Manufacturing can develop only if labour is released from the land, and labour will not be released from the land unless agricultural productivity is increasing faster than the demand for food.

So far we have been thinking of a closed community. We shall now broaden the picture to take in relations between countries. The rural exodus within one country now takes the form of international migration, but its role in economic development remains the same. In the great era of unrestricted movement, international migration was in essence a vast secular transfer from agriculture to industry facilitated by the rise in agricultural productivity which was the indispensable condition of economic growth. This can be seen most clearly if we forget national boundaries and regard the Atlantic community of nations as one large economy made up of interdependent regions. The growth of this Atlantic economy during the century ending in 1914 entailed a redistribution of labour and capital as between its component parts. Between 1846 and 1914 about 43 million persons migrated to the Americas, mainly from the continent of Europe; the

---

[1] The amount of wheat flour consumed per head in the United States declined from 222 lb. in 1898 to 175 lb. in 1929. Real output per man-year in agriculture in the United States more than doubled between 1870 and 1930. (See Colin Clark, *The Conditions of Economic Progress*, 2nd edition, Macmillan, London, 1950, p. 209.)

average rate of growth of population each decade in the nineteenth century was 29 per cent. in the United States, 34 per cent. in Argentina, and 8 per cent. in Europe. The world's leading exporter of capital was Great Britain, and by 1913 nearly 70 per cent. of the £3,500 million which she had invested abroad were located in North America, South America, and Oceania. The transfer of population and capital from countries where they were relatively abundant to countries where they were relatively scarce was a necessary condition of the expansion of the international economy.

This movement did not proceed at an even pace. There were four outstanding transatlantic outflows of migrants from Europe—1844–54, 1863–73, 1881–8, and 1903–1913, and in each of these periods there was a corresponding outflow of capital from Great Britain. A close analysis of these massive upsurges of emigration brings out some revealing facts. Each of them was for the most part a rural exodus. Of the 2 million Europeans arriving in America in the years 1849–54, no fewer than 80 per cent. came from Ireland and Germany. The tragic story of the Irish peasant in those years is well known, but in Germany, too, the driving force was the breaking-up of the obsolete rural economy of the south-west. During the two following periods—1867–73 and 1881–8—two-thirds of the European migrants to America were from Ireland, Scandinavia, and Germany. In the eighties no less than 1¼ million left Germany and over half a million were uprooted from Scandinavia; it was early in that decade that the first heavy impact of technical progress in American agriculture was felt by the old agrarian economies of Europe. In Schumpeter's striking words, 'the story of the way in which civilized humanity got and fought cheap bread is the story of American railroads and American machinery'.[1] With the introduction of the harvester in 1872 and the binder in 1880, the efficiency of American farming rose rapidly, and added to this was the technical revolution in transport by land and sea. A contemporary writer reported that '. . . on the wheat farms of the North-Western United States it was claimed in 1887 that, with wages at twenty-five dollars per month and board for permanent employees, wheat could be produced for forty cents per bushel; while in Rhenish Prussia, with wages at six dollars per month, the cost of production was reported to be eighty cents per bushel'.[2] This brought a crisis to agriculture in most European countries and caused

[1] J. A. Schumpeter, *Business Cycles*, McGraw-Hill, New York, 1931, vol. i, p. 319.
[2] D. A. Wells, *Recent Economic Changes*, Appleton, New York, 1889, p. 59.

further waves of emigration.[1] The greatest of these occurred in the early years of this century. Between 1903 and 1913 nearly 10 million migrants crossed from Europe to the United States and 71 per cent. of them came from Italy, Russia, the Baltic countries, and central Europe. Commenting on this influx, the United States Immigration Commission wrote:

Before coming to the United States the greater proportion were engaged in farming or unskilled labor and had no experience or training in manufacturing industry or mining. As a consequence their employment in the mines and manufacturing plants of this country has been made possible only by the invention of mechanical devices and processes which have eliminated the skill and experience formerly required in a large number of occupations.[2]

Exactly the same had been true of the 1,200,000 Irish migrants who landed in America in the years 1847–54.

An interesting feature of the international economy of the nineteenth century was the inverse relation between fluctuations in the rate of capital formation in Great Britain and the countries of new settlement overseas.[3] During periods when emigration and foreign lending were booming, i.e. 1847–54, 1866–73, 1881–8, and 1903–13, the receiving countries, particularly the United States, experienced a vigorous upswing in capital construction such as railways and buildings. At such times the export sector in Great Britain was very busy, with home construction relatively depressed. During the intervening downswings in emigration and foreign lending, the United States went through a phase of stagnating capital construction, while simultaneously Great Britain had a boom in her own capital construction. Over the long period there was clearly a community of interest between the lending and borrowing countries. In one phase the borrowing country went ahead briskly with investment in capital equipment, aided by loanable funds, migrants, and capital goods from the creditor country; in the next phase it was the turn of the creditor

---

[1] Writing in 1889, D. A. Wells gave this illustration: 'Indian corn can be successfully and has been exclusively raised in Italy. But Indian corn grown in the valley of the Mississippi, a thousand miles from the seaboard, has been transported in recent years to Italy and sold in her markets at lower cost than the corn of Lombardy and Venetia, where the wages of the agriculturist are not one third of the wages paid in the United States for corresponding labor. And one not surprising sequel of this is that 77,000 Italian laborers emigrated to the United States in 1885' (Ibid., p. 91).

[2] United States Immigration Commission, *Abstract of Reports*, vol. i. Senate Document No. 747, 61st Congress, 3rd Session, 1911–12, p. 494.

[3] For a detailed analysis see Brinley Thomas, *Migration and Economic Growth*, Cambridge University Press, 1954, chaps. vii, viii, x, and xi.

country to add substantially to its own capital equipment, aided by a copious flow of food and raw materials imported from the debtor country.

These inverse long swings in capital construction were partly governed by population movements. We have already seen that each wave of transatlantic emigration was in essence a rural exodus. When capital exports to the United States were booming and home construction in Great Britain was languishing, surplus labour on the land tended to migrate to America instead of to urban counties at home; in the next phase, when investment in Britain increased substantially, the workers released from agriculture flocked into the rapidly growing towns and emigration declined. There was thus an inverse relation between internal and external migration. A wave of home construction drew on the agricultural reserve army for urban employment at home; and a wave of foreign investment drew on the agricultural reserve army for urban employment abroad.[1]

We shall now try to fit Wales into this evolving international system. The lack of separate Welsh statistics of income, investment, exports, and imports puts severe limits on the analysis, but we can manage with the help of the population census and the main indexes of industrial and agricultural production since the middle of the nineteenth century.

2. Wales's external migration balance since 1851

We shall begin by comparing the external migration experience of Wales with that of England, Scotland, Ireland, and Sweden over the century 1851–1951. In almost every decade in this era most countries in Europe lost a portion of their natural increase through migration; the amplitude and time-shape of these losses are an interesting index of the growth and fluctuations of their economies. The net loss or gain by migration may be fairly accurately calculated for periods between population censuses by taking the increase in the enumerated

[1] The old idea that huge waves of immigrants were attracted to the American West by the lure of free land has been discredited by modern research. The following conclusion by Professor Fred A. Shannon is worth noting: 'For that matter, outside the cotton belt, the majority of the westward moving population did not settle on farms. Farmers from farther East took up the Western lands, but they also swarmed to Western cities and towns. When the Eastern city laborer managed to pay his fare or "ride the roads" westward, he also was most likely to establish himself in a mining camp, town or city' (Fred. A. Shannon, *The Farmer's Last Frontier*, Farrar & Rhinehart, New York, 1945, p. 357). Professor Shannon suggests a new hypothesis: instead of Western agriculture being a safety valve for the Eastern industrial worker, the rise of the city was a safety valve for rural discontent.

population from one census to the next, say 1851–61, and subtracting from it the excess of births over deaths in the same period. A net loss by migration occurs when the excess of births over deaths exceeds the increase in the enumerated population; a net gain by migration occurs when the excess of births over deaths is less than the increase in the enumerated population. The experience of different countries may be compared by expressing the migration balance, positive or negative, as a rate per 10,000 of the mean decennial population; it is sometimes useful to show the migration losses as a percentage of the natural increase.

The net migration rates since 1851 for Wales and the other countries are set out in Table 1.

TABLE 1

Wales, England, Scotland, Ireland, Sweden, and U.S.A.: Rate of net loss (−) or gain (+) by migration, decennially, 1851–1957

Period	Wales	England	Scotland	Ireland North	Ireland South	Sweden	U.S.A.[a]
				Annual rate per 10,000 mean population			
1851–61	− 28	−16	−101	−194[b]		− 7	+98
1861–71	− 47	− 7	− 44	−169		−37	+67
1871–81	− 35	− 5	− 28	−119	−127	−32	+51
1881–91	− 11	−23	− 58	−108	−163	−74	+80
1891–1901	− 5	− 2	− 13	− 55	−118	−37	+37
1901–11	+ 45	−19	− 57	− 52	− 82	−36	+63
1911–21	− 21	−16	− 50	− 47	− 88[c]	−11	+32
1921–31	−102	+ 3	− 80	− 82	− 56[d]	−15	+27
1931–9	− 72	+24	− 8	− 5	− 63[e]	+ 9[f]	+ 0·8
1939–46	+ 1[g]	+ 6	− 3	− 23		+12[h]	
1946–51	− 18[i]	+ 6	− 92	− 63	− 84	+28[j]	
1951–7	− 19	+12	− 53	− 70	−134[k]	+13[l]	

a The U.S.A. decades are 1850–60, 1860–70, &c.

b Based on G. Sundbärg, *Den Svenska och Europeiska Folköknings- och Omflyttningsstatistiken*, *Emigrationsutredningen*, Kungl. Boktryckeriet, Stockholm, 1910, Bilaga IV, p. 99.

c 1911–26. d 1926–36. e 1936–46. f 1931–40. g 1939–48. h 1941–45. i 1948–51 j 1945–50. k 1951–6. l 1951–5.

SOURCES:

Wales: Population Tables of Census Reports, 1851–1951; Registrar-General's Annual Statistical Reports, 1851–1951; Registrar-General's Quarterly Returns, 1931, 1939, and 1951. The original figures are set out in Table 2. Allowance has been made for under-registration of births in 1851–61 and 1861–71.

England and Wales, Scotland and N. Ireland: N. H. Carrier and J. R. Jeffery,

The pattern traced by Wales diverges sharply from that of the rest
of the British Isles; this is brought out clearly in Fig. 1. Let us first
examine the period 1851–1911. From a peak in the sixties the rate of
loss by migration in Wales declined steadily until in the first decade of
this century there was a substantial gain through immigration. The

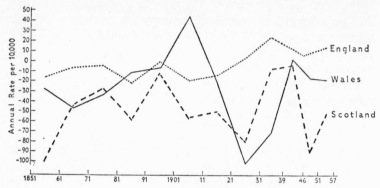

FIG. 1. Wales, Scotland, and England: Decennial net gain or loss by migration,
1851–1957. (Annual rates per 10,000 mean population.)

SOURCE: Table 1, p. 7.

half-century 1861–1911 in the history of Wales was a period of sustained and rapid economic growth. The contrast with other countries
is most evident in the 1880's when there was an emigration peak in
the figures for England, Scotland, Ireland, and Sweden. In that
decade these countries contributed substantially to the large volume
of transatlantic emigration, but the rate of outflow from Wales
was negligible. The difference is again marked in the years 1901–11
when Wales was unique in having an annual rate of immigration of
45 per 10,000 population, whereas all the other neighbouring
countries experienced large losses through emigration. At the beginning of this century Wales was absorbing population at a rate not
much less than the United States.

A violent reaction came in the inter-war period. In 1921–31 Wales

External Migration: A Study of the Available Statistics, 1815–1950, General
Register Office, 1953, Table 2, p. 14.

Sweden: *Historisk Statistik för Sverige, Befolkning, 1720–1950* (Statistiska
Centralbyrån, Stockholm, 1955), p. 37. *Statistisk Årsbok för Sverige*, 1958, p. 47.

United States: S. Kuznets and E. Rubin *Immigration and the Foreign Born*,
National Bureau of Economic Research, New York, 1954, p. 94.

Southern Ireland: *Statistical Abstract of Ireland*, 1958, Table 7, p. 17.

suffered by far the heaviest loss by migration—an annual rate of
102 per 10,000 population; the suddenness of the change is illustrated
in Fig. 1. In the years 1921-39 the population of Wales actually fell
from 2,656,000 to 2,465,000; the net loss by migration was 450,000.

TABLE 2

*Wales: Natural increase and net loss or gain by migration, decennially,
1851-1957*

Period	Initial enumerated population of area as constituted at end of period	Final enumerated population of area	Intercensal increase or decrease	Natural increase in period	Net loss or gain by migration
					('000)
1851–61	1,186,697	1,312,834	+126,137	+162,408	− 36·3
1861–71	1,296,001	1,421,670	+125,669	+188,674	− 63·0
1871–81	1,420,408	1,577,559	+157,151	+209,290	− 52·1
1881–91	1,577,533	1,776,405	+198,872	+216,666	− 17·8
1891–1901	1,774,810	2,015,012	+240,202	+249,552	− 9·3
1901–11	2,033,287	2,442,041	+408,754	+310,262	+ 98·5
1911–21	2,420,921	2,656,474	+235,553	+290,043	− 54·5
1921–31	2,656,474	2,593,332	− 63,142	+205,565	−268·7
1931–mid-1939	2,593,332	2,465,200	−128,132	+ 53,153	−181·3
mid-1939–51	2,465,200	2,585,908	+120,708	+129,721	− 9·0
1951–7	2,584,000	2,611,000	+ 27,000	+ 54,538	− 27·5

NOTES:

(i)   In arriving at the natural increase for the periods 1851–61 and 1861–71, allowance has been
      made for the under-registration of births.

(ii) Up to and including 1910, figures relate to the registration counties of Wales. Since 1911
      figures relate to the administrative area of Wales.

(iii) To prevent boundary changes distorting the estimates of migration flows, it has been neces-
      sary to relate changes in enumerated population to the same area at both the beginning and
      end of the intercensal period.

(iv) Natural increase for the intercensal periods before 1911 cannot be calculated. The natural
      increase figures for these periods relate to the decades beginning 1 Jan. preceding the census
      (normally taken in April).

SOURCES: Population Tables of each Census Report, 1851–1951. Registrar-General's Annual
Statistical Reports, 1851–1951. Registrar-General's Quarterly Returns, 1931, 1939, and 1951.

The whole of the natural increase of 259,000 was lost together with an
extra 191,000. Scotland and Northern Ireland were also hard hit in
the twenties, but, unlike Wales, their losses were relatively low in the
thirties. England registered a net gain in the years 1931-9 as a result
of the influx from Ireland and the depressed areas and even from
some oversea countries.

Further interesting divergences are to be seen since 1939. Over the
years 1939-48 Wales had a slight gain through immigration, which
meant a remarkable recovery from her depressed condition before the
war. On the other hand, Scotland in 1945-51 suffered a very heavy

loss by migration, her highest in the century under review, namely, an average annual rate of 92 per 10,000 population.

The recent course of the external balance for Wales may be given in more detail.[1] Between mid-year 1939 and 13 March 1951 there was a net loss by migration of 9,000. If we split up this period we find that from 1939 to 1948 there was a net gain of about 3,000 through migration, but from 1948 to 1951 a net loss of 12,000 was sustained. The latter was an annual rate of about 18 per 10,000 population. Since 1951 the external balance has continued at roughly the same rate; between 1951 and 1957 the net loss by migration was 27,500. In contrast to Scotland, Northern Ireland, and Eire, the aggregate demand for labour in Wales since 1939 has been high enough to enable her to retain four-fifths of her natural increase.[2]

An example of a more brisk pace of development is seen in Scandinavia. After many decades of net losses, Sweden since 1931 has become more and more an immigration country with a rate of 28 per 10,000 in 1945–51. She has recently been going through a rapid phase of economic growth; her national product *per capita* increased in the first fifty years of this century at the average rate of 29 per cent. each decade.

Table 1 shows that in the period 1851–1911 there were long swings in emigration from England and Scotland, with peaks in 1851–61, 1881–91, and 1901–11; this fluctuation coincided with the long swings in international investment and in net immigration into the United States. The course of Wales's migration balance does not fit in to this pattern; in the whole period there was only one peak in emigration and that was in 1861–71, whereas in 1901–11 Wales joined the ranks of the countries of new settlement, such as the United States and Canada, and absorbed population at a remarkable rate. Ireland, both north and south, suffered a succession of enormous losses far in excess of the natural increase; the population of Ireland fell from 8,175,000 in 1841 to 4,390,000 in 1911.

British statistics have never distinguished between Welsh and English emigrants going overseas; for information on this subject we have to go to the receiving countries. Fortunately, the most important of these, the United States, published as from 1875 a series showing the number of immigrants from Wales as distinct from

---

[1] I am grateful to the General Register Office, Somerset House, for their kindness in supplying the figures used in this paragraph.

[2] Between mid-year 1939 and mid-year 1957 Wales had an excess of births over deaths of 184,300 and a net loss by migration of 36,600.

England. The figures for Wales, England, Scotland, and Ireland for
the period 1881-1930 are summarized in Table 3; in order to compare
the incidence of emigration to the United States from each country

TABLE 3

United States: Number of immigrants (with and without occupation)
from Wales, England, Scotland, and Ireland, decennially, 1881-1930

Period and country of origin	Mean population of country of origin ('000)	Immigrants to U.S.A. (with occupation)	Annual rate per 10,000 mean population	Total immigrants to U.S.A. (with and without occupation)	Annual rate per 10,000 mean population
Wales					
1881–90	1,677	5,682	3	12,640	8
1891–1900	1,895	5,005	3	11,219	6
1901–10	2,238	11,708	5	18,631	8
1911–20	2,538	9,988	4	15,379	6
1921–30	2,629	8,402	3	16,267	6
England					
1881–90	25,812	319,118	12	644,680	25
1891–1900	28,861	128,107	4	224,350	8
1901–10	32,061	237,227	7	387,005	12
1911–20	34,440	271,181	8	419,526	12
1921–30	36,290	258,523	7	472,873	13
Scotland					
1881–90	3,881	79,342	20	149,869	39
1891–1900	4,249	28,006	7	60,046	14
1901–10	4,617	86,976	19	133,333	29
1911–20	4,822	100,824	21	164,131	34
1921–30	4,862	177,476	36	293,764	60
Ireland					
1881–90	4,940	382,368	77	655,482	133
1891–1900	4,582	280,054	61	404,045	88
1901–10	4,429	316,340	71	371,772	84
1911–20	4,372	187,902	43	240,041	55
1921–30	4,269	278,794	65	362,921	84

SOURCES: Original data taken from returns issued by the United States Bureau of
Statistics of the Treasury Department and the *Annual Report of the Commissioner
General of Immigration.*

in the British Isles, we have expressed the outflow as an annual rate
per 10,000 of the mean population in each decade. The source dis-
tinguishes between immigrants who reported an occupation and those
who did not, the latter consisting mainly of wives and children.

The popular impression that Welsh workers flocked to the United
States in the latter half of the nineteenth century is a myth. In the
decade 1881–90, when the absorptive power of the United States was

at a peak, the effect on Wales was hardly noticeable. In proportion to population, English emigrants to America (with occupation) were four times as numerous as the Welsh, and the Scots were seven times as numerous. The sharpest contrast is with Ireland, where the rate was 77 per 10,000 as against 3 per 10,000 in Wales. The internal demand for labour in Wales in the eighties must have been relatively stronger than in the rest of the British Isles. In the nineties there was a sharp fall in the rate of emigration to America from England and

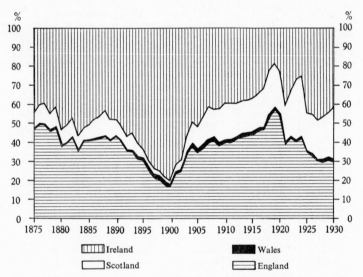

Fig. 2. The United States: Percentage distribution of immigrants from the United Kingdom by national origin, annually, 1875–1930 (total reporting occupation).

Source: Brinley Thomas, *Migration and Economic Growth*, Cambridge, 1954, p. 66.

Scotland (from 25 per 10,000 to 8 per 10,000 and from 39 per 10,000 to 14 per 10,000 respectively), but the rate from Wales showed barely any change. Welsh emigration to America was not only very small but also remarkably steady throughout the period 1881–1930. Fig. 2 sets out the percentage distribution of occupied immigrants to the United States from the British Isles by national origin each year from 1875 to 1930. Fig. 3 shows the occupational distribution of Welsh emigrants who went to the United States between 1875 and 1930. Throughout the period skilled workers were in the majority, and the proportion of farmers was very low. In quality, but not in quantity, the Welsh emigrants were similar to those who left Scotland to settle in America.

The figures in Table 3 are gross, not net; they do not take into account any return movement there may have been from the United States. These emigration rates are thus not comparable with the *net* rates given in Table 1. We can, however, infer the part played by emigration to America in the total net loss for certain countries. For example, in the depressed 1920's the total net outflow from Scotland

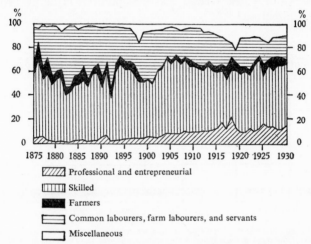

FIG. 3. The United States: Percentage distribution of immigrants from Wales by occupational group, annually, 1875–1930.

SOURCE: Brinley Thomas, *Migration and Economic Growth*, Cambridge, 1954, p. 66.

was at an annual rate of 80 per 10,000, and the gross movement to America was at an annual rate of 60 per 10,000. It is reasonable to conclude that a majority of the Scottish emigrants in that decade went to America rather than to England. On the other hand, the aggregate net outflow from Wales was no less than 102 per 10,000, while the gross rate of outflow to the United States was only 6 per 10,000. The workers driven from Wales by the depression went mainly to England.

Population trends in various parts of the British Isles may be put in a nutshell as follows. In the period 1871–1951 the proportion of the natural increase lost through migration was 3 per cent. in England, 29 per cent. in Wales, 47 per cent. in Scotland, 97 per cent. in Northern Ireland, and 171 per cent. in Eire.

3. *Wales's internal migration balance since 1851*

The evolution of the Welsh economy in the century 1851–1951 falls into three phases—rapid growth in the period 1851–1911, a severe set-back between the wars, and further expansion since 1939. We shall now examine the changing pattern of internal migration in each of these phases. The data for the period 1851–1911 are set out in Tables 4 and 5. The groundwork for this analysis was provided by the researches of T. A. Welton and the additions made by Professor A. K. Cairncross.[1]

TABLE 4

England and Wales: Internal migration, decennially, 1851–1911

Net loss by migration (−). Net gain by migration (+)

Area	1851–61	1861–71	1871–81	1881–91	1891–1901	1901–11
Rural residues	− 742,573	− 683,031	− 837,452	− 845,444	− 660,440	− 294,641
Towns	+ 516,789	+ 532,615	+ 604,680	+ 137,760	+ 520,822	− 321,095
Colliery districts	+ 103,467	+ 90,860	+ 84,474	+ 90,303	+ 85,158	+ 113,999
England and Wales*	− 327,000	− 206,000	− 164,000	− 601,000	− 69,000	− 501,000

* The migration balance for England and Wales is based on N. H. Carrier and J. R. Jeffery, *External Migration: A Study of the Available Statistics 1815–1950*, General Register Office, 1953, p. 14. The figures for 1851–61 and 1861–71 allow for under-registration of births, as estimated by Dr. Farr, *1871 Census of England and Wales*, vol. iv, p. 55. See also D. V. Glass, 'A Note on the Under-registration of Births in the Nineteenth Century', *Population Studies*, vol. v, no. 1, July 1951. This allowance for under-registration of births is the explanation of the big discrepancy between the net losses by migration from England and Wales in 1851–61 and 1861–71 given above and the net losses which would be obtained by taking the algebraic sum of the figures in the first two columns of the table which are based on *recorded* births.

Sources: T. A. Welton, *England's Recent Progress: an Investigation of the Statistics of Migration, Mortality, &c., in the Twenty Years from 1881 to 1901 as indicating Tendencies towards the Growth or Decay of Particular Communities*, and A. K. Cairncross, 'Internal Migration in Victorian England', *The Manchester School*, vol. xvii, no. 1, Jan. 1949, pp. 82–86.

Welton grouped the registration districts of England and Wales into three classes—Towns, Colliery Districts, and Rural Residues, and he calculated net gains and losses by migration in each decade. Professor Cairncross uses the same groupings in his extension of the investigation to cover the period 1841–1911. It has been possible to disentangle the Welsh areas so as to present in Table 5 the internal balance of gains and losses by migration.

[1] T. A. Welton, op. cit., Chapman & Hall, London, 1911 and his 'Note on Urban and Rural Variations according to the English Census of 1911', *Journal of the Royal Statistical Society*, vol. lxxvi, 1913. A. K. Cairncross, art. cit., pp. 67–87.

A bird's-eye view of internal migration in England and Wales is given in Table 4. In the fifties and sixties nearly 1½ million people were released by the rural areas; the expanding towns and coalfields absorbed about two-thirds of them and net emigration accounted for about one-third. From the seventies to the 1900's there was a clear inverse relation between internal and external migration. The

TABLE 5

Wales: Internal migration, decennially, 1851–1911

Net loss by migration (−). Net gain by migration (+)

Area	1851–61	1861–71	1871–81	1881–91	1891–1901	1901–11
Welsh rural areas . .	− 63,322	− 58,967	− 64,646	− 106,087	− 57,413	− 37,909
Glamorgan–Monmouth- shire colliery area .	+ 39,627	+ 11,033	+ 12,213	+ 87,225	+ 40,326	+ 129,295
Wrexham colliery area .	+ 2,661	− 1,984	− 1,907	− 1,122	− 618	− 2,875
Llandudno and Rhyl areas . . .	+ 1,259	− 2,268	+ 2,339	+ 2,190	+ 8,289	+ 5,715
Wales* . . .	− 36,271	− 63,005	− 52,139	− 17,794	− 9,350	+ 98,492

* The migration balance for Wales is based on Table 2. The estimated migration balance for 1851–61 and 1861–71 has been arrived at after making allowance for under-registration of births in those decades. The recorded number of births was 4 per cent. too low in 1851–61 and 2 per cent. too low in 1861–71, according to D. V. Glass's estimates for England and Wales in *Population Studies*, vol. v, no. 1, July 1951. The figures of net gains or losses by migration in the body of the above table, derived from the work of Welton and Cairncross, are based on the number of *recorded* births. Hence the discrepancy in the first two columns of the table. See note to Table 4.

SOURCE: T. A. Welton, op. cit., and A. K. Cairncross, loc. cit.

very high net outflow of 837,000 from the country-side in 1871–81 was matched by a powerful absorptive capacity in the urban areas, with net emigration relatively low (164,000). The reverse took place in 1881–91; corresponding to the heavy rural exodus of 845,000 there was a net inflow of only 228,000 into the towns and coalfields, whereas net emigration amounted to 601,000. In the nineties there was a swing of the pendulum in favour of domestic industrial expansion which absorbed nearly all the labour released by the rural districts. In the decade 1901–11 even the towns taken as a whole had a net loss by migration of 321,000, and net emigration soared again to 501,000.

Turning to the picture for Wales given in Table 5, we are immediately struck by the fact that the industrial sector of Wales (the Glamorgan–Monmouthshire area) expanded most in those very decades when the industrial sector of England and Wales as a whole expanded least, i.e. in 1851–61, 1881–91, and 1901–11. The progress of the South Wales coalfield in the sixties and seventies was comparatively slow, and during that period only a small part of the Welsh rural exodus could be absorbed in Wales. Net emigration mainly to England took away about 115,000 people. In the eighties the net outflow from the country-side in Wales reached a peak of 106,000, but most of it was absorbed by the vigorously expanding South Wales coalfield. Thus, in this decade when emigration from England was

TABLE 6

Colliery districts and migration balances, 1851–1911

Decade	Welsh colliery districts* Net gain (+) or loss (−) by migration	English colliery districts* Net gain (+) or loss (−) by migration	Wales† Net migration (annual rate per 10,000 population)	England† Net migration (annual rate per 10,000 population)
	('000)	('000)		
1851–61 . . .	+ 42	+63	−28	−16
1861–71 . . .	+ 9	+82	−47	− 7
1871–81 . . .	+ 10	+74	−35	− 5
1881–91 . . .	+ 86	+ 4	−11	−23
1891–1901 . .	+ 40	+45	− 5	− 2
1901–11 . . .	+126	−12	+45	−19

* SOURCE: Cairncross, loc. cit., p. 86.
† SOURCE: Table 1 above.

very heavy, emigration from Wales was negligible. During the nineties, when England was having a home-investment boom, the net absorptive capacity of industry in South Wales was less than half of what it had been in the previous decade. However, the spectacular growth of new towns such as Llandudno and Rhyl, and the striking fall in size of the rural surplus, enabled Wales to retain almost the whole of its natural increase. At no time was the contrast more evident than in the decade 1901–11 when a net Welsh rural exodus of 38,000 was matched by a net absorption of 129,000 in the Glamorgan–Monmouthshire coalfield; Wales had become an immigration country.

How did the rate of development of the Welsh coalfields compare with that of the English coalfields? Some light on this is thrown by Table 6, which gives the shape of the fluctuations in the growth of the mining labour force in the two countries, and the figures are illustrated in Fig. 4. There is a marked inverse relation between the rate of growth of the Welsh and the English colliery districts. In the sixties and seventies the main expansion in coal-mining was in England; in the eighties Wales almost monopolized the advance, whereas England took the lead in the nineties. The decade 1901–11 saw a vast development in Wales and an actual loss by migration in the English coalfields taken as a whole. Fig. 4 also shows the parallel inverse relation between the course of external migration in Wales

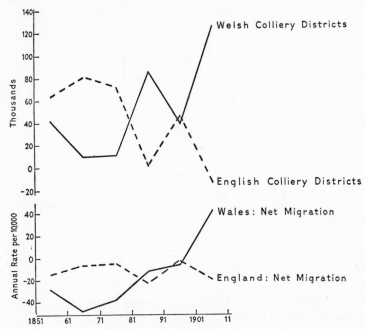

FIG. 4. Welsh and English colliery districts: Net migration movements, 1851–1911.

SOURCE: Table 6.

and in England. In the sixties the main coalfield expansion was in Durham; in the seventies it was in Durham, Wigan, Chesterfield, Nuneaton and Barnsley; and in the nineties it was in Durham, Chesterfield, Nuneaton, and Barnsley. Welsh coal was chiefly for export, and the opening up of the Welsh colliery districts fluctuated with the wider export sector of the United Kingdom; on the other hand, the output of English coals consumed on the home market was sensitive to the long swing in the rate of home capital construction. Since the industrial sector of Wales consisted almost entirely of the coalfields, it is not surprising that the rate of growth (as measured by net migration) in Wales was inverse to that of England.

The drastic change in the balance of internal migration in the twenty years after the First World War is brought out in Table 7.

TABLE 7

Wales: Internal migration, decennially 1921–39

Net loss by migration (−). Net gain by migration (+)

Area	1921–31	1931–9
Rural areas . . .	− 30,337	− 23,592
Non-industrial towns .	+ 6,896	+ 16,524
Industrial areas . .	−246,463	−174,092
Wales*	−269,904	−181,160

* The discrepancies between these figures for 1921–31 and 1931–9 and those in Table 2 are explained by the fact that in Table 2 the decennial excess of births over deaths had to be estimated for calendar years.

SOURCES: *Annual Reports of the Registrar-General*, Civil Tables.

In the depression of the inter-war period the net outflow from the country-side continued on about the same scale as before the First World War, but it was now accompanied by an immense efflux of 421,000 people from the hard-hit industrial areas. The only bright spot in these gloomy years was the net inflow into the non-industrial towns, mostly in North Wales, such as Bangor, Caernarvon, Colwyn Bay, Llandudno, Rhyl, Conway, Prestatyn, and Abergele. Between 1921 and 1939 Wales lost on balance 450,000 people through emigration; the natural increase in this period was 259,000, and so there was an absolute fall of 191,000 in the population.

4. *Long swings in investment.*

So far we have used population data to trace the shape of Welsh economic development since the middle of the nineteenth century, and some interesting differences between Wales and other parts of the British Isles have emerged. We shall now examine the growth and fluctuations of industry and agriculture. Since there are no indexes of income and investment in Wales, we must make the best of the few time-series available for the period under review. The object is to relate the long swings in industrial growth in Wales to the pattern of development in the rest of the United Kingdom and the Atlantic economy. We shall take the volume of coal exports from South Wales ports (from 1850) and the output of crude steel in South Wales (from 1879) as indexes of the growth of the industrial sector. The average price of steam coal, f.o.b. Cardiff (from 1850), can be regarded as an indication of fluctuations in income, and the course of agriculture will be reflected in the index of total livestock (from 1867).

The long swings in the Atlantic economy are shown in Fig. 5. British foreign investment and merchandise exports fluctuated in unison with railway building and bituminous coal output in the United States. On the upward course of the long swing, when investment in capital equipment in the United States was booming, the export sector in the United Kingdom expanded rapidly. Fig. 5 shows that the industrial investment sector of Wales (as revealed in the course of coal exports and steel output) fluctuated in harmony with the British export sector.[1] We can now see the phenomenon of the eighties in Wales in its true perspective. There was an upsurge in British foreign investment and exports, related to the construction boom overseas and particularly in the United States; the Welsh economy participated fully in this upswing. It would not be too much to say that the whole of the industrial zone of Wales (the coalfields of Glamorgan and Monmouthshire) was a part of the British export sector. Fig. 5 shows, too, that the long swings in Welsh emigration to the United States were parallel to the long swings in the international economy; paradoxically, this meant—in the long period as distinct from the short period—that emigration went up and down with prosperity in Wales. We have already seen that over the entire period the volume of emigration from Wales was negligible; and now we can see that this trickle of emigration varied with the ups and downs in the long cycle in foreign investment and exports. These emigrants were not forced out by the impoverishment of the economy as happened in Ireland and Scotland; it was a complementary export of labour on a very minor scale induced by the export-biased nature of the Welsh economy. In the short cycle, however, emigration, as one would expect, was inverse to fluctuations in income in Wales, as shown in Fig. 6. Sharp and frequent changes occurred in the price of coal; when the price rose there was prosperity and the incentive to

---

[1] The dip in the South Wales coal export series in the early seventies when the British export series were going up is easily explained. There were serious industrial stoppages in 1871, 1873, and 1875. In the prolonged struggle of 1875 the pits were idle for five months. Hence the sharp trough in the series. A similar one is to be found in 1898.

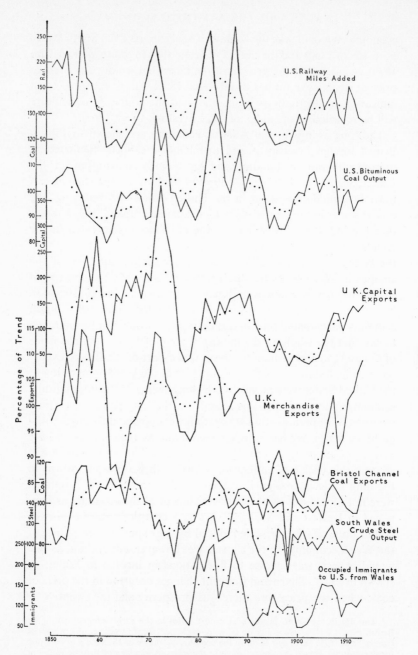

Fig. 5. Indexes of long swings in Wales and the Atlantic economy, 1850–1913.

emigrate weakened, and vice versa when the price fell. These short cyclical ups and downs are to be distinguished from the long swing.

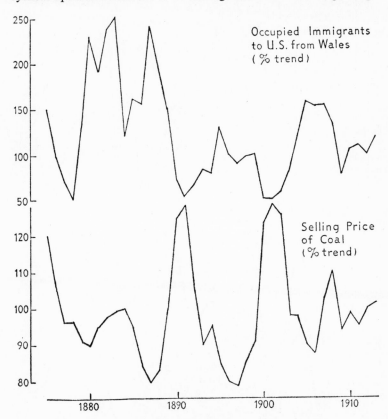

FIG. 6. Wales: Emigration and the price of coal, 1875–1913.
SOURCES: Brinley Thomas, op. cit., Table 84; Finlay Gibson, op. cit., p. 174.

Fig. 7 brings new evidence to bear on the thesis developed earlier in this chapter. As already explained, the coal industry in South Wales was seriously disturbed by stoppages during the seventies; it is therefore better to concentrate on the period 1880–1913. Here we find

SOURCES OF FIG. 5: Brinley Thomas, op. cit., Tables 84, 97, 98, 101, and 102; 'The South Wales Steel Industry', *Bulletin of the British Iron and Steel Federation*, Dec. 1955; Finlay Gibson, *The Coalmining Industries of the United Kingdom* (Cardiff, 1921), p. 84; D. A. Thomas, 'The Growth and Direction of our Foreign Trade in coal during the Last Half Century', *Journal of the Royal Statistical Society*, vol. lxvi, Sept. 1903, p. 71.

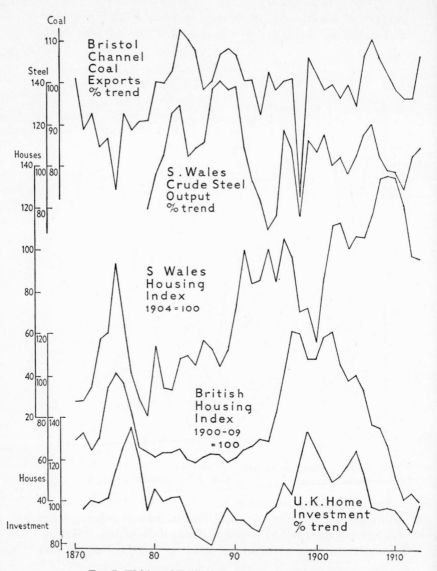

FIG. 7. Welsh and British investment indexes, 1870–1913.

SOURCES: Finlay Gibson, op. cit., p. 84; D. A. Thomas, loc. cit.; *Bulletin of British Iron and Steel Federation*, Dec. 1955; J. Hamish Richards and J. Parry Lewis, 'House Building in the South Wales Coalfield, 1851–1913', *The Manchester School*, vol. xxiv, Sept. 1956, Table II; B. Weber, 'A New Index of Residential Construction, 1835–1950', *Scottish Journal of Political Economy*, vol. ii, June 1955, pp. 104–32; Brinley Thomas, op. cit., Table 100.

the movements of Welsh coal exports, steel output, and building[1] inverse to those of home investment and building in the United Kingdom. In the eighties the Welsh coal and steel indexes rise sharply relatively to trend, and building reached a high peak in 1891; meanwhile house building and home investment in the United Kingdom were declining relatively to trend. In the nineties relative stagnation in the Welsh industrial sector coincided with a marked boom in home investment and housing in Britain as a whole. After the turn of the century a vigorous expansion in housing and in the coal and steel industries of South Wales was accompanied by a rapid decline in British home investment and housing in relation to trend.

When the Welsh economy was going ahead briskly the English export sector was simultaneously expanding, while home capital construction was in relative decline. Our population analysis indicated that during such phases Welsh economic growth was strong enough to retain nearly the whole of the country's natural increase or even to attract a net inflow of labour from outside, whereas in England the weakness of the home-construction sector caused a large part of the rural surplus to emigrate overseas. Thus low emigration from (or immigration into) Wales coincided with high emigration from England. On the other hand, when the Welsh economy was stagnating relatively to trend, the English home-construction sector was simultaneously expanding and the export sector declining relatively to trend. In this phase the workers displaced from the land in Wales, facing a weak demand for labour in their own country, migrated over the border to England where there was a brisk demand for labour in the prosperous home-construction sector. Thus, high emigration from Wales coincided with low emigration from England. The agricultural surplus in Wales was recruited either for the export-geared Welsh industrial sector or for the English home-construction sector: there was comparatively little recruitment for overseas. The time-series in Fig. 7 confirm the conclusion reached in sections 2 and 3 of this chapter.

The lack of statistics of income makes it difficult to trace internal reactions of industrial fluctuations in Wales, but an attempt has been made in Fig. 8 to approach the problem indirectly. The selling price of coal is a good guide to variations in income during the period. It

---

[1] For an analysis of the Welsh building cycle, see J. Hamish Richards and J. Parry Lewis, 'House Building in the South Wales Coalfield, 1851–1911', *The Manchester School*, vol. xxiv, Sept. 1956, pp. 289–301.

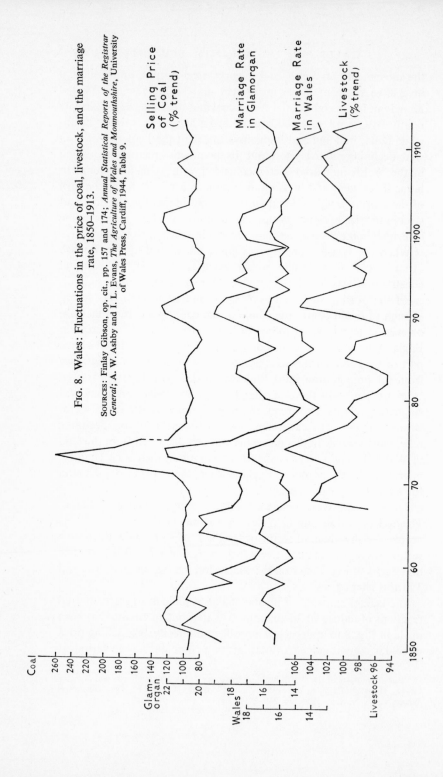

Fig. 8. Wales: Fluctuations in the price of coal, livestock, and the marriage rate, 1850–1913.

Sources: Finlay Gibson, op. cit., pp. 157 and 174; *Annual Statistical Reports of the Registrar General*; A. W. Ashby and I. L. Evans, *The Agriculture of Wales and Monmouthshire*, University of Wales Press, Cardiff, 1944, Table 9.

Selling Price of Coal (% trend)

Marriage Rate in Glamorgan

Marriage Rate in Wales

Livestock (% trend)

is interesting to note that the marriage rate per 1,000 population in Glamorgan and in Wales as a whole showed a marked correlation with the price of coal. The year 1873 saw the highest peak in coal prices, and in the following year the marriage rate in Glamorgan reached a maximum of 22·2 per 1,000 and the birth-rate 44·3 per 1,000. There was also close agreement between fluctuations in total livestock (in stock units) and the movements in coal prices, the former lagging slightly after the latter. Changes in income were accompanied by variations in the marriage rate and changes in investment in agriculture. The ups and downs in purchasing power in the coalfield had a direct effect on the agricultural sector.

The year 1891 may be regarded as a watershed in the fortunes of the Welsh rural economy; it marked the culmination of a rapid growth in livestock, with two prominent cyclical peaks in 1874 and 1891. Between the early seventies and the beginning of the nineties there was an increase of 25 per cent. in the total of livestock (in stock units) on Welsh farms and of 33 per cent. in the acreage in permanent grass. Meanwhile the number of men engaged in farming fell from 129,200 in 1851 to 86,300 in 1901, as shown in Table 8.

TABLE 8

Wales: Number of males engaged in farming, 1851–1911

Year	Farmers	Relatives	Labourers	Bailiffs	Total
	('000)	('000)	('000)	('000)	('000)
1851 . . .	35·3	20·0	73·3	0·6	129·2
1871 . . .	35·2	14·3	53·0	1·1	103·6
1891 . . .	32·3	12·5	44·9	1·2	90·9
1901 . . .	32·0	15·1	37·8	1·4	86·3
1911 . . .	32·1	15·9	39·5	1·6	89·1

SOURCE: Census returns. See A. W. Ashby and I. L. Evans, op. cit., pp. 74–75.

After the mid-nineties a recovery in world prices helped the farmers and in the decade 1901–11 when, as we have seen, Wales was absorbing population from outside her borders, there was actually an increase in the number engaged in agriculture—males from 86,300 to 89,100, and females from 12,300 to 20,100. However, this was a passing phase; after the First World War difficulties multiplied, and by the eve of the Second World War the area under cultivation was down to what it was seventy years before.[1]

[1] For a detailed analysis see Ashby and Evans, op. cit.

5. *Industrialization and the Welsh language*

It is a commonplace of the nationalist creed that the economic growth of Wales in the last century was seriously inimical to the nation's language and culture. Industrialism, while it brought ample material gain, is seen as a powerful anglicizing force which swept over most of the country, leaving the rural counties of the north and west as the last fastnesses of the Welsh-speaking tradition. The country-side is the backbone of all that is enduring in the national culture, and the flight from the land has been a paralysing disease: this has become an article of faith for poets and politicians, preachers, and pedagogues alike. The Council for Wales and Monmouthshire made a special study of the depopulation of Welsh rural areas over the last 100 years, and drew a gloomy picture of 'the seriousness of the problem'.[1] High academic authority can be cited and the thesis is now part of the conventional wisdom of the standard textbooks. Professor David Williams puts it in the following words.

In the course of the nineteenth century the industrialization of Wales added a further division in so far as it brought in a large non-Welsh population which has never been assimilated. Besides, industrialism linked Wales with England as never before in its history. While Wales was isolated geographically, and was almost self-sufficing economically, the influence of England was not strong. But the building of roads and railways, and the enormous growth of Welsh industry as part of the economic development of Britain, profoundly affected Welsh life; so much so that there is a marked tendency to regard Welsh culture as being in essence the culture of rural Wales and not of the industrial areas.[2]

One often gets a clearer view of a country's history by looking at it from the outside. That is what this chapter has tried to do—to see Wales in perspective against the wider world of which it was a tiny part. Is it really true that industrialization and the accompanying rural exodus undermined the language and culture of Wales in the period 1850–1913? The telling fact, which historians have not noticed, is that *the Welsh language was saved by the redistribution of a growing population brought about by industrialism*. By implication this has already been demonstrated in earlier sections of this chapter. We can now make it explicit. In the sixty years, 1851–1911, there was a net loss of 388,000 people by migration out of Welsh rural areas; in the same period the Glamorgan–Monmouthshire colliery districts

[1] Cmd. 8060, p. 20.
[2] David Williams, *A History of Modern Wales*, John Murray, 1950, p. 269.

and the North Wales towns absorbed on balance 336,000 by inward migration. It is true that a good proportion of the latter were non-Welsh. A detailed analysis of the census figures for Glamorgan enables us to estimate that 160,000[1] of the migrants to that country between 1861 and 1911 came from Welsh counties.[2] To these one would need to add the number of children and grandchildren they had after settling down in Glamorgan.[3] If a similar analysis had been made of the inflow into the rest of the South Wales coalfield in Carmarthenshire and Monmouthshire, we could arrive at a rough estimate of the total number of people received into the industrial areas from the rest of Wales which was largely rural. We do know, however, that in 1911 there were in the three counties of Glamorgan, Monmouthshire, and Carmarthenshire (containing the coalfield) 556,000 people would could speak Welsh and these comprised 57 per cent. of the total number of Welsh-speakers in Wales at that time. The vast majority of these people would not have been there but for the pull of industrialism. The census figures are given in detail in Table 9.

If Wales had been an agricultural country like Ireland, the whole of her surplus rural population, which was Welsh to the core (nearly 400,000 in the sixty years up to 1911), would have had to go to England or overseas; these people, together with their descendants, would have been lost to the land of their birth for ever. This would have been a major disaster to the Welsh language; the number speaking it would probably have been well below half the figure recorded in 1911. The reason why this did not happen was the vigorous growth of the South Wales coalfield.[4] Industrial development was on such a scale that Wales was able to retain a large proportion of the indigenous stock which was displaced from the country-side. The young men and women who left the farms and flocked into the mining townships carried the Welsh way of life with them and brought up their children to speak the mother tongue. Indeed, many of these closely packed and isolated communities acted as melting-pots; they were so intensely

---

[1] To allow for the anglicized parts of Monmouthshire, only half of the migrants from that county have been included.

[2] Brinley Thomas, 'The Migration of Labour into the Glamorganshire Coalfields 1861–1911', *Economica*, Nov. 1930, pp. 292–4.

[3] The addition to the population of Glamorgan through the excess of births over deaths increased from 61,000 in 1861–70 to 169,000 in 1901–10.

[4] Professor David Williams (op. cit., pp. 290–1) says that the absolute number of those who could speak Welsh went on increasing '. . . because of the natural increase of the population'. This is a misconception. It was not the natural increase (which by itself would have been a menace) but the fact that industrialism enabled so much of the natural increase to remain in Wales.

Welsh that a number of the English immigrants—not to mention the
Italian shopkeepers—were quickly assimilated and picked up the
language. It is worth noting that, even in 1951, 54 per cent. of the
715,000 who were Welsh-speaking were in the South Wales industrial
area.

TABLE 9

*Wales: Number of Welsh-speaking persons aged 3 and over, 1901,
1911, and 1951*

County	Number of Welsh-speaking persons aged 3 and over			Proportion speaking Welsh per 1,000 population aged 3 and over		
	1901	1911	1951	1901	1911	1951
Mainly rural						
Anglesey . . .	43,554	42,666	38,443	917	887	798
Brecknock . .	23,119	22,896	16,339	459	415	303
Caernarvon . .	105,301	101,247	85,115	896	856	717
Cardigan . . .	53,638	51,077	40,642	930	896	795
Denbigh . . .	75,604	76,861	62,502	619	567	385
Flint . . .	37,290	36,533	29,121	491	422	211
Merioneth . . .	42,755	38,976	29,966	937	903	754
Montgomery . .	24,341	22,406	15,340	475	448	351
Pembroke . . .	28,333	27,390	23,227	344	324	269
Radnor . . .	1,360	1,139	857	62	54	45
	435,295	421,191	341,552	648	602	448
Mainly industrial						
Glamorgan . .	344,892	393,692	231,722	435	381	203
Carmarthen . .	113,947	127,236	127,295	904	849	773
Monmouth . .	35,690	35,247	14,117	130	96	35
	494,529	556,175	373,134	415	359	218
TOTAL . . .	929,824	977,366	714,686	499	435	289

SOURCES: *Census of England and Wales.* 1901, *Summary Tables*, Table LII. 1911,
County Reports, Table 33. 1951, *Report on Welsh-speaking Population*, Table D, p. xiv.

The romanticist will no doubt reply that the heritage would have
been much safer in the hands of a small homogeneous nation of
culture-loving peasants. But what would have been its fate in the
great agricultural depression of the eighties? Given a miracle, Wales,
like Denmark, might have found her Grundvig; but it is much more
likely, when we think of the physical disabilities of Welsh agriculture,
that she would have been caught, like Ireland, in the vicious circle of
mass emigration. We saw that the fortunes of the Welsh farmer
largely depended on the purchasing power in the coalfields. Thanks to
the abnormally high rate of industrial growth and particularly its
time-shape in relation to that of England, the rate of emigration

from Wales to the United States was negligible as compared with the flow from other parts of the United Kingdom. Moreover, without the wealth and productivity of the industrial sector, is it conceivable that resources could have been found for that trinity of modern institutions expressing the national consciousness—the University, the Library, and the Museum?

Instead of bemoaning the rural exodus, the Welsh patriot should sing the praises of industrial development. In that tremendous half-century before the First World War, economic growth in Wales was so vigorous that her net loss of people by emigration was a mere 4 per cent. of her bountiful natural increase over the period. Few countries in Europe came anywhere near to that. The unrighteous Mammon in opening up the coalfields at such a pace unwittingly gave the Welsh language a new lease of life and Welsh Nonconformity a glorious high noon.

II

POST-WAR EXPANSION

By BRINLEY THOMAS

THE depression of the thirties was so severe in Wales that there seemed to be no alternative to a prolonged contraction and large-scale emigration. Government policy did little to mitigate the painful adjustment borne by the depressed areas; in so far as investment in housing was stimulated by cheap money, the benefits were reaped mainly in areas which had been hit least. There was so much unemployment in the coal industry that recruitment had to be limited to sons of miners. It looked as if the coal and steel industries were suffering from secular stagnation. No one in 1939 could foresee the profound effects which the Second World War was destined to have on the Welsh economy.

1. *The impact of the war*

It did not take long for the war effort to absorb redundant labour and equipment, and by July 1941 the number of unemployed in Wales was only 35,000. Westerly locations were favoured on grounds of relative security from air attacks, and a number of plants were transferred from vulnerable areas in England. The redistribution which had been sought in vain in the thirties was now brought about by strategic necessity; the full implications of the all-out war economy were to be seen in 1944. In the middle of that year there were 219,000 insured women workers in Wales compared with only 94,000 in 1939, an increase of 134 per cent.: in Great Britain as a whole the corresponding addition of female labour at the peak of the war effort was only 30 per cent. The number of male insured workers in Wales fell from 602,000 in 1939 to 480,000 in 1944, so that women made up nearly one-third of the labour supply. The distribution over various occupations was significant. Nearly 50 per cent. of the men were in mining, iron and steel, and transport; and 50 per cent. of the women were in manufacturing (chemicals, engineering, and vehicles), metals, and transport.

At its height the war had twisted the Welsh economy into an unfamiliar mould. Between 1939 and 1944 there was an increase in the labour supply in chemicals, paints, and oils from 4,000 to 69,000; in engineering from 11,000 to 48,000; in vehicle construction from 7,000 to 30,000; and in agriculture from 23,000 to 29,000. Much of this expansion was necessarily temporary, but a base was created for a genuine growth of manufacturing. Meanwhile, the labour force in mining contracted from 183,000 to 132,000, and in building from 90,000 to 22,000. The sharp decrease in the latter, coming on top of the substantial loss of skilled craftsmen through emigration in the thirties, was to lead to difficulties in the rebuilding phase after the war.

So far we have been looking at the insured population attached to various industries in 1944 compared with 1939. As soon as victory was assured some parts of the war economy underwent rapid change. In order to bring out the more significant consequences of the war, we shall now glance at the distribution of workers in employment (i.e. insured population minus the unemployed) in 1946 as compared with 1939. The figures are shown in Table 10.

Before the war 40 per cent. of the insured population of Wales were employed in the heavy industries, chiefly coal-mining and iron and steel: by 1946 the share of this group had contracted to 32 per cent. Employment in coal-mining fell from 144,400 to 116,400 and in tinplate manufacture from 23,000 to 12,600. The outstanding fact brought out by Table 10 is the increase of 80 per cent. in the number employed in general manufacturing from 69,800 to 125,400. However, a great deal of this was an artificial expansion. When the war ended there were no less than 48,700 (24,900 men and 23,800 women) making explosives in Wales, but by the middle of 1946 the number had diminished to 11,750. Employment in engineering and the construction and repair of vehicles had also been stimulated. The main reason was that Wales had been a favoured location for industrial activity, which had had to be decentralized on strategic grounds. General manufacturing accounted for one-fifth of total employment in 1946 as against one-ninth before the war. Another new feature was that one out of every ten persons employed in Wales was either a national or a local civil servant; the absolute increase between 1939 and 1946 was 129 per cent. compared with 93 per cent. in Britain as a whole, the difference being due to the transfer of civil servants from London. It is interesting to note that building, transport, public utilities, distribution, and government service together were responsible for exactly the same share of total employment as before the war, namely, 37 per cent. General manufacturing had come in to redress the balance in the heavy industries.

TABLE 10

Wales: Industrial classification of insured persons in employment in 1939 and 1946

Industry	1939	1946	1939	1946
	('000)	('000)	(%)	(%)
Agriculture and fishing . . .	23·3	30·4	3·9	4·8
Coal-mining	144·4	116·4	24·2	18·2
Other mining, quarrying, non-metal mining products, bricks, &c. . .	24·4	17·2	4·1	2·7
Metal manufacture . . .	66·1	62·3	11·0	9·8
Shipbuilding and repairing . . .	3·4	8·4	0·6	1·3
General manufacturing* . . .	69·8	125·4	11·7	19·7
Building and civil engineering . .	61·2	38·3	10·2	6·0
Gas, water, and electricity . .	7·4	7·9	1·2	1·2
Transport and communications . .	41·1	53·6	7·0	8·4
Distributive trades	82·0	68·7	13·7	10·8
National and local government . .	28·3	64·8	4·7	10·2
Miscellaneous services† . . .	45·9	44·0	7·7	6·9
TOTAL	597·4	637·5	100·0	100·0

* Chemicals, paints, oils, &c., engineering, &c., earthenware, glass, leather, leather goods, fur, construction and repair of vehicles, other metal industries, textiles, clothing, food, drink, tobacco, wood working, paper, printing, and miscellaneous.

† Including commerce and finance.

SOURCE: *Tables relating to Employment and Unemployment in Great Britain, 1939, 1945, and 1946*, H.M.S.O., 1947, pp. 26–27. Mid-year estimates to nearest hundred.

Probably the most significant effect of the war was to bring women into the factories in unprecedented numbers. In 1946, when things were beginning to settle down, female employment in Wales was still 158,000, i.e. 83 per cent. more than in 1939, whereas in Great Britain it was only 14 per cent. more. Welsh women workers were distributed mainly as follows: 31 per cent. in manufacturing, 23 per cent. in distributive trades, 17 per cent. in miscellaneous services, and 16 per cent. in national and local government. Four out of every ten people engaged in manufacturing were women.

The war did three things which were to have an enduring effect on the Welsh economy: it eliminated unemployment, the core of a potentially strong manufacturing sector was established, and hitherto unknown employment opportunities for women were created.

2. Pains of transition, 1946–7[1]

For a time in 1946, Welsh people began to fear the worst; there were signs that the curse of unemployment which had darkened their lives in the thirties was again rearing its head. In February 1946 as many as 10 per cent. of the insured males were out of work, and it looked as if freedom from enforced idleness had been a purely war-time phenomenon. Government departments did what they could by giving liberal allocations of scarce raw materials and helping firms to switch quickly from war-time to peace-time activities. However, they seemed to lack faith in these expedients, for they began to resort once more to the policy of industrial transference, euphemistically called a Voluntary Temporary Transfer Scheme; in the year ending July 1946 nearly 10,000 men and women from Wales were placed in jobs elsewhere.

Fortunately, the forebodings of the pessimists proved groundless. Between June 1946 and June 1947 the number of unemployed in Wales fell by over 20,000; the transition to peace-time production was gathering momentum. In the middle of 1947 there were 44,000 persons out of work, or 6 per cent. of the insured population: this compared very favourably with the situation in 1938 when no less than 22 per cent. were unemployed. A close analysis of the unused labour shows the influence of special circumstances. Of the 27,636 males wholly unemployed in June 1947, 12,102 were registered as disabled; and of the 15,534 who were fit 4,083 were over 55 years of age, leaving 11,451 aged 15–55. Subtracting the 3,314 who had been without work for less than four weeks, we obtain a figure of 8,137 genuinely unemployed, or 29 per cent. of the total returned as wholly unemployed. Some unfit men may not have registered as disabled because they felt it would spoil their chances of getting a job; this probably goes far to explain the fact that 2,107 of the fit men aged 15–55 had been out of work for over a year. From these figures it is

[1] I am grateful to the Editors of the London and Cambridge Economic Service for permission to use in this section material published in my article, 'Wales, Development Area Policy and the Crisis', published in *London and Cambridge Economic Service*, vol. xxv, bulletin iv, 10 Nov. 1947, pp. 124–7.

clear that the redundant part of the effective supply of male labour in Wales in 1947 was comparatively small.

Thus far we have been considering problems of immediate post-war adjustment which were specifically Welsh. In common with the rest of the United Kingdom, Wales was involved in the struggle to overcome the deficit in the balance of payments. One of the conditions of the American loan of 3,750 million dollars, which replaced lend-lease, was that sterling earned in current transactions should become convertible within one year after the date when the Agreement came into force. The ill-fated experiment in full convertibility lasted only five weeks and had to be suspended on 21 August 1947. At the rate at which gold was flowing out during the last week, the whole of the dollar loan would have been exhausted by September of that year. Nothing could have demonstrated more dramatically the grim fact that Britain needed far more than a year or two to recover from the strains and distortions inflicted on her economy by the war. In 1945 the volume of her exports was only 40 per cent. of what it had been in 1938, and the merchant shipping fleet of the United Kingdom and the colonies was smaller by 30 per cent. It was then calculated that to attain international viability the volume of exports would have to reach a level at least 75 per cent. higher than in 1938. In these circumstances it was pertinent to ask whether the measures to promote activity in the development areas were consistent with what had to be done to solve the problem of the balance of payments. The purpose of the development area policy was to insure certain regions against recurrence of the mass unemployment which had afflicted them between the wars. But, in view of the radical change in Britain's economic condition, could this policy of *regional* discrimination be reconciled with the overriding necessity to redistribute manpower *functionally* in order to eliminate the chronic weakness revealed by the failure of convertibility in 1947?

There appeared to be a real conflict. Commenting on the policy towards development areas, *The Economist* (27 September 1947) argued that '. . . more than half the Board of Trade's post-war factory building programme has been located in these areas. . . . To date only 11,000 jobs have yet been created, and though this is only the first instalment of an estimated ultimate total of 192,000, even that seems a very small return for such a large slice of post-war capital resources.' This conclusion, however, was based on a misleading interpretation of the facts. The Board of Trade's programme of new factories was in four parts: A, new firms occupying existing government-owned premises, B, new firms housed in existing privately owned premises, C, firms housed in temporary buildings while waiting for new factory space to be built, and D, firms occupying newly completed post-war buildings. The total mentioned by *The Economist* referred to category D, only. The full picture for the South Wales development area is given in Table 11.

TABLE 11

South Wales: Persons employed in post-war factory jobs in the Development Area at 30 August 1947

Category	Males	Females	Total
	('000)	('000)	('000)
A. New firms occupying existing government-owned space built before or during the war	20·2	10·6	30·8
B. New firms housed 'permanently' in existing privately owned space . .	1·5	1·3	2·9
Firms for whom new post-war factories and extensions had been approved:			
C. In temporary premises awaiting completion of new buildings . . .	0·4	1·7	2·0
D. Actually in occupation of newly completed post-war buildings . .	2·3	1·4	3·7
TOTAL	24·4	15·0	39·4

NOTE: The figures cover all developments (excluding non-factory employment between mid-1944, when the Board of Trade assumed responsibility, and 30 August 1947). Clerical and administrative workers are included.

SOURCE: Board of Trade.

Up to August 1947 39,400 persons had found jobs in the four categories of post-war factories in South Wales, and only 3,700 of these (category D) were in newly completed post-war buildings. This is striking proof that at that crucial stage the development area's programme of new factory building was not digging into the country's scarce capital resources. Practically the whole of the expansion in the newer industries was achieved by making the maximum use of existing premises. No doubt some of the firms producing things like clothing, electric fires, cookers, and refrigerators were preparing for a restocking boom in the home market; but, where they were flexible enough, they could turn to the export market. In so far as textile production was growing in South Wales and not in traditional areas, it served the national interest; an area where female employment had increased by 83 per cent. since 1939 (compared with 14 per cent. in the country as a whole) had special advantages to offer to certain export trades. Some of the new firms provided substitutes for imports, e.g. synthetic chemicals, and others supplied agricultural machinery. In the labour market there was no doubt some competition between the new trading estate factories and the coal-mines, though it is impossible to give a quantitative estimate. A necessary consequence of the establishment of new industries simultaneously with efforts to expand the old was a relative growth of transport; on the other hand, in the early post-war years the building and distributive trades remained well below their pre-war size. On the whole, we may conclude that, in the most difficult stage of the post-war transition, the development area and the 'crisis' policies were not seriously in conflict.

3. *Expanding and contracting industries, 1948–58*

A study of trends in the decade 1948–58 will reveal the more permanent changes which have occurred in the industrial structure of Wales. The groupings which were used in the previous section were revised in 1948, but fortunately the new industrial classification introduced by the Ministry of Labour and National Service in that year has remained unchanged for a whole decade. It is thus possible to present a fairly accurate and detailed picture.

The distribution of the insured population by industry group in 1948 and 1958 is given in Table 12. In these ten years the number of insured workers grew from 919,500 to 952,000. The biggest relative contraction took place in agriculture, fishing, and forestry (from 38,300 to 26,400) and coal-mining (from 134,100 to 119,600). If it had not been for forestry where the labour force rose sharply from 2,960 to 4,250, the decline in the agricultural group would have been even greater. Coal-mining, which absorbed 14·6 per cent. of the working population in 1948, accounted for only 12·9 per cent. in 1958, and there was also a marked decrease in the number engaged in slate quarrying. The sector devoted to primary production—agriculture, fishing, forestry, mining, and quarrying—shrank from one-fifth to one-sixth of the total.

The labour force in building fell from 46,000 to 39,900, but this was to a small extent mitigated by a moderate growth in civil engineering and electrical wiring and contracting. Transport as a whole released labour, but the component parts fared variously. Whereas the number in railway service fell from 36,470 to 33,320, the rise in employment in buses and trams was very slight—from 12,670 to 13,160. Goods transport by road grew from 5,930 to 7,260, while

TABLE 12

Wales: Distribution of insured population by industry group in 1948 and 1958

Industry group	Number of insured workers		Percentage distribution	
	July 1948	May 1958	1948	1958
	('000)	('000)	(%)	(%)
Contracting groups				
Agriculture, fishing, and forestry .	38·3	26·4	4·2	2·7
Coal-mining	134·1	119·6	14·6	12·9
Slate quarrying . . .	4·7	3·3	0·5	0·3
Other mining and quarrying . .	6·9	5·7	0·7	0·6
Shipbuilding and repairing . .	9·0	7·1	0·9	0·7
Building and contracting . . .	66·0	62·1	7·2	6·5
Transport and communication . .	91·4	85·1	9·9	9·0
National government . . .	30·3	21·1	3·3	2·2
Miscellaneous services . . .	73·5	66·8	8·0	7·0
Expanding groups				
Metal manufacture	80·7	85·9	8·8	9·0
General manufacturing* . . .	171·6	219·6	18·6	23·0
Gas, water, and electricity . .	13·7	20·6	1·5	2·2
Distributive trades	82·7	93·4	9·0	9·8
Local government	39·8	45·3	4·3	4·8
Professional services† . . .	68·9	89·4	7·4	9·4
Ex-service personnel not classified .	8·3	0·8	1·1	—
TOTAL	919·5	952·0	100·0	100·0

* Comprising chemicals, engineering, treatment of non-metalliferous products other than coal, vehicles, other metal, precision instruments, textiles, leather, clothing, food, wood and cork, paper and printing, and other manufacturing.

† Including insurance, banking, and finance.

SOURCE: *Digest of Welsh Statistics*, No. 4, H.M.S.O., 1957. We are indebted to the Wales Office of the Ministry of Labour, Cardiff, for their kindness in supplying the figures for 1958.

sea transport declined from 9,490 to 7,270. The postal, telegraph, and wireless services decreased from 14,760 to 13,500.

There was a reduction of 30 per cent. in the staffs employed in national government; this was exactly the same as in Great Britain as a whole. It was half compensated by an expansion in local government. The contraction in miscellaneous services was brought about mainly by a huge fall in the number of insured resident domestic servants from 10,410 to 3,660 (i.e. by 65 per cent.) and non-resident from 8,840 to 6,910 (28 per cent.). As a partial offset there was an increase in the hotel and catering industry from 31,920 to 35,130.

In the expanding sector the outstanding feature is the growth of

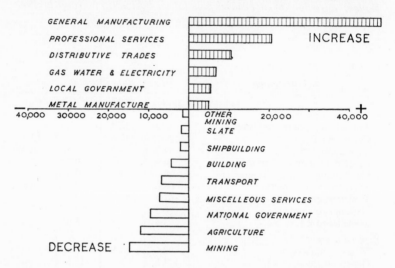

FIG. 9. Wales: Increases and decreases in numbers of insured workers by industry group, 1948 and 1958.

SOURCE: Table 12.

general manufacturing from 171,600 to 219,600; in 1958 about one out of every four workers in Wales was in these industries. The nature of this development may be seen by looking at the numbers in the various trades shown in Table 13.

The industries growing fastest were miscellaneous manufacturing, precision instruments, engineering, paper and printing, and textiles—on an average by 50 per cent. In manufacturing as a whole there was an absolute increase of 28 per cent. over the decade.

The far-reaching changes in the iron and steel industry are shown by the figures for metal manufacture. The number of blast-furnace workers rose from 1,660 to 4,530, iron and steel melting, rolling, &c., expanded from 28,060 to 37,080, and steel-sheet manufacture from 13,250 to 15,040; on the other hand, labour employed in tin-plate manufacture decreased from 16,960 to 9,910, or by 41 per cent.

Employment in metal manufacture as a whole went up by 6 per cent. A good index of economic development is the consumption of electrical power; in the decade under review the labour force engaged in supplying electricity in Wales grew by 68 per cent., from 8,570 to

TABLE 13

Wales: Number of insured workers in various manufacturing industries in 1948 and 1958

Industry	1948	1958	Rate of Growth 1948–58
	('000)	('000)	(%)
Other manufacturing	5·5	10·5	91
Precision instruments, &c. . . .	3·2	5·0	56
Engineering (excluding shipbuilding) .	27·1	40·7	50
Paper and printing	6·6	9·5	46
Textiles	12·3	16·3	33
Clothing	11·4	14·7	29
Chemicals, &c.	19·7	25·1	27
Food, drink, and tobacco . . .	20·8	25·3	22
Miscellaneous metal	17·6	21·0	18
Leather	1·7	2·0	18
Vehicles	28·2	31·2	11
Wood and cork	6·3	6·6	5
Treatment of non-metalliferous mining products	11·2	11·7	4
TOTAL MANUFACTURING . . .	171·6	219·6	28

SOURCE: See Table 12.

14,530. In distribution, which expanded by 13 per cent., the number working in retail stores selling food and drink hardly increased at all: a spectacular advance took place in retail stores selling non-food goods, from 32,970 to 40,610. Another interesting sign of the times is the substantial growth of professional services from 68,900 to 89,400; in 1958 nearly 10 per cent. of the insured population of Wales were in this group. Outstanding was the expansion of 54 per cent. in the number engaged in medical and dental services, from 21,530 to 32,920; education grew by 24 per cent. and insurance, banking, and finance by 25 per cent.

To sum up, the expanding industries of Wales taken as a whole grew at the rate of 21 per cent. between 1948 and 1958, and at the end of the decade they comprised 58 per cent. of the insured population. As compared with before the war the fraction of the working population in coal-mining had fallen from over one-quarter to one-eighth, while that in general manufacturing had risen from about one ninth to just under one-quarter.

The extent of the change in the balance of various industries may be appreciated by making a comparison with Great Britain in the decade 1948–58. The relevant figures are set out in Table 14.

TABLE 14

Great Britain: Distribution of insured population by industry group, 1948 and 1958

Industry group	Number of insured workers		Percentage distribution	
	1948	1958	1948	1958
	('000)	('000)	(%)	(%)
Contracting groups				
Agriculture, fishing, and forestry	951·7	659·0	4·6	3·0
Coal-mining	795·4	785·4	3·9	3·6
Other mining and quarrying .	81·6	76·2	0·4	0·3
Shipbuilding and repairing .	234·8	211·7	1·2	1·0
Building and contracting . .	1,373·8	1,389·5	6·7	6·4
Transport and communication .	1,787·9	1,686·4	8·7	7·7
National government . .	699·4	538·6	3·4	2·5
Miscellaneous services . .	1,936·2	1,598·0	9·7	7·3
Expanding groups				
Metal manufacture . . .	503·1	577·1	2·5	2·7
General manufacturing . .	7,215·9	8,343·4	35·2	38·2
Gas, water, and electricity .	297·4	379·9	1·5	1·7
Distributive trades . . .	2,157·9	2,493·6	10·5	11·4
Local government . . .	775·7	782·1	3·8	3·6
Professional services . . .	1,588·1	2,288·1	7·7	10·5
Ex-service personnel not classified	101·0	11·3	0·5	0·1
TOTAL	20,499·9	21,820·3	100·0	100·0

NOTE: The industrial groups in this table are identical with those in Table 12 except that 'Other mining and quarrying' in this table includes slate quarrying.

SOURCES: *Ministry of Labour Gazette*, Feb. 1949 and Feb. 1959.

The contracting and expanding sectors are the same in both countries. The striking fact is that the *relative* growth of manufacturing was much greater in Wales than in the country as a whole (18·6 per cent. to 23·0 per cent. as against 35·2 per cent. to 38·2 per cent.). The absolute rate of increase in the labour force in general manufacturing between 1948 and 1958 was 28 per cent. in Wales as against 15 per cent. in Great Britain. General manufacturing and metal manufacture contain 32 per cent. of the insured population of Wales, the corresponding proportion in Great Britain being 41 per cent.

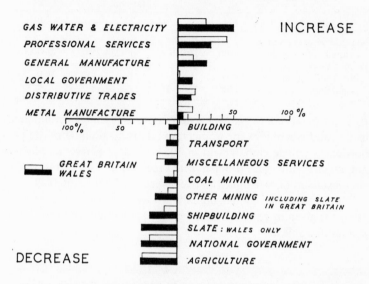

FIG. 10. Wales and Great Britain: Percentage change in insured workers by industry group, 1948 to 1958.
SOURCES: Tables 12 and 14.

The distributive trades have shown a modest relative expansion in the country as a whole—from 10·5 per cent. to 11·4 per cent. of the total, and in Wales the degree of increase was similar—from 9·0 per cent. to 9·8 per cent of the total. Some of the special features of distribution in Wales will be analysed in Chapter VIII. An important sign of a rising standard of living and a more diverse social structure is the fact that the proportion engaged in professional services in Wales (9·4 per cent.) is almost as high as in the country as a whole (10·5 per cent.). The basic specialization remains; in Wales 22 per cent. earn their living in coal-mining and iron and steel as compared with only 6 per cent. in Great Britain.

4. *Female employment*

The wider scope for women in industry, which was achieved in Wales during the war, did not prove to be a temporary phase. In 1958 there were 269,000 women in insured occupations as compared with 219,400 at the peak of the war effort in 1944. The growth in female employment has been as follows.

Wales	Mid-year			
	1939	1944	1948	1958
Number of women in insured occupations	93,900	219,400	234,750	269,000
Women as percentage of total insured population . .	13·5	31·3	25·6	28·3

If recent trends continue, Wales may come to resemble certain areas in England where jobs for women are relatively abundant. The proportion of female employment in 1958 was 28·3 per cent., which is not much below the 31·3 per cent. reached in the extraordinary circumstances of war-time and over twice the fraction in 1939.

The distribution of female labour over different occupational groups is given in Table 15, and the corresponding picture for Great Britain in Table 16.

TABLE 15

Wales: Distribution of insured women workers by industry, 1948 and 1958

Industry group	Number of insured workers		Percentage distribution	
	1948	1958	1948	1958
	('000)	('000)	(%)	(%)
Contracting groups				
Agriculture, forestry, and fishing .	5·6	2·6	2·4	1·0
Metal manufacture	7·9	6·2	3·4	2·3
National government . . .	10·0	6·1	4·3	2·3
Miscellaneous services . . .	55·6	51·5	23·7	19·1
Expanding groups				
General manufacturing . . .	53·1	70·0	22·6	26·0
Distributive trades	39·2	50·5	16·7	18·8
Professional services . . .	37·4	50·0	15·9	18·6
Insurance, banking, and finance .	3·2	5·3	1·3	2·0
Local government	9·3	10·3	3·9	3·8
Transport and communication . .	9·4	9·5	4·0	3·5
Others	4·2	7·0	1·8	2·6
TOTAL INSURED	234·8	269·0	100·0	100·0

SOURCE: See Table 12.

In common with the rest of the country there has been a marked
narrowing of the field for female labour in national government,
miscellaneous services, and agriculture. The main factors have been

TABLE 16

*Great Britain: Distribution of insured women workers by industry,
1948 and 1958*

Industry group	Number of insured workers		Percentage distribution	
	1948	*1958*	*1948*	*1958*
	('000)	*('000)*	*(%)*	*(%)*
Contracting groups				
Agriculture, forestry, and fishing	146·2	93·5	2·1	1·2
National government	231·3	159·2	3·4	2·1
Local government	234·9	208·3	3·5	2·7
Miscellaneous services	1,362·9	1,171·7	20·0	15·4
Expanding groups				
General manufacturing	2,561·9	2,852·4	37·7	37·5
Distributive trades	998·9	1,278·7	14·7	16·8
Professional services*	891·2	1,380·3	13·1	18·2
Transport and communication	233·3	249·6	3·4	3·3
Metal manufacture	59·1	66·3	0·9	0·9
Others	80·3	140·0	1·2	1·9
TOTAL INSURED	6,800·0	7,600·0	100·0	100·0

* Including insurance, banking, and finance.
SOURCES: *Ministry of Labour Gazette*, Feb. 1949 and Feb. 1959.

the dismantling of controls and the substantial decrease in the number
of insured domestic servants working part-time. In the country as
a whole the proportion of women engaged in general manufacturing
was no greater in 1958 than it was in 1948, but in Wales the fraction
rose from 22·6 per cent. to 26·0 per cent. An interesting difference
may be seen between the two patterns of employment in 1958. If
we take services in the widest sense—miscellaneous and professional
services, national and local government, and the distributive trades—
we find that they account for 64·6 per cent. of the gainfully employed
women in Wales as against 55·2 per cent. in Great Britain. On the
other hand, the proportion in general manufacturing was 26·0 per
cent. in Wales as compared with 37·5 per cent. in the country as a
whole.

Since the expansion of the Welsh labour force has taken the
form of an addition of women, one might suppose that the most

progressive parts of the economy are those where it has been profitable to substitute female labour for male. Such an inference would be misleading. A test can be made by looking at the sex ratio in the individual industries. No less than 75 per cent. of the total number of

TABLE 17

Wales: Changes in sex ratio of labour supply in industries where intake of females increased, 1948–58

Industry	Number of female employees		Rate of change in total labour force	Sex ratio (females per 100 males)	
	1948	1958	1948–58	1948	1958
			(%)		
Other manufacturing . .	3,350	4,950	+91	157	89
Precision instruments, &c.. .	1,560	2,480	+60	94	100
Engineering (excluding shipbuilding)	8,150	11,210	+50	53	37
Paper and printing . . .	2,040	2,990	+46	46	46
Textiles	4,360	5,520	+33	55	51
Clothing	8,700	12,240	+29	325	597
Chemicals, &c. . . .	3,490	3,700	+27	22	17
Food, drink, and tobacco .	6,750	10,340	+22	48	69
Miscellaneous metal . . .	7,190	8,100	+18	69	63
Leather	650	890	+18	65	82
Vehicles	4,930	5,180	+11	21	20
Wood and cork . . .	720	940	+ 5	13	17
Treatment of non-metalliferous mining products . . .	1,210	1,450	+ 4	12	14
Total manufacturing . .	53,100	69,990	+28	45	47
Professional services . . .	37,410	49,980	+31	178	190
Insurance, banking, and finance	3,200	5,280	+25	44	68
Distributive trades . . .	39,220	50,500	+13	90	118
Local government . . .	9,270	10,340	+14	30	30
Transport and communication .	9,350	9,490	− 7	11	13
Others	4,030	6,980	− 7	2	3

women employees in Wales in 1958 were in the groups which had expanded in the previous decade. A detailed scrutiny of these groups will reveal where women have been increasing their foothold. The data are set out in Table 17.

An interesting conclusion emerges from this analysis. Contrary to popular belief, the rapid growth of the new manufacturing industries is not based on a more intensive use of female labour. The number of females per 100 males engaged in general manufacturing hardly changed at all between 1948 and 1958; indeed, in some of the most buoyant trades, such as miscellaneous manufacturing, engineering, nylon and rayon, and chemicals, there was a distinct tendency to employ relatively less women. If we exclude clothing, which is traditionally a women's trade, we find that the sex ratio in the expanding manufacturing sector has remained constant. During the war and immediately afterwards the relative abundance of women workers was part of the attraction, but this has not been a factor promoting the expansion in recent years. On the whole there has been an increase in the scale of manufacturing without a substitution in favour of female labour. It is in the various service occupations that women have increased their sway. The number of females per 100 males rose from 178 to 190 in professional services, from 44 to 68 in insurance, banking, and finance, and from 90 to 118 in the distributive trades. The ratio moved sharply in favour of women in the retail (food and drink) trade (83 to 125), the retail (non-food) trade (162 to 202), and catering and hotels (348 to 384). In so far as the relative cheapness of women's labour is a factor affecting demand, it is to be seen in the growth of professional and distribution services but not in the expansion of manufacturing production.

5. *Manufacturing in non-industrial areas*

The most spectacular and publicized examples of diversification are the new factories located in the Development Areas under the influence of the Distribution of Industry Act. The picture would not be complete, however, if we ignored what has been happening in areas which are 'non-industrial' or 'rural'. Chapter I emphasized the fact that the flight from the land is part of the process of economic growth; left to itself this process makes a country richer by decreasing the proportion of the population earning its living in agriculture. If Parliament thought this was undesirable on non-economic grounds, measures could be introduced to retain a larger population on the land at the cost of forgoing some of the fruits of economic progress. There is, however, another way in which the economic life of the country-side can be strengthened, namely, by the establishment of rural industries. New factors influencing the location of firms have emerged in recent years, and it is of interest to discover to what extent there has been a movement away from the traditional areas.

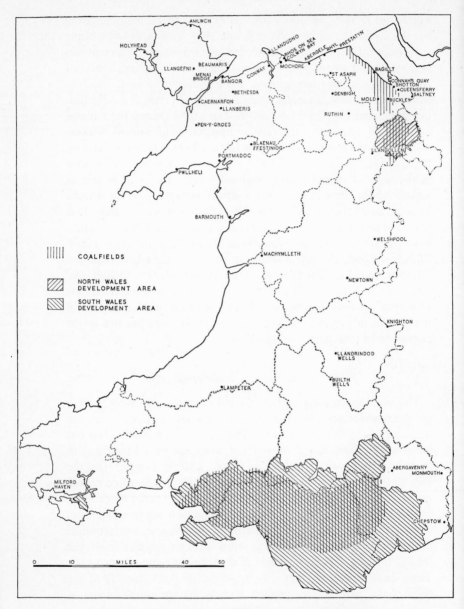

FIG. 11. Wales: Centres of post-war industrial development.

The only way of ascertaining the facts was to collect them, since there are no published statistics on the subject.[1]

By non-industrial or 'rural' areas we mean those lying outside the development areas of Glamorgan, west Monmouthshire, east Carmarthenshire, the southern fringe of Brecknockshire, and the area centred on Wrexham. In May 1959 there were eighty-five firms which started in these areas of Wales some time since the beginning of 1945; they were to be found in or near forty-seven towns in eleven counties. The distribution by county is as follows: sixty firms, or 70 per cent. of the total, were in the four counties of Monmouthshire, Caernarvonshire, Denbighshire, and Flintshire; ten were in Anglesey, and fifteen scattered over the other six counties. Those in Monmouthshire are near the large market in the coalfield and have good communications with the Midlands, London, and the south of England. The advantages of being close to a coalfield apply also in Denbighshire and Flintshire, whereas Caernarvonshire has a more industralized background than the rural counties of North and mid-Wales.

The eighty-five new manufacturing firms employed 7,515 persons, of whom at least 2,819, or 39 per cent., were females.[2] The distribution of the number employed by county is shown in Table 18, and the size of firm by county in Table 19.

In only two counties are more women than men employed. In Merioneth, with three new factories, 73 per cent. of the employees are females, and in Anglesey there are 370 women to 334 men. The county with the largest number of female workers is Caernarvonshire, but it is under a third of the total employed in that county. Two-thirds of the employment provided by post-war manufacturing in 'rural' Wales is located in the three counties of Caernarvonshire, Flintshire, and Monmouthshire.

Only two of the new factories employ more than 500 people, and one of them has over 1,000; both are engineering firms. Six firms

---

[1] All firms with eleven or more employees have to register with the Board of Trade and the Ministry of Labour. In May 1959 we made a survey of ninety-two manufacturing firms in the non-industrial areas of Wales. The response was excellent; only one firm refused to supply statistics, and six had closed down. We wish to record our appreciation of the assistance given by the Research Department of the Board of Trade at Cardiff and our thanks to the firms who were kind enough to supply the information asked for. The statistical results are set out in such a way that no individual firm can be identified.

A review of the position in 1947 may be seen in Professor A. Beacham's *Industries in Welsh Country Towns*, Oxford University Press, 1951.

[2] Three firms did not state the number of male and female employees separately. The 39 per cent. relates to the total where this information was given.

have a payroll of between 200 and 499, thirteen have 100 to 199, forty-five have 25 to 99, and fourteen have 11 to 24. Further information is obtained by classifying the firms according to type of product,

TABLE 18

Wales: Employment in manufacturing in non-industrial areas, 1958, by county

County	Number of towns	Number of firms	Numbers employed				Percentage distribution
			Males	Females	Not classified by sex	Total	
Anglesey . .	5	10	334	370	—	704	9·4
Caernarvon .	10	17	1,544	686	—	2,230	29·7
Cardigan and Brecknock .	2	2	121	22	—	143	1·9
Denbigh . .	7	13	298	287	—	585	7·8
Flint . .	10	17	787	458	145	1,390	18·4
Montgomery .	3	5	330	334	—	664	8·8
Merioneth .	2	3	40	108	—	148	2·0
Radnor . .	2	2	48	18	—	66	0·9
Pembroke .	2	3	239	205	—	444	5·9
Monmouth .	3	13	720	331	92	1,143	15·2
TOTAL . .	46	85	4,461	2,819	237	7,517	100·0

SOURCE: Survey undertaken by the Economic Research Unit, Economics Department, University College, Cardiff, in May 1959.

TABLE 19

Wales: Size of manufacturing firms, in non-industrial areas, 1958, by county

County	Numbers employed							Total
	Under 10	11–24	25–49	50–99	100–99	200–499	Over 500	
Anglesey . . .	1	2	1	4	2	—	—	10
Caernarvon . . .	1	2	3	7	2	1	1	17
Denbigh . . .	—	4	5	2	2	—	—	13
Cardigan and Brecknock	—	—	1	—	1	—	—	2
Flint . . .	1	2	3	6	3	2	—	17
Montgomery . .	1	1	1	1	—	—	1	5
Merioneth . . .	—	—	2	1	—	—	—	3
Monmouth . . .	1	3	4	2	1	2	—	13
Radnor . . .	—	—	2	—	—	—	—	2
Pembroke . . .	—	—	—	—	2	1	—	3
TOTAL . . .	5	14	22	23	13	6	2	85

SOURCE: See footnote to Table 18.

TABLE 20

Wales: Size of manufacturing firms in non-industrial areas, 1958, by type of product

	Size of firm (numbers employed) by type of product											Total employed	
	Under 10	11–24	25–49	50–99	100–99	200–99	300–99	400–99	500–99	Over 1,000	Total	Number	Percentage distribution
Milk	—	—	1	1	1	—	—	—	—	—	3	187	2·5
Clothing	—	2	3	8	3	—	—	—	—	—	16	1,051	14·0
Metal manufacturing	—	2	—	1	—	—	—	—	—	—	3	95	1·3
Engineering	2	2	5	7	1	1	1	—	1	1	21	2,863	38·1
Optical instruments, rubber, and electronics	1	—	1	1	1	1	—	—	—	—	5	494	6·6
Chemicals	—	—	1	1	2	—	—	—	—	—	4	425	5·7
Plastics	—	—	3	—	—	—	1	—	—	—	4	447	5·9
Toys and games	—	2	—	1	1	—	—	—	—	—	4	294	3·9
Woodwork	1	4	—	—	—	—	—	—	—	—	5	77	1·0
Food	1	—	2	2	—	—	—	—	—	—	5	221	2·9
Paper, pulp, &c.	—	—	1	—	3	—	—	—	—	—	4	442	5·9
Miscellaneous manufacturing	—	2	2	—	1	1	—	—	—	—	6	452	6·0
Tiles, concrete, &c.	—	—	3	1	—	1	—	—	—	—	5	469	6·2
TOTAL	5	14	22	23	13	4	2	—	1	1	85	7,517	100·0

E

as shown in Table 20. By far the most important group is engineering which accounts for 38 per cent. of the total employment in these post-war 'rural' firms; the next prominent group is clothing, comprising 14 per cent. The relatively large firms are those turning out engineering products, optical instruments, plastics, and cement. Of the sixteen clothing firms, eleven have a pay roll of 50 to 199; two of the five new factories in Montgomeryshire—a county associated with the old Welsh cloth industry—manufacture clothing. All four firms using wood as their raw material employ less than twenty-four people, and they are found not in the heart of the country-side but close to industrialized areas.

The extent of the post-war growth in manufacturing in 'rural' Wales in relation to previous development can be roughly estimated. Our survey did not include firms which were in existence before 1 January 1945. According to Professor Beacham's analysis there were 110 firms employing 12,181 persons in Welsh country towns at the end of 1946.[1] Our survey has shown that in May 1959 there were at least eighty-five firms employing 7,517 workers which had been located in 'rural' Wales since 1945. This has been part of the relative growth of manufacturing analysed earlier in this chapter, and it is of unique interest as a diversifying element and a contribution towards maintaining the level of activity in areas where employment in agriculture is receding. The Mid-Wales Industrial Development Association, covering the five counties of Brecknock, Cardigan, Merioneth, Montgomery, and Radnor, is doing an important service in giving publicity to the advantages of these areas to industrialists. Recent research has demonstrated that rural labour is at least as efficient as urban labour;[2] from the strictly economic point of view, apart from social considerations, it is essential that entrepreneurs should have the fullest information about the potentialities of rural locations.

A NOTE ON POST-WAR PRODUCTIVITY

By J. PARRY LEWIS

THERE have been considerable changes in the relative productivity of Wales and the rest of the United Kingdom, and it is possible to examine some of these by considering the value of net output per

[1] A. Beacham, op. cit., p. 18.
[2] C. D. Harbury, *The Efficiency of Rural Labour*, University of Wales Press, Cardiff, 1958.

employee which is given for a large number of industries in the Censuses of Production for 1948, 1951, and 1954. We must bear in mind that only larger establishments are included, and that for some important industries (such as nylon) Welsh information is not given. Another important point is that a single name will often cover a multitude of operations, only a few of which may be performed in Wales. For example, the industry officially described as 'motor vehicles and cycles (manufacturing)' in Wales does not produce finished cars. Thus we must expect productivity to vary between regions for reasons that are often to do with the nature of the product rather than anything else, a low figure indicating simply that the region concerned is specializing in less remunerative branches of the industry rather than that it is less efficient.

With these points in mind we may consider the coal-mining industry. According to the Censuses of Production, the net outputs per employee in the three years 1948, 1951, and 1954 were valued at £385, £474, and £601. These data relate to average annual outputs at current prices and take no account of either price changes or of changes in the number of shifts worked. The importance of these factors which the census data neglect is shown by comparing these values with the actual output per man-shift in the three years concerned, namely, 0·85 ton, 0·92 ton, and 0·93 ton. Coal-mining is one of the very few industries for which absolute production figures are available on a regional basis. National figures for the value of output can often be deflated by the use of price indexes in order to assess real changes in productivity, but without making unwarranted assumptions about the exact nature of the product it is usually impossible to apply this technique to regional production figures. It is, however, possible to make some inter-regional comparisons by expressing the Welsh net output per employee as a percentage of the national net output per employee, and then examining the changes in this ratio (which we shall call the *productivity ratio*) between different years. The results are set out in Table 20A.

The net output per employee in coal-mining in 1948 was £385 in Wales and £478 in Great Britain. This gives a productivity ratio of 81 per cent. for that year; the Welsh miner added to the gross national product only four-fifths of the amount added by the British miner. In 1951 the ratio was 84 per cent., and in 1954 90 per cent. Both the product and the problems of coal-mining vary from one region to another, but the fact that the ratio was steadily increasing means that between them capital, management, and men combined to bring about a more rapid growth in productivity in Wales than in Great Britain as a whole.

TABLE 20A

Wales and Great Britain: Net output per employee in larger establishments of selected industries, 1948, 1951, and 1954

Industry	Wales Net output per employee (£)			Ratio of Welsh net output per employer to British net output per employee*		
	1948	1951	1954	1948	1951	1954
Coal-mining . .	385	474	601	81	84	90
Non-metalliferous mines and quarries other than coal, salt, and slate .	615	669	812	95	84	83
Slate quarries and mines	386	420	470	100	98	97
Brick and fire-clay .	502	580	661	100	96	88
Chemicals (general)† .	727	1,014	1,412	90	92	96
Iron and steel (melting and rolling) . .	610	910	1,563	103	108	144
Iron foundries	489	603	714	87	90	94
Steel sheets . . .	664	984	1,094	105	106	114
Tinplate . . .	620	949	1,244	101	101	102
Non-ferrous metals (smelting, rolling, &c.) .	647	1,016	909	97	112	97
Shipbuilding and repairing	597	597	714	120	113	111
Mechanical engineering (general)† . .	501	647	837	90	94	98
Electrical engineering .	312	546	873	63	87	110
Radio and telecommunications . . .	466	503	693	101	94	104
Motor vehicles and cycles (manufacturing). .	439	632	674	78	86	70
Railway carriages, wagons and trams† . .	564	576	728	128	115	120
Chain, nail, screw, and miscellaneous forgings	436	557	680	80	84	89
Hardware, hollow-ware, metal furniture, and sheet metal . .	400	567	679	80	92	93
Tailoring, dressmaking, &c.	261	297	379	70	76	84
Bread and flour confectionery . . .	590	575	649	102	106	103
Gas supply . . .	530	698	800‡	87	103	107‡
Electricity supply .	797	1,005	1,076‡	89	100	79‡

* The ratio compare Wales with Great Britain in 1948 but with the United Kingdom in 1951 and 1954.

† Changes in definition make comparisons less reliable in these industries.

‡ Excessive rounding in the Census of Production tables results in possible large errors in these terms.

SOURCE: Census of Production.

In the iron and steel (melting and rolling) industry, Welsh net output per employee rose from £610 in 1948 to £910 in 1951 and to £1,563 in 1954. These figures, of course, take no account of price changes, and their implications are fully discussed in Chapter VI; but it is interesting to note that the productivity ratios in these years were 103 per cent., 108 per cent., and 144 per cent. Changes of this kind may be due to greater effort, the introduction of more efficient plant, changes in the nature of the product, or a price increase of the Welsh product out of all proportion to that of the rather different English product. In this particular case the change was largely due to the introduction of superior technical methods.

Welsh iron foundries produce less per man, but once again the course of the productivity ratio, from 87 per cent. in 1948 to 90 per cent. in 1951 and then to 94 per cent. in 1954 shows that the difference is being steadily narrowed. In steel sheets the ratio was 105 per cent., 106 per cent., and 114 per cent. in the years concerned.

'Mechanical engineering (general)' is a term that obviously covers a vast range of activities, and the definition of the industry changed during the period under review. Even so, it is interesting to note from Table 20A that the ratio increased from 90 per cent. through 94 per cent. to 98 per cent. In electrical engineering the change was quite startling: from 63 per cent. in 1948, through 87 per cent. in 1951 to 110 per cent. in 1954. Whatever may be the reasons, the fact remains that the workers who in 1948 were adding to the gross national product only two-thirds of the amount added by their English counterparts were outpacing them six years later.

Table 20A shows similar data for the twenty-two industries (covered by the Census of Production) which employed at least 3,500 workers in larger establishments in 1951 and for which Welsh information is available. It will be seen that in 1954 the net output per employee was higher in Wales than elsewhere in ten of these twenty-two industries. Furthermore, in eleven of them productivity grew more rapidly in Wales than elsewhere, both between 1948 and 1951 and between 1951 and 1954. There were only four industries in which the productivity ratio fell during the two periods. Whether a Welsh worker has a higher productivity than an English worker producing exactly the same kind of good is a problem which is largely academic and can rarely be answered. What does seem clear is that in the majority of its sizeable industries Welsh productivity is growing more rapidly than elsewhere, and that already in many of these industries the net output per employee exceeds that of the English worker.

III

THE UNEMPLOYMENT CYCLE

By BRINLEY THOMAS

THE unemployment which aroused anxiety in 1958 and the early part of 1959 has to be seen in perspective against the background of the previous decade and, even more so, of the inter-war years.

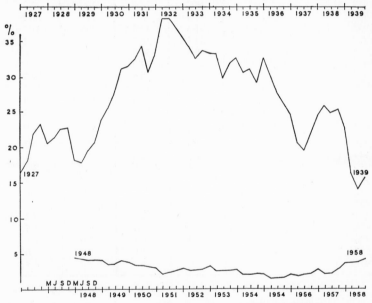

FIG. 12. Wales: Unemployment rates, 1927–39 and 1948–58.
SOURCE: Table 21.

The number recorded as out of work in Wales in December 1958 was 39,463, almost exactly the same as in December 1948, when it was 39,122. At the height of the boom in June 1955 the figure was 14,942, the lowest in the post-war period; as a proportion of the insured population this was 1·6 per cent. as against 1·0 per cent. for Great Britain.

The profound contrast with what happened between the wars is illustrated in Fig. 12, which puts the years 1948–58 in juxtaposition to the years 1929–39. The pre-war cycle in Wales went from 18 per cent. unemployment in the 'boom' of 1929 to 38 per cent. at the bottom of the depression in 1932, and then down to 14 per cent. in 1939. Since 1945 we have been living in a totally different world. In the slump of

TABLE 21

Wales: Percentage unemployment rates, 1927–39 and 1948–58

Year	March	June	September	December
1927	16·5	18·1	22·2	23·3
1928	20·7	21·3	22·7	22·8
1929	18·2	17·9	19·6	20·7
1930	23·9	25·5	27·7	31·2
1931	31·5	32·5	34·4	31·7
1932	33·1	38·2	38·2	37·2
1933	35·6	34·3	32·5	33·6
1934	33·3	33·2	29·7	31·9
1935	32·6	30·6	31·1	29·2
1936	32·6	30·1	27·6*	26·3
1937	24·7	20·7	19·6	21·9
1938	24·4	25·8	24·8	25·3*
1939	22·6	16·5	14·0	15·6
1948	4·6	4·4	4·2	4·3
1949	4·2	3·6	3·7	4·1
1950	3·9	3·5	3·5	3·4
1951	3·0	2·3	2·4	2·8
1952	3·0	2·7	2·7	3·0
1953	3·4	2·8	2·7	2·7
1954	2·8	2·1	2·1	2·3
1955	2·2	1·6	1·6	1·7
1956	2·0	1·9	2·0	2·3
1957	2·9	2·1	2·3	3·0
1958	3·6	3·7	3·7	4·1

* From Sept. 1936 until Dec. 1938 the unemployed covered by the Agricultural Scheme have been excluded.

SOURCE: Wales Office, Ministry of Labour.

1958 the rate of unemployment was only one-tenth of what it was in the slump of 1932; the cycle in 1948–58 had a very narrow amplitude between full employment (with 98·4 per cent. in work) and a 96 per cent. utilization of the labour supply.

As against a total of 39,463 persons out of work in Wales in the first week of December 1958 there were 6,107 unfilled vacancies; but 40 per cent. of the latter were for agricultural workers.[1] 27,245

[1] These were not genuine unfilled vacancies, for reasons given in section 3 of this chapter.

TABLE 22

Wales: Quarterly average percentage rates of unemployment and unfilled vacancies and excess demand for labour, 1948–58

Year	Quarter	Unemployment		Unfilled vacancies		Excess demand (4–2) (negative)
		Quarterly average percentage rate	Seasonally adjusted	Quarterly average percentage rate	Seasonally adjusted	
		1	2	3	4	5
1948	3	4·33	4·60	1·18	1·13	3·47
	4	4·30	4·32	1·00	1·09	3·23
1949	1	4·43	4·08	1·02	1·11	2·97
	2	3·87	3·94	1·17	1·04	2·90
	3	3·62	3·89	1·18	0·99	2·90
	4	4·08	4·10	0·89	0·98	3·12
1950	1	4·18	3·83	0·85	0·94	2·89
	2	3·70	3·77	1·03	0·90	2·87
	3	3·51	3·78	1·01	0·96	2·82
	4	3·49	3·51	0·96	1·05	2·46
1951	1	3·31	2·96	1·21	1·31	1·65
	2	2·52	2·59	1·48	1·35	1·24
	3	2·35	2·62	1·36	1·31	1·31
	4	2·75	2·77	1·16	1·25	1·52
1952	1	3·15	2·80	1·00	1·09	1·71
	2	2·86	2·93	1·19	1·06	1·87
	3	2·67	2·94	1·07	1·02	1·92
	4	2·96	2·98	0·93	1·02	1·96
1953	1	3·51	3·16	0·84	0·93	2·23
	2	3·11	3·04	0·92	0·79	2·25
	3	2·66	2·93	0·89	0·84	2·09
	4	2·73	2·75	0·77	0·86	1·89
1954	1	3·04	2·69	0·72	0·81	1·88
	2	2·48	2·55	0·98	0·85	1·70
	3	2·11	2·38	0·88	0·83	1·55
	4	2·25	2·27	0·84	0·93	1·34
1955	1	2·31	1·96	0·88	0·97	0·99
	2	1·73	1·80	1·28	1·15	0·65
	3	1·52	1·79	1·18	1·13	0·66
	4	1·76	1·78	1·05	1·14	0·64
1956	1	1·98	1·63	1·03	1·12	0·51
	2	1·91	1·98	1·21	1·08	0·90
	3	2·04	2·31	1·01	0·96	1·35
	4	2·22	2·24	0·75	0·84	1·40
1957	1	2·89	2·54	0·69	0·78	1·76
	2	2·45	2·52	0·90	0·78	1·74
	3	2·23	2·50	0·75	0·70	1·80
	4	2·79	2·81	0·55	0·64	2·17
1958	1	3·67	3·32	0·55	0·64	2·68
	2	3·80	3·87	0·62	0·49	3·38
	3	3·64	3·91	0·46	0·41	3·50
	4	4·12	4·14	0·40	0·49	3·65

NOTE: The unfilled vacancies exclude agricultural replacement needs.
SOURCE: Wales Office, Ministry of Labour.

men were registered as unemployed, or 3·98 per cent. of the insured population. Subtracting 2,996 temporarily stopped and casuals, we obtain a total of 24,249 wholly unemployed. Of these, 4,571 were disabled, accounting for 17 per cent. of the total on the register. If we take out the men who were 55 and over (4,389), we are left with 15,289 unemployed who were fit and under 55 years of age. These comprised just under two-thirds of the wholly unemployed or 2·2 per cent. of the insured population. Subtracting the 3,980 who had been without a job for less than four weeks, we arrive at a total of 11,309 men who were fit, under 55, and had been unemployed for four weeks or over; these accounted for 47 per cent. of the wholly unemployed. The corresponding proportion in June 1947 was 29 per cent., mainly because at that time as many as 12,102 men were registered as disabled.

1. The cycle of 1948–58

Fig. 13 gives a close view of unemployment and unfilled vacancies in Great Britain and Wales from 1948 to 1958. The spread between these two indexes can be regarded as a rough measure of the pressure in the labour market; when the percentage of unfilled vacancies is greater than the percentage of unemployed we have 'excess demand for labour'.[1] The indexes for Great Britain and Wales are shown in Fig. 14.

The shape of the curve for Wales reflects partly the successive balance of payments crises and partly the structural changes within the Welsh economy itself. The early years were dominated by the devaluation of sterling in September 1949 and the outbreak of the Korean War in June 1950. The British economy was stimulated to a high pitch of activity, with unemployment at 1·5 per cent. and falling to 1 per cent. at the peak of the boom; the effect in Wales was to bring unemployment down from 4·6 per cent. to 2·6 per cent. This potent stimulus was followed by a sharp reaction. In the second half of 1951 the overseas Sterling Area countries, with incomes swollen by high raw-material prices, were importing from North America at double the 1950 rate. Meanwhile the United States cut stockpiling purchases and took measures to check inflation; there was a sharp fall in the prices of raw materials. Between the first and second half

---

[1] The adjustments that need to be made to the primary data are explained by J. C. R. Dow and L. A. Dicks-Mireaux in 'The Excess Demand for Labour. A Study of Conditions in Great Britain, 1946–56', *Oxford Economic Papers*, vol. x, no. 1 Feb. 1958.

of 1951 there was a decrease of 50 per cent. in the dollar earnings of the outer Sterling Area. Swift measures to restrict imports and reduce home demand were taken by the British Government in order to stop the heavy drain on the gold and dollar reserves; the disinflation showed itself in a sharp rise in the British unemployment percentage

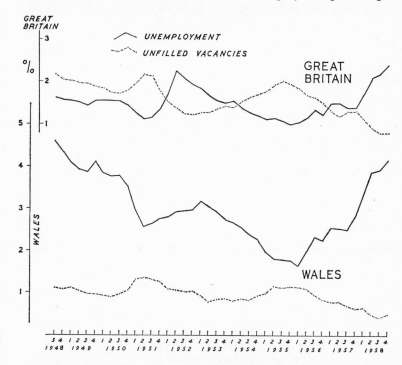

FIG. 13. Wales and Great Britain: Unemployment and unfilled vacancies as a percentage of insured population, 1948–58

SOURCE: Table 22.

in the first half of 1952. In Wales, however, the increase in unemployment was relatively slight. The main reason was that the bulk of the contraction in demand was felt by textiles and clothing, which accounted for almost two-thirds of the drop in total industrial production in 1952. A general slump in textile demand had set in all over the world in the early part of 1951 as a reaction to the abnormal buying caused by the outbreak of the Korean War; the labour employed in this industry in Britain was reduced from 1,747,000 in June 1951 to 1,553,000 in July 1952. This readjustment had hardly any effect on

Wales. Whereas British unemployment (allowing for seasonal influences) rose from 1·1 per cent. to 2·25 per cent. between the second quarter of 1951 and the second quarter of 1952, the Welsh figure moved from 2·6 per cent. to only 2·9 per cent. in the same period. For the rest of 1952 until the first quarter of 1953 Welsh unemployment continued to rise while the British figure was falling sharply.

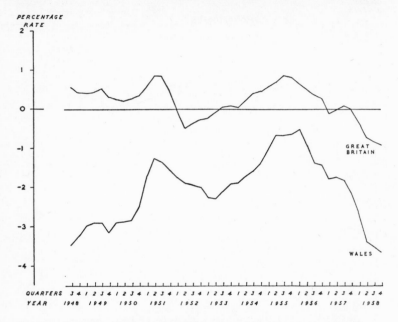

FIG. 14. Wales and Great Britain: Excess demand for labour, 1948–58

SOURCE: Table 22.

NOTE: The Great Britain figures are corrected for maldistribution of labour and misstatement of vacancies. SOURCE: Dow and Dicks-Mireaux, loc. cit., and continued in *The National Institute Economic Review*, vol. i, no. 1, 1959. The Wales figures are NOT corrected for maldistribution of labour or misstatement of vacancies apart from the elimination of agricultural replacement demand.

The interval in 1952–3 saw the disappearance of excess demand in Britain as a whole; an international margin was restored and the stage was set for further expansion. The Government gave a special fillip to private industrial investment through tax concessions on capital equipment and a relaxing of restrictions on industrial building. By 1955 a rapid expansion in private capital formation superimposed on heavy outlays in the public sector caused strong inflationary pressure; in the middle of that year unemployment in

Britain was down to 1 per cent. and in Wales it was 1·6 per cent., the lowest on record. Fig. 14 shows that the excess demand for labour in mid-1955 was of the same intensity as before the crisis of 1951. Once again the Government intervened to check demand by re-imposing hire-purchase restrictions, increasing purchase tax, and stiffening credit conditions. The Suez crisis in 1956 led to a strong wave of speculation against the pound which was repelled through prompt action by the International Monetary Fund in granting large drawing facilities. In the summer of 1957 there was another run on the pound and the bank-rate was raised to 7 per cent. and substantial curbs on public and private investment were introduced. By the end of 1958 unemployment in the country as a whole was up to 2·4 per cent. and in Wales to 4·1 per cent. The recession of 1957–8 was international in scope and was particularly marked in the United States.

There was an important difference between the experience of Wales and that of Great Britain. Almost every two years the British economy has been experiencing a see-saw within the narrow limits of 1 per cent. and 2·5 per cent. unemployment; a boom in home invest-ment with a sharp rise in imports and stocks brings inflationary pressure and sends the gold and foreign reserves down to danger point, and then domestic demand has to be checked, unemployment increases, imports and stocks are reduced, and exchange reserves rise again. These are short-run oscillations of a brimful economy. In Wales, on the other hand, there has been something faintly resembling the pre-war business cycle; the curve of demand for labour has a more pronounced swing than the corresponding curve for Great Britain. Starting from a trough of unemployment in 1948–9 coincid-ing with excess demand in Britain as a whole, the Welsh economy expanded rapidly in 1950, reacted slightly in 1951–2, surged forward to a peak of full employment in mid-1955, and then ran into a sharp depression which brought unemployment at the end of 1958 up to the level of ten years previously.

Since there was much slack to be taken up, the curve of labour demand rose much more steeply in Wales than in Great Britain in 1950–1; unemployment (seasonally adjusted) went down from 3·7 per cent. in June 1950 to 2·6 per cent. in June 1951, the absolute number falling by as much as 36 per cent. This first stage of the upswing had a strong effect on manufacturing, building, and iron and steel. The set-back between June 1951 and March 1953, when the number of unemployed rose by 52 per cent., was marked by a drastic decline in the demand for tinplate which sent unemployment in metal manufacture up from 719 to 5,503. The second stage of the upswing started in the middle of 1953 and reached a high peak in mid-1955. Demand for labour was intense in iron and steel (where unemployment fell from 5,503 to 587), manufacturing, miscellaneous services, and distribution. The 1951 peak of excess demand in the British economy as a whole was as intense as the peak of 1955, but in 1951 Wales still had a fair amount of surplus. It was not until the middle of 1955 that Wales reached a state of full employment, when excess supply of male labour disappeared. The recession between 1955 and 1958 was more severe in Wales than in the country as a whole.

2. Incidence of unemployment by industry and area

The rates of male and female unemployment in various industries at three significant dates—December 1948, June 1955, (the top of the boom), and December 1958 are shown in Tables 23 and 24.

TABLE 23

Wales: Rates of male unemployment in various industries, 1948, 1955, and 1958

Industry	Male unemployment as percentage of insured population		
	December 1948	June 1955	December 1958
Agriculture . . .	4·3	1·9	4·9
Mining and quarrying .	0·4	0·5	1·1
Metal manufacture . .	1·6	0·6	4·7
Engineering . . .	6·0	1·6	5·5
Building	9·2	3·0	9·2
Transport	3·0	1·2	2·6
TOTAL	4·1	1·4	4·0

Between December 1948 and June 1955 the number of men out of work in Wales fell from 28,400 to 9,400, and the number of women from 10,700 to 5,500; from the peak of the boom to December 1958 male unemployment rose from 9,400 to 27,200 and female from 5,500 to 12,200. Even when the demand for labour was most acute, as many as 3 per cent. of the men in the building trades were still out of work; indeed, one in five of the unemployed both in boom and slump have been building workers, the vast majority of whom are unskilled. Unemployment in the mining industry has been negligible. The outstanding feature brought out in Table 23 is the emergence of surplus labour in the iron and steel industry between 1955 and 1958, mainly caused by the closing of the old-fashioned tinplate mills. Unemployment among women remained fairly high in clothing, food, drink, and tobacco, and miscellaneous services even when the economy was

TABLE 24

Wales: Rates of female unemployment in various industries, 1948, 1955, and 1958

Industry	Female unemployment as percentage of insured population		
	December 1948	June 1955	December 1958
Clothing	4·0	2·8	6·3
Food, drink, and tobacco .	4·1	2·1	8·1
Distributive trades . .	3·0	1·7	3·5
Miscellaneous services .	5·0	2·4	5·7
TOTAL . .	4·6	2·1	4·5

running at a brisk pace; in these three industry groups the female unemployment rates in December 1958 had risen to 6·3 per cent., 8·1 per cent., and 5·7 per cent. respectively. These rates were higher than any of those for the male groups except building. The slump in Wales in 1958 was thus accentuated by three factors—the displacement of labour by technical reorganization in the iron and steel industry, the hard core of redundant building labour, and the cyclical sensitivity of certain occupations in which women were mostly employed.

The burden of unemployment has been very unevenly distributed over various parts of Wales. Table 25 shows the rate in each county in 1948, 1955, and 1958. In June 1948, when 4·5 per cent. of the total insured population were unemployed, the counties of Montgomery, Radnor, Flint, Merioneth, Caernarvon, Denbigh, and Pembroke had rates well below the Welsh average, whereas the counties of Carmarthen and Brecknock were well above. With the exception of Montgomery and Radnor, every county in Wales had heavier unemployment than the average for Great Britain. At the top of the boom in mid-1955, when the Welsh rate was 1·6 per cent., not much above

TABLE 25

Wales: Unemployment rates by county, 1948–58

County	June 1948			June 1955			June 1958			December 1958		
	% Unemployment	% of mean for Wales	% of mean for G.B.	% Unemployment	% of mean for Wales	% of mean for G.B.	% Unemployment	% of mean for Wales	% of mean for G.B.	% Unemployment	% of mean for Wales	% of mean for G.B.
Anglesey .	4·8	106	240	7·1	443	710	9·5	257	475	12·5	305	521
Caernarvon	3·1	68	155	3·1	192	310	7·0	189	350	9·2	224	383
Merioneth	2·8	56	140	2·1	131	210	3·2	86	160	6·4	156	267
Denbigh .	3·0	66	150	1·2	75	120	2·9	78	145	4·2	102	175
Flint .	2·2	48	110	0·8	50	80	3·1	84	155	3·8	93	158
Montgomery and Radnor .	1·0	22	50	1·4	87	140	3·4	92	170	2·8	68	117
Cardigan .	2·8	56	140	2·5	155	250	3·2	86	160	4·3	105	179
Carmarthen	5·7	126	285	1·8	112	180	6·4	173	320	5·7	139	238
Pembroke .	2·6	57	130	1·5	93	150	4·7	127	235	5·0	122	208
Glamorgan	5·1	113	255	1·7	106	170	3·8	102	190	4·1	100	170
Monmouth	3·8	84	190	1·1	68	110	3·1	84	155	3·7	90	154
Brecknock	5·8	129	290	2·4	150	240	3·8	102	190	4·6	112	192
Wales .	4·5	100	225	1·6	100	160	3·7	100	185	4·1	100	170
Great Britain .	2·0	—	100	1·0	—	100	2·0	—	100	2·4	—	100

the 1·0 per cent. for Great Britain, the experience of some counties diverged markedly. The rate of unemployment in Anglesey (7·1 per cent.) was four times the average for Wales and seven times the average for Great Britain. Whereas in 1948 Anglesey and Caernarvon together accounted for 5 per cent. of the Welsh unemployed, in 1955 they had as many as 13 per cent. of them. In the slump conditions of December 1958, the counties of Glamorgan and Monmouth, which used to be the black spots, did better than most other areas.

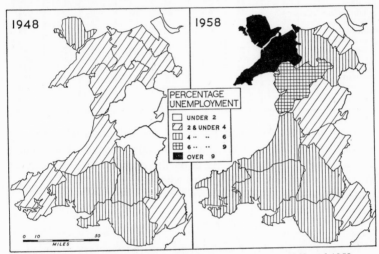

FIG. 15. Wales: Percentage unemployment by county, 1948 and 1958.

There have also been significant differences between various regions of Great Britain as shown in Table 26. In 1948, when there was strong demand for labour in Britain as a whole, the old depressed areas—the North, Scotland and Wales—were still lagging well behind; the rate of unemployment in Wales was actually nine times higher than in the booming Midlands and 2¼ times the national average. When the British economy was at full stretch in mid-1955, the spread of regional unemployment rates became much narrower, and the Welsh rate (at 1·6 per cent.) was fairly near the national average and only three times the figure for the Midlands. The growing strength of the Welsh economy became evident in the depression of 1958; at the end of that year when British unemployment was almost at its post-war maximum, the figure in Wales was only twice as high as in the Midlands, whereas it had been nine times

TABLE 26

Great Britain: Unemployment rates by region, 1948–58

Division	June 1948		June 1955		June 1958		Dec. 1958	
	% unemployment	% of mean for G.B.	% unemployment	% of mean for G.B.	% unemployment	% of mean for G.B.	% unemployment	% of mean for G.B.
London and South-east	1·5	75	0·6	60	1·2	60	1·4	58
Eastern	1·0	50	0·7	70	1·4	70	1·7	70
Southern	1·5	75	0·7	70	1·4	70	1·8	75
South-western	1·5	75	0·9	90	1·8	90	2·6	108
Midland	0·5	25	0·5	50	1·5	75	1·8	75
North Midland	0·5	25	0·5	50	1·5	75	1·8	75
East and West Ridings	1·0	50	0·7	70	1·9	95	2·3	95
North-western	2·0	100	1·4	140	2·6	130	3·3	137
Northern	3·0	150	1·6	160	2·1	105	3·2	133
Scotland	3·0	150	2·2	220	3·5	175	4·4	183
Wales	4·5	225	1·6	160	3·7	185	4·1	170
Great Britain	2·0	100	1·0	100	2·0	100	2·4	100

as high in 1948. Although the old depressed areas were still relatively unlucky, there were signs that adversity was being more equally shared by different parts of the country. The capacity of Wales, Scotland, and the North to withstand cyclical set-backs had materially improved.

3. The problem of Anglesey

Anglesey, with 13 per cent. of its insured workers recorded as unemployed at the end of 1958, stood out as the new depressed area in Wales. Its pattern of occupations is, of course, different from that of the country generally.

From Table 27 we see that in Anglesey agriculture employs 10 per cent. of the labour as against 3 per cent. in Wales, and transport absorbs 17 per cent. as against 9 per cent. in Wales. Miscellaneous services are relatively well represented, but manufacturing is not. There are no metal or mining industries.

A major cause of surplus labour is the rapid growth of productivity due to mechanization in agriculture. Since 1946 tillage acreage has declined steadily and there has been a shift to livestock and milk production. The expansion of output between 1945 and 1958 was associated with a fall of 20 per cent. in the number of persons engaged in agriculture (including farmers' sons and daughters)—from 2,927 to 2,300. In December 1958 16 per cent. of the unemployed were agricultural workers, i.e. 234 in number, and yet at the very same time there were 217 unfilled vacancies in the farms of the county. The reason for this odd state of affairs is interesting and deserves to be explained in full. When a farmworker reached the age for National Service, he was granted deferment of call-up until a *suitable* replacement was found, and the Ministry of Labour recorded an unfilled

TABLE 27

Anglesey and Wales: Industrial distribution of the insured
population, 1958

Industry	Anglesey	Wales
	(%)	(%)
Agriculture	9·9	2·7
Shipbuilding and repairing . .	3·3	0·7
Building and contracting . .	9·1	6·5
Gas, water, and electricity . .	3·0	2·2
Transport	16·6	9·0
National and local government .	9·8	7·0
Miscellaneous services . . .	11·3	7·0
General manufacturing . .	19·0	23·0
Distributive trades . . .	8·4	9·8
Professional services . . .	8·2	9·4
Mining and quarrying . . .	0·9	13·8
Metal manufacturing . . .	. .	9·0
TOTAL	100·0	100·0

vacancy in agriculture. As the army recruit was often the farmer's son, the farmer was keen to keep the vacancy 'unfilled'; thus any agricultural worker submitted by the Employment Exchange was found to be *unsuitable*. The procedure could be repeated at intervals, but the vacancy remained until the young worker reached the upper age limit for National Service. Thus, the unfilled vacancies recorded in agriculture are not vacancies at all: they record the number of young farmworkers eligible for National Service. An adjustment for this anomaly brings the rate of unemployment in Anglesey in December 1958 down from 13 per cent. to 11 per cent. Some of the implications of this situation may be noted. If the young workers had to do National Service, the number of older men unemployed would be reduced accordingly. It is possible that, in order to justify his claims to keep his son at the farm, the farmer may understaff. If there were no National Service, some agricultural labourers out of work would in fact be employed. Some young workers remained on the land merely to avoid National Service: in the absence of such commitments some may have sought more remunerative jobs in industry, thus leaving vacancies to be filled by older agricultural workers.

The rest of the unemployment was mainly in building (23 per cent. of the total), manufacturing (17 per cent.), and miscellaneous services (15 per cent.). No less than one-third of the men attached to the building trade were out of work. One in four of all the unemployed men in the island had been without a job for over a year.

Anglesey's population fell from 51,700 in 1921 to 46,100 in 1954; since then it has slowly increased and reached 52,100 in 1958. There was a net gain by migration of 1,700 in the years 1931-57 as against a net loss of 7,000 in the period 1911-31. The county is classified as an area of high unemployment under the Distribution of Industry (Industrial Finance) Act of 1958, which empowers the Treasury to make grants or loans to assist industrialists who wish to locate in such areas. A number of new firms employing about 2,400 persons have been established in the county since 1939.

TABLE 28

Employment in firms located in Anglesey, 1939–58, classified by industry

| | Number of insured workers | | |
Industry	Males	Females	Total
Agriculture	89	33	122
Forestry	37	. .	37
Engineering, chemicals, &c. . . .	1,061	155	1,216
Toys	57	164	221
Clothing	11	168	179
Distribution (milk marketing) . .	61	10	71
War Office and Air Ministry establishments	589	8	597
TOTAL	1,905	538	2,443

SOURCE: Anglesey County Council, *Memorandum on the Unemployment Position in the County of Anglesey—December, 1958.*

The island has been able to attract a moderate amount of private investment in engineering and chemicals, and the other mainstay has been the work provided by military establishments. The relatively high incidence of genuine unemployment may be partly due to greater immobility of labour than before the war. Anglesey lacks the location advantages of, say, Flintshire; it has to take the consequences of increased efficiency in agriculture without having enough manufacturing to redress the balance.

4. *Labour mobility and excess demand*

Under full employment there can be extreme scarcity of labour in some areas and a dearth in others. In the post-war period the pressure of excess demand has been felt most in the Midlands, London, and

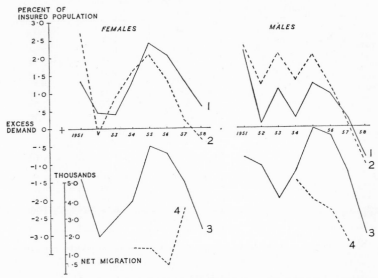

FIG. 16. Indexes of regional excess demand for male and female labour, 1951–8.
1. London, South-eastern, and Southern Regions. 2. Midlands and North Midlands. 3. Wales. 4. Net migration from Wales.
SOURCE: Table 29.

the South-east, while in Wales and Scotland 'excess supply' has been the rule. We know far too little about the adjustment that takes place through movements of labour between areas of low and high pressure in the course of short-period oscillations in a high-employment economy. In Fig. 16 we have plotted the indexes of excess demand for male and female labour in the Midlands, London–South-east, and Wales over the period 1951–8, with the net outward migration from Wales, 1954–7. The figures are shown in Table 29.

Throughout the years 1951–8 there was excess demand for females in London–South-east and excess supply in Wales. From 1952 to 1955–6 the upswing in Wales brought about a sharp reduction in

TABLE 29

(a) Regional indexes of excess demand for male and female labour, 1951-8

		Females		
Year		London, South-east, Eastern, and Southern	Midlands and North Midlands	Wales
		(%)	(%)	(%)
1951	. . . . .	+1·33	+2·70	−1·41
1952	. . . . .	+0·46	−0·18	−3·04
1953	. . . . .	+0·40	+0·81	−2·54
1954	. . . . .	+1·26	+1·57	−2·00
1955	. . . . .	+2·36	+2·09	−0·51
1956	. . . . .	+2·11	+1·34	−0·74
1957	. . . . .	+1·33	+0·22	−1·58
1958	. . . . .	+0·62	−0·29	−2·86
		Males		
1951	. . . . .	+2·20	+2·30	−0·82
1952	. . . . .	+0·14	+1·22	−1·10
1953	. . . . .	+1·15	+2·08	−2·00
1954	. . . . .	+0·26	+1·30	−1·21
1955	. . . . .	+1·21	+2·00	−0·01
1956	. . . . .	+0·87	+1·18	−0·25
1957	. . . . .	+0·25	+0·14	−1·30
1958	. . . . .	−0·84	−1·02	−3·04

NOTE: Indexes of excess demand expressed as a percentage of insured population.

(b) Net migration of insured labour from Wales to London, South-east, Southern, and Eastern England and Midlands

		London, South-east, Eastern, and Southern	Midlands, and North Midlands	Total
Period		Females ('000)		
1953–4	. . . . .	−0·8	−0·5	−1·3
1954–5	. . . . .	−0·6	−0·6	−1·2
1955–6	. . . . .	−1·1	+0·7	−0·4
1956–7	. . . . .	−3·6	+0·1	−3·5
		Males ('000)		
1953–4	. . . . .	−3·6	−1·4	−5·0
1954–5	. . . . .	−1·1	−2·8	−3·9
1955–6	. . . . .	−1·3	−2·0	−3·3
1956–7	. . . . .	−1·9	+0·4	−1·5

SOURCES: *Ministry of Labour Gazette*. Wales Office, Ministry of Labour.

unemployment and almost eliminated excess supply, and the net efflux of women declined. It is interesting to note that there was a big and uninterrupted increase in the excess demand for women in the Midlands–South-east region from 1952 to 1955, whereas for male labour there was a break in the pressure of demand in 1954. Then, as the downswing proceeded, there was a sudden rise in the net outward migration from Wales mainly to London and the South-east in 1956–7. This may be explained by the fact that the receiving area in that year had a fairly substantial excess demand, while conditions for female employment were relatively deteriorating in Wales. We have already seen that in some of the most buoyant manufacturing industries in Wales there was a substitution in favour of male labour.

The trough in demand for male labour in Wales in 1953, coinciding with a peak in the Midlands–South-east, is explained by the tinplate slump in South Wales. By 1955 excess supply was virtually eliminated in Wales and the level of activity remained almost as high in 1956. In the years 1951 to 1955 the pressure of demand in the Midlands was more acute than anywhere else in the country, and the reaction afterwards was correspondingly sharp. The statistics of net migration show that the outward movement of males from Wales to the Midlands–South-east decreased steadily from 1953–4 to 1956–7. We must not read too much into these figures, but for what they are worth they indicate that, by the time the general recession came, Wales had developed considerable powers of resistance.

IV

AGRICULTURE

By ANNE MARTIN

THE contribution which agriculture makes to the Welsh economy is not, in quantitative terms, very different from that which it makes to the economy of the United Kingdom as a whole. In 1950 the agricultural sector contributed about 5 per cent. of the National Product, both in Wales and in the whole United Kingdom.[1] The industry in Wales, however, absorbed 7·4 per cent. of the working population in 1951 compared with 4·7 per cent. in England. The relative size of the Welsh agricultural sector, measured by the employment it provides is, then, considerably larger than the English, but smaller than the Scottish (9·8 per cent.), and much smaller than the Northern Irish (nearly 17 per cent.). By this criterion, Wales must be considered not only a more advanced economy than Scotland or Northern Ireland, but also than Belgium or the United States, where agriculture still absorbs some 12 per cent. of the working population. If, however, we exclude the industrial area of South Wales, we see more justification for the popular belief that the Celtic populations are much more preoccupied with guarding their flocks and tilling their soil than is the English population. Excluding Glamorgan and Monmouthshire, 15·8 per cent. of the working population in Wales were engaged in agriculture in 1951.

Wales contains some 9 per cent. of the land in agricultural use in the United Kingdom, although under 6 per cent. of the arable area. In 1951, the Welsh agricultural labour force (including farmers) accounted for 7 per cent. of the total numbers employed in agriculture in the United Kingdom. The Welsh contribution to the agricultural output of the United Kingdom is greatest in the sphere of livestock production; in 1950 nearly 10 per cent. of all the cattle in the kingdom were in Wales and nearly 19 per cent. of the sheep. In total, however, Wales probably contributes under 4 per cent. of the value of the total

[1] The figure for Wales is based on E. Nevin, *The Social Accounts of the Welsh Economy, 1948 to 1952*, University of Wales Press, Cardiff, 1956.

agricultural output of the United Kingdom,[1] since much of her soil is relatively poor and the altitude and high rainfall of much of the country makes it unsuitable for the production of cereals for human consumption.

It is not, of course, possible to put any quantitative measure on the contribution which the rural way of life makes to the whole complex of Welsh culture. The common experience of all industrial economies is that, as the proportion of the working population engaged in agriculture falls, so the townsman becomes more concerned, on non-economic grounds, to slow down the rate of exodus from the country-side. It seems clear that the existence of a rural sector of a certain minimum size results in very real external benefits to the community as a whole; and the smaller the sector becomes, the lighter is the burden on the rest of the community entailed by maintaining it at its present size, even if this be too large if judged by purely economic criteria. Without being unduly romantic, it appears true that farming is a profession which encourages self-reliance and independence of judgement; and these two qualities are worth making considerable effort to preserve in a primarily industrial economy where relatively few people retain the power of responsible decision in their working lives. Such arguments apply with particular force to Wales, partly because the typical pattern of Welsh agriculture is of the isolated farmstead rather than the nucleated village. Such a pattern emphasizes even more strongly the quality of self-reliance, both in work and in leisure, and also makes the way of life of many Welsh farmers more distinctive than that of their English counterparts. There may be those who feel that to attempt to retard the rural exodus under such conditions is to try to preserve an 'ethnological Whipsnade', but, on the whole, Welsh public opinion appears to take a more positive view of its rural culture, valuing particularly highly both its strongly religious character, and its preservation of Welsh as a living language.

Between the census dates of 1931 and 1951, the total numbers engaged in agriculture in Wales fell from about 91,000 to about 77,000, i.e. by 15 per cent. The proportion of the working population in agriculture in the whole of Wales fell from 10 per cent. to 7 per cent. while, excluding Glamorgan and Monmouthshire, the fall was from 21 per cent. to 16 per cent. This is a smaller decline than in England in the same period, where the numbers in farming fell by

[1] Calculation based on Nevin, op. cit.

23 per cent., partly, no doubt, reflecting the better prospects of industrial employment in England during this period. The rate of emigration from the land, as Professor Thomas has shown,[1] is ultimately dependent on the rate at which other sectors of the economy are expanding, whether in Wales, England, or overseas. This is an illustration of a world-wide phenomenon. Incomes per head in agriculture are nearly always below those in other sectors of the economy, so that the long-term trend, in a mobile economy, is towards a transfer of labour from farming to other occupations. The rate at which the transfer proceeds, however, is seldom steady, since, in time of depression, industrial jobs are not available for new-comers. In times of prosperity, even though prices and incomes rise faster in the agricultural sector than in the industrial, the drift off the land gathers speed because alternative employment is plentiful. We may, in fact, get the apparently paradoxical result that, in times of severe agricultural depression, the numbers on the land actually increase, as the unemployed from the towns return to the farms with which they retain some family connexion. In other words, the pull of the industrial sector (expressed negatively as a push in times of depression) is of more effect in transferring labour than the push off the land.[2]

Since 1931 the total number of agricultural holdings in Wales has fallen from 60,410 to 52,816 in 1958, i.e. by nearly 13 per cent. The fall in the total amount of land in agricultural use (including rough grazings) was just under 13 per cent. in the same period; the exodus from the land over the past twenty-five years has resulted in some amalgamation of holdings into larger units as well as in the abandonment of farm land or its surrender to other uses. If the acreage of agricultural land at each date is divided by the total number of holdings, the resulting acreage available per holding is about 75 in 1931, as against 73 in 1958.

The most striking difference between the agriculture of Wales and that of England is in the relative importance of grassland and of livestock production. Wales is, by comparison, a country of high rainfall, high altitude, low insolation, and poor soil. About 41 per cent. of the land area of Wales lies under 500 ft. above sea-level, 32 per cent. between 500 and 1,000, 20 per cent. between 1,000 and 1,500, and 7 per cent. above 1,500. Most of the country has an annual rainfall of over 40 in., while about 45 per cent. of the area has over

[1] Chapter I.
[2] Cf. T. W. Schultz, *Agriculture in an Unstable Economy*, McGraw-Hill, New York, 1945, pp. 129–30, for comparable American experience.

50. In the highland areas, rainfall rises to 80 in. and above. Generally speaking, in British conditions, only areas with 30 in. of rainfall or less are favourable to cereal production, so that the rainfall pattern of Wales, together with its altitude, which implies a correspondingly short growing season, accounts for the very great dependence of the Welsh farmer on grass and on livestock.

Table 30 shows clearly the similarity between the basic structure of farming in Wales, Scotland, and Northern Ireland, and the difference between the Welsh and the English pattern.

TABLE 30

Wales, Scotland, Northern Ireland, and England: Use of agricultural land, 1959

| | Percentage of total agricultural land | | | |
	Wales	Scotland	Northern Ireland	England
Tillage	8·9	9·2	12·4	35·9
Rotation grass . . .	12·9	10·7	19·4	16·5
TOTAL ARABLE . . .	21·8	19·9	31·8	52·4
Permanent grass . . .	45·7	6·0	40·0	38·1
Rough grazings . . .	32·5	74·1	28·2	9·5

Table 31 shows the great importance in Wales of oats and mixed corn, both used mainly for livestock feeding. In the high proportion of these crops in the total tillage area, Welsh agriculture is again much more akin to that of Scotland and Northern Ireland than to that of England.

TABLE 31

Wales, Scotland, Northern Ireland, and England: Use of tillage area, 1959

| | Percentage of tillage area* | | | |
	Wales	Scotland	Northern Ireland	England
Wheat	5·0	5·5	0·6	28·1
Barley	10·0	14·7	7·7	31·9
Oats	35·4	46·6	56·2	11·4
Mixed corn	10·9	0·4	1·2	2·1
Potatoes	6·8	9·6	27·2	6·3
Turnips, swedes, and mangolds	7·0	16·4	1·6	3·8

* These percentages do not total 100, since only the major crops are included.

The most striking feature in Table 32 is the much higher density of sheep on the agricultural land of Wales than in that of the other three countries. Table 33 is of particular interest in showing the large rise in cattle numbers since the 1930's, due in part to the stimulus to milk production given by the Milk Marketing Board schemes.

TABLE 32

Wales, Scotland, Northern Ireland, and England: Density of livestock carried, 1959

	Acres (including rough grazings) per unit			
	Wales	Scotland	Northern Ireland	England
Cattle	3·1	8·1	2·6	2·1
Sheep	0·7	1·8	2·5	1·2

TABLE 33

Wales: Changes in cattle and sheep populations, 1920–59

	Cattle		Sheep	
Year	Numbers	Acres per unit*	Numbers	Acres per unit*
	('000)		('000)	
1920	774	5·6	3,331	1·3
1930	785	5·7	4,102	1·1
1939	856	5·3	4,648	1·0
1946	928	4·8	4,050	1·1
1959	1,127	3·4	5,196	0·7

* Including rough grazings.

Table 34 illustrates the effect on the pattern of Welsh agriculture of the changes in the general economic situation over the past thirty-nine years. During the depressed period of the 1920's and 1930's, the proportion of arable land fell by nearly one-half, most of the gain being in the area devoted to rough grazing. The fall was much greater in the area devoted to tillage than in that used for rotation grass. This change implies a movement out of relatively highly-capitalized enterprises into 'dog-and-stick' farming as the farmer's economic position worsened and his accumulated reserves vanished. The wartime ploughing-up campaign, together with the high prices for agricultural products, more than doubled the proportion of the arable area between 1939 and 1946. It is clear from the figures that this increase was achieved entirely by ploughing up permanent grassland. By 1959 the arable area was just a little above the 1920 proportion,

TABLE 34

Wales: Changes in the use of agricultural land, 1920–59

Year	Percentage of total agricultural land				
	Tillage	Rotation grass	Total arable	Permanent grass	Rough grazing
1920 . . .	13·6	6·8	20·4	45·9	33·7
1930 . . .	8·0	6·7	14·7	47·0	38·3
1939 . . .	6·5	5·4	11·9	47·9	40·2
1946 . . .	16·1	10·3	26·4	31·0	42·6
1959 . . .	8 9	12·9	21·8	45·7	32·5

and the reversion of some 78 per cent. of Welsh farmland to permanent grass and rough grazing reflects the waning of the war-time objective of the production of the maximum number of calories per acre, and its replacement, to some extent, by the laws of comparative advantage. It has been estimated that, in the 1930's, sales of livestock and its produce accounted for some 95 per cent. of the total receipts of the Welsh farmer,[1] and it may be that much the same figure would be true today.

The amount of agricultural land available per holding is very much the same in Wales as in England, being 79 and 80 acres

TABLE 35

Wales and England: Size distribution of agricultural holdings, 1958

Size of holdings (acres)	Wales		England	
	% of holdings	% of acreage*	% of holdings	% of acreage*
Under 20	40·1	6·9	44·8	4·1
20–100	45·2	46·5	32·1	23·5
100–500	14·6	45·8	21·6	58·8
500–1,000	0·07	0·8	1·3	9·7
1,000 and over . . .	..	..	0·2	3·9

* Excluding rough grazings. This percentage relates to 1957.

[1] A. W. Ashby and I. L. Evans, *The Agriculture of Wales and Monmouthshire*, University of Wales Press, Cardiff, 1944, p. 72.

respectively. The size distribution of the holdings is, however, markedly different in the two countries. In Wales, 55 per cent. of the agricultural land, excluding rough grazings, is distributed amongst the 85 per cent. of the holdings of under 100 acres. In England, on the other hand, the 77 per cent. of holdings of under 100 acres covers only 27 per cent. of the agricultural area, while nearly 72 per cent. of the land is distributed amongst the 23 per cent. of holdings of over 100 acres. Table 36 shows that there has been little change in the size-pattern of Welsh holdings since before the war, although there has been a slight tendency for farms to become larger. In 1939, 88·3 per cent. of Welsh holdings were of less than 100 acres, whereas the corresponding figure for 1958 is 85·4 per cent.

TABLE 36

Wales: Changes in the size distribution of holdings, 1939–58

Size of holding (acres)	% of total holdings	
	1939	1958
1–5	13·8	12·5
5–20	31·5	27·6
20–50	24·0	24·5
50–100	19·0	20·8
100–150	6·3	8·7
150–300.	5·2	5·4
300–500	0·3	0·5
Over 500	0·03	0·07

As might be expected from the smaller average size of farm, Welsh farming is much less dependent on hired labour than is English. According to the *1951 Census of Population*, there were about 41,500 farmers in Wales at that date, and 29,800 farm workers, or 14 farmers for every 10 farm workers. In England there were about 249,400 farmers and 551,000 farm workers, or 22 workers for every 10 farmers.

The distribution of holdings between tenants and owner-occupiers is much the same in Wales as in England. In 1941 63 per cent. of the holdings in Wales, covering 61 per cent. of the area, were farmed by tenants; the corresponding figures for England were 66 per cent. of the holdings and 67 per cent. of the area. Since the war, there has been a considerable movement towards owner-occupancy in both countries, as the low level of rents, compared with the costs of maintenance, has made land-ownership a steadily less attractive proposition; it is probable that about half the holdings and half the land are now farmed by owner-occupiers, in Wales as in England.

It is difficult to generalize meaningfully about the efficiency of any country's agriculture. It is certain that Welsh land is, on the whole, poor, the Welsh climate and topography relatively unfavourable to agriculture, and that hill farming is a relatively unprofitable occupation. These facts do much to explain why, although Wales provides nearly 7 per cent. of the agricultural employment in the United Kingdom, her agriculture contributes less than 4 per cent. to the total value of British agricultural output.

TABLE 37

Wales and England: Crop yields (cwt. per acre), 1920–9 to 1948–55

Period	Wheat		Barley		Oats		Potatoes	
	Wales	Eng-land	Wales	Eng-land	Wales	Eng-land	Wales	Eng-land
1920–29 . . .	14·9	17·7	13·1	15·7	14·4	14·9	5·3	6·3
1934–43 . . .	16·5	18·5	14·1	16·8	14·0	16·5	6·3	7·1
1939–48 . . .	16·9	18·8	14·6	17·6	14·4	17·0	5·9	7·1
1948–55 . . .	18·4	21·6	17·0	20·2	16·0	19·1	5·8	7·5
Percentage increase from beginning to end of period . . .	23·0	22·0	31·0	29·0	23·0	28·0	9·0	19·0

Table 37 shows clearly the inferiority of the Welsh yields per acre to the English, for the four crops chosen. It also shows, however, considerable improvement in yields since the 1920's. This should be attributed mostly to increased use of lime and fertilizers and to improved methods of harvesting. The Welsh farmer has certainly not been slow to invest in machinery. Measured by the number of tractors in use, Welsh farming is now more mechanized than English. In 1959 Wales had one tractor for every 20 acres of arable area, against one for every 33 in England. Between 1942 and 1959 the number of tractors in Wales increased six times compared with a rise of four times in England. It is, indeed, likely that some Welsh farmers have mechanized not wisely but too well. The Welsh Agricultural Land Sub-Commission, in its report on mid-Wales, stated: 'it was found during the investigation that most farmers who had any cultivations to perform had their own tractors. In many cases this meant gross over-capitalisation in machinery. There is a pride of possession attached to a tractor which impels a farmer to acquire one even if this means restricting other expenditure on the farm.'[1] It should be added, however, that in an area of high rainfall and restricted periods of good weather at harvest-time, a tractor in individual ownership may represent a very sound insurance; under such conditions, there are obvious difficulties in the way of the co-operative use of machinery or of the development of private contracting.

It is a general belief that Welsh (and Scottish) farmers are relatively poor compared with those in England. Indeed, to the layman the term 'marginal farm' has acquired a geographical overtone, implying farms in the western and northern 'margins' of the United Kingdom. In parenthesis, we may pause to deplore the use of the word 'marginal' to mean, roughly, 'poorest'. In economic usage, the term should apply to the land which will first go out of agricultural use when the industry's fortunes take a turn for the worse. It is, however, well known that much of the poorest land in the United Kingdom is likely to remain in some agricultural use, of however unambitious a kind, even through the most severe economic depression. This is simply because such land, being relatively remote from industrial centres, is likely to have no profitable alternative use. Also, the man who farms it is likely to have relatively little free capital and little non-agricultural experience or aptitude, and will therefore be likely to tighten his belt and stay in farming for as long as possible. It may well be the richer farmer, with more capital behind him, and possibly possessing wider experience, more education, and greater adaptability, who will, in fact, leave farming first in times of adversity. And, when the balance tilts in favour of the industrial use of land against the agricultural, it is the land nearest to large centres of population which is usually absorbed first, irrespective of its agricultural advantages of fertility or of location. Rather oddly, the layman and the administrator appear to have swallowed whole the notion of perfect mobility of factors of production which is found, as an expository device, in economics textbooks. This has led them to equate poor land, in terms of its infertility, and poor farmers, in terms of their net income, with that land which is only just worth cultivating, and those farmers who only just find it worth their while to stay in agriculture; forgetting, in both cases, to ask what the

[1] Welsh Agricultural Land Sub-Commission, *Mid-Wales Investigation Report*, H.M.S.O., Cmd. 9631, 1955, p. 32.

alternative employments are, and what are the difficulties in the way of diverting the land, or the farmers, to them. Indeed, if the word 'marginal' were really appropriate, implying the possibility of instant movement to another industry, the poverty of farmers, in Wales or elsewhere, would scarcely be a proper matter for social concern, since it could be assumed that those farmers who remained in agriculture at a considerably lower reward than that of industrial workers, did so entirely voluntarily.

TABLE 38

Net income per farm in various farming areas, 1958

Type of farming area	Net income per farm	
Dairying	(£)	(£)
England and Wales . . .	1,262	
Wales		987
Livestock, with substantial dairying		
England and Wales . . .	1,180	
Wales, poor land		663
Wales, better land		1,340
Predominantly livestock		
England and Wales . . .	1,270	
Wales, poor land		994
Wales, better land		1,281
All types of farms		
England and Wales . . .	1,555	

It is difficult, with the data that are available, to arrive at any accurate measure of the relative poverty of the Welsh farmer. However, using Nevin's figure for the Welsh income from self-employment in agriculture in 1950,[1] and dividing it by the number of farmers in Wales at 1951, it appears that the average return to the Welsh farmer was about £346. At that date, the average annual earnings of a non-specialized farm worker in Wales were probably not below £300. If we treat the available figures for the United Kingdom in the same way, we find that the average farmer's return was £1,233[2] or rather over three times the Welsh figure. A further impression of the Welsh farmer's unfavourable position can be obtained from the figures based on the Farm Management Survey,[3] giving the

---

[1] E. Nevin, op. cit. This figure includes rents.
[2] Also including rents.
[3] *Farm Incomes in England and Wales, 1958*, H.M.S.O., 1960.

financial results from a sample of farms in different areas and of different types. In interpreting these figures it must be remembered that livestock farming takes up by far the greater part of the Welsh agricultural area, and that the poor land is much in excess of the better. The National Farm Survey figures (Table 39) also enable us to see how net income per farm increases rapidly with farm size. Some 94 per cent. of Welsh farms are of under 150 acres, compared with 85 per cent. of English, so that some of the blame for the relative poverty of the Welsh farmer can be ascribed to the small size of his farm, although more is due to the poverty of his land.

TABLE 39

Wales and England: Average net income per farm, 1958

Size of farm	Net income per farm	% of holdings in each size group	
		Wales	England
(acres)	*(£)*		
50 and under .	548	64·6	61·4
50–100 . .	885	20·8	15·6
100–150 . .	1,197	8·7	8·5
150–300 . .	1,667	5·4	10·1
300–500 . .	2,786	0·5	3·1
500 and over .	3,669	0·07	0·3

The policy of the United Kingdom Government towards agriculture, in particular towards the smaller and poorer farms, has played, since the 1930's, a vital part in determining the economic situation of Welsh agriculture. For Wales the most significant legislation of the pre-war period was the creation of Milk Marketing Boards in 1933. 'The turn of the economic tide for Welsh agriculture generally came with the establishment of the Milk Marketing Board and the commencement of the collection of liquid milk from farms previously dependent on the rearing of cattle and sheep and the sale of butter.'[1] The basis of the Milk Marketing Scheme was the division of the milk market into two separate compartments, for liquid milk and milk for manufacture, the establishment of a minimum price within each market in each area, and the payment to producers of a 'pooled' price from the receipts in the two markets, irrespective

[1] *Mid-Wales Investigation Report*, p. 16.

of the use to which the individual producer's milk was put. This system resulted in the dairy farmers of the east of Britain, who sold on the liquid market, subsidizing those of the west whose output normally went largely for manufacture. The increased profitability of dairy farming in the western regions, including Wales, caused a sharp increase in the amount of milk sold off farms in these areas. Apart from this effect of regional income redistribution, the virtually guaranteed price which each farmer now received for his milk, irrespective of the size of his own output, naturally acted as a stimulus to milk production all over the country. Between 1934 and 1939, the number of registered milk producers in Wales nearly doubled, rising from 10,510 to 20,223. By 1947 the figure had risen by a further 40 per cent. to 28,000. During the 1950's the number has declined slightly, to under 25,000 in 1959, reflecting, in part, the success of the Government's efforts to encourage beef production at the expense of milk. As in other parts of Britain, the security of the monthly milk cheque, and the attraction of a farm enterprise with a relatively fast turnover of capital, may have induced a greater concentration in milk production than is in the farmer's long-term interests. Referring to mid-Wales, the Welsh Agricultural Land Sub-Commission reported that 'there has in recent years been a widespread development of milk production on small poorly equipped farms, many of them on wet land not suited to dairying. The occupiers are by now dependent on the larger turnover and the monthly milk cheque and it would, therefore, be hard for them to revert to their previous practice of livestock rearing.'[1]

The Welsh farmer may derive considerable benefit from the joint attempt of the Fatstock Marketing Corporation and the National Farmers' Union to provide the beef-producer with some equivalent to the monthly milk cheque. In 1958 they started jointly a new company known as Fatstock Finance Ltd. This company operates two credit schemes: firstly, it grants short-term credit to finance the buying of store cattle, whereby the grazier may receive a loan of up to 75 per cent. of the purchase price; and, secondly, it will make advances, paid in monthly instalments, of up to 60 per cent. of the cost of fattening the cattle. The two forms of credit together may amount to an advance to the individual farmer of anything between £100 and £5,000 over a period of three to twelve months. The advances, together with an interest payment which varies with the

[1] *Mid-Wales Investigation Report*, p. 24.

general level of interest rates, and a sum to cover administrative costs, are deducted from the farmer's price for his cattle when he comes to sell it to the Fatstock Marketing Corporation. Since Welsh farmers have been very quick to see the advantages of trading through the Corporation, it is likely that they will be equally quick to obtain the benefits of these new credit schemes.

The agricultural legislation passed since 1945 has beyond question been of enormous benefit to Welsh agriculture, whether or not we consider that the total sum spent on supporting agriculture in the United Kingdom has been apportioned as wisely as it might have been. Under the Agriculture Act of 1947, guaranteed prices, or minimum prices, announced in advance, have been assured for most farm products; and under a wide variety of Acts, grants have been payable to farmers in respect of specific operations or investments and, in some cases (e.g. the Hill Farming Subsidies), in respect of their relatively unfavourable situation. The British system of support to agriculture has often been criticized on the grounds that to rely largely on subsidizing the prices of the farmer's output inevitably means that most of the taxpayer's money goes to the farmers with the highest production, and the highest net income, who least need the help. In 1955 it was estimated that farmers in the top third income group in the United Kingdom received some 60 per cent. of the total subsidies on cereals, milk, pigs, and eggs; applying the same proportion to the other subsidies and grants, it appeared that the 'upper third', whose net income averages £2,000 per head, received an average total of subsidy payments of £1,125, while the remaining two-thirds, with an average net income of only £417, received an average of £375 in subsidies.[1] These figures also bring out, however, the relatively much greater importance of the subsidies to the poorer groups, to whose net income they contribute nearly 90 per cent. compared with 56 per cent. to that of the richer groups. In any case, British agricultural policy since the war has not been primarily intended to redistribute income between farmers: the emphasis has been largely on stimulating production, both in total and of particular products, and, where this is the aim, subsidy payments made on the basis of output achieved is a logical way of achieving it. Grants for particular farming operations, or investments, may also achieve this end, but are inevitably costly to administer, as well as being rather uncertain in result. However, it must be stressed

[1] E. M. H. Lloyd, *The Times*, 20 and 21 July 1955.

that the greater *security* which post-war legislation has given to agriculture has, in itself, been of the greatest benefit to the poorer farmer, since it is he who finds the burden of economic uncertainty hardest to bear. The smaller are the farmer's reserves, the greater is his caution when faced with price uncertainty, and the more likely he is to restrict investment in his farm below the economic optimum, whether this investment be made by using his own resources or by borrowing. Wherever this is so, the community as a whole, as well as the producer, suffers from the consequent misallocation of resources between the various sectors of the economy. Thus, any system of forward prices in agriculture is likely to be particularly helpful in stimulating investment by those farmers who were formerly particularly vulnerable to the keen and unpredictable winds of the free market.

It seems probable that total payments to Welsh farmers in 1958–9, in the form of direct subsidies and production grants, came to almost £14 million or some 6 per cent. of the total of agricultural support in the United Kingdom.[1] Of this total, about 52 per cent. was in the form of grants for particular purposes, or to farms in particular areas, and 48 per cent. in the form of direct subsidy payments on production. In recent years, agricultural legislation has been designed to help in particular the poorer farmer, or at least those farmers who are considered capable, with assistance, of raising their net income to a level not below that of an agricultural worker. The Agriculture Act, 1957, provided for the payment of grants to farmers to cover up to one-third of the cost of the major permanent improvements which were not already covered by other legislation. Theses grants are intended particularly for the erection and improvement of farm buildings, the building and improvement of farm roads, and the reclamation of land. A major aim of these grants is to make small farms 'viable', i.e. capable of yielding a net income to the farmer which, after reasonable provision for the return on his capital, will not be less than that of a farm worker, and, in the White Paper preceding the Act, special emphasis was laid on the possibility of amalgamating small holdings into units of an economically efficient size. Between 1957 and 1959 the number of Farm Improvement Schemes approved in Wales rose from 281 to 5,492 and the total cost from £162,000 to £2,897,000.

In 1959 the new Small Farmers' Scheme came into operation,

---

[1] See note at the end of this chapter for the method of calculation.

designed to make once-for-all capital grants to farmers for approved schemes which, it is hoped, will permanently raise their economic efficiency. The Scheme lays particular emphasis on the improvement of grassland farming, in order to reduce the heavy dependence of British agriculture on imported feeding-stuffs, and is thus of particular significance for Wales. To be eligible for grants under this Scheme, farms must be of between 20 and 100 acres (excluding rough grazing), provide fewer than 450 'standard man-days' of labour at present, but be capable, after completion of the Farm Plan, of providing at least 275. These restrictions serve to exclude both very small farms (many of which will be farmed as a part-time occupation) and highly intensive enterprises, such as horticulture or poultry farming. The Farm Plans, which must be approved by officers of the National Agricultural Advisory Service, are to cover a period of three to five years, and the total of grant is limited to a maximum of £1,000 to any one farm, payable in instalments over a three-year period. The present system of Marginal Production Grants is to be abolished, but temporary assistance will be given to farmers who previously received these grants, but are ineligible for payments under the new scheme. It has been estimated that some 9,000 Welsh farms will be eligible, out of a total of some 90,000 in the United Kingdom as a whole. It is hoped that the Scheme will be a more productive way of helping small farmers than the alternative of continuing to spend very large sums on the price support of milk, pigs, and eggs, the typical mainstays of the small farmer, which have all been in surplus supply in recent years.

It should not be thought that the Welsh farmer has been content to sit back and allow the Government to spoon-feed him. On the contrary, the Welsh record in agricultural co-operation is outstanding, and Welsh farmers have given strong support to the Fatstock Marketing Corporation, a non-profit-making company which organizes the slaughter and sale of fatstock on the farmer's behalf. In 1955 the Agricultural Co-operative Societies in Wales had a total membership of over 54,000, about one-fifth of the membership in the whole United Kingdom.[1] Membership had risen by 93 per cent. since 1939. The total value of sales by all Welsh Co-operative Societies was nearly £12 million in 1955, nearly six times their value in 1939. In 1955 Wales had forty-five general purpose societies, twenty-seven

[1] Some farmers are members of more than one society, so that this figure considerably over-states the number of individual members.

specialized marketing societies, eleven service societies (including five for grass-drying), and five farming societies. The importance of the Fatstock Marketing Corporation to the Welsh farmer may be illustrated by the fact that in 1956–7 the Fatstock Marketing Corporation slaughtered some 40 per cent. of all cattle killed in Wales, and some 25 per cent. of all sheep. Wales supplied about 14 per cent. of the total cattle killed by the Fatstock Marketing Corporation in the United Kingdom, and about 25 per cent. of the sheep.[1]

What, then, are the prospects for Welsh agriculture? We should expect the movement out of farming to continue, as agricultural productivity per head continues to rise and, on purely economic grounds, we should welcome such a movement, particularly if it is accompanied by the amalgamation of the smallest holdings into larger and better-planned farms. The rate at which this exodus proceeds will depend, very largely, on the level of employment maintained in the industrial sector of Great Britain in general and of Wales in particular. The prospects for those who remain in agriculture should be promising, since the demand for home-produced beef, in particular, is a buoyant one, and one which the Government is particularly anxious to see met. However, there is a very real problem of agricultural poverty in Wales, to which it is difficult to see a short-term answer: reduction in the number of farmers does not come mainly through established farmers abandoning their occupation, but through a reduction in the number of recruits to agriculture, mostly farmers' sons, an essentially long-term trend. Wales must have a high proportion of those farmers who cannot, within the limits of reasonable assistance, achieve a net income equivalent to that of an agricultural employee.[2] This may be because their farms are too small, and unsuitable for amalgamation, too infertile, or too unfavourably located, or because they lack the personal capacity to make good in an industry which is not subject to rapid technical change. If our agricultural policy continues in its present direction, towards restoring contact with normal economic forces, some of these 'problem farmers' may well be squeezed off their farms. Since the Government's policy for the past twenty years has been, in

[1] These figures are estimates, since it is necessary to exclude some English counties from the Corporation's North-western area.

[2] In the area studied by the Welsh Agricultural Land Sub-Commission, covering parts of the counties of Cardigan, Montgomery, and Radnor, it was found that, of a total of 1,404 farms, 57 per cent. were too small to yield any net profit over and above the agricultural wage and interest on invested capital. *Mid-Wales Investigation Report*, p. 25.

effect, to encourage these farmers to stay on the land, despite the high cost of their production, their fate is a proper matter for social concern, and should be recognized as a national responsibility.

This responsibility could not be handled by the Ministry of Agriculture as such. It would concern employment; it would concern pensions; it would concern housing; it would concern, obviously, finance. It would call for close collaboration, across departmental demarcation-lines, in a general national scheme. The Agriculture (Small Farmers) Bill is a small, bright beacon which may eventually light the way for a new and more sensible agricultural policy. For that very reason it calls for a pendant measure to help off the land men who are still farmers only because they have benefited so long from a much less sensible one.[1]

NOTE

Method of estimation of total subsidy payments to Welsh agriculture, 1958–9

I.	Direct subsidy payments	£'000
	Cereal deficiency payments	1,081
	Egg subsidy	1,500*
	Fat cattle subsidy	146
	Fat sheep subsidy	3,090
	Pigs subsidy	445
	Milk subsidy	408†
		£6,670

II.	Production grants (1959)	
	Ploughing grants	859
	Agricultural lime scheme	737
	Fertilizer subsidies	1,311
	Marginal production grants	190
	Calf subsidy	1,616
	Hill cattle	183*
	Hill cows	533
	Hill farming and livestock rearing improvement schemes .	1,415
	Farm water-supply	42
	Farm ditching	59
	Tile drainage	62
	Silo subsidy	203
		£7,210
	TOTAL OF I AND II	£13,880

SOURCE: Unless otherwise stated, *Digest of Welsh Statistics, 1959,* H.M.S.O., 1960.

* Ministry of Agriculture, Fisheries, and Food.

† Estimated by applying to the total United Kingdom subsidy the ratio of Welsh to total milk sales off farm.

[1] *The Economist,* 8 Nov. 1958.

V

COAL

LESLIE JONES

THE South Wales coalfield, covering an area of about 800 square miles, extends from Pontypool in the east to St. Bride's Bay in the west, varying in width from 16 to 20 miles in the east to about 2 miles at its western end. The reserves are estimated at 9,500 million tons in seams of 24 inches and upwards at depths of not more than 4,000 ft. South Wales is richly endowed with anthracite, steam, and bituminous varieties. The latter occur in a narrow belt along the eastern and southern outcrops mainly in Glamorgan and Monmouthshire, steam coals are found in the central region, and anthracite is in the western zone, which is the only major source of supply in the United Kingdom. About one-quarter of the output now comes from seams of under 3 ft., 45 per cent. from those of between 3 and 5 ft., and the remainder from those over 5 ft. Most of the coal is mined at a depth of between 2,000 and 3,000 ft.

The review of long-run trends in Chapter I brought out an inverse relation between phases of growth in the Welsh and the English coalfields. Periods of intensive investment in steam-coal pits in South Wales coincided with major upswings in the export sector of the British economy, and the most pronounced expansion in bituminous coalfields in England took place during major upswings in home construction. This pattern disappeared after the First World War. Between the wars all British coalfields suffered stagnation and instability, with low wages, and bitter strife. Output in South Wales, which had been 57 million tons in 1913, was 35 million in 1939. After the fall of France in 1940 and the suspension of exports, there was a dramatic contraction, and by 1945 production was down to 20 million tons. The number employed, which had been 270,000 in 1920, was barely 100,000. The amount of coal exported from South Wales was down to where it was in 1860; in the lifespan of one man it had gone full circle from 1·7 million tons to a peak of 35 million and then down again to 1·6 million, as illustrated in Fig. 18.

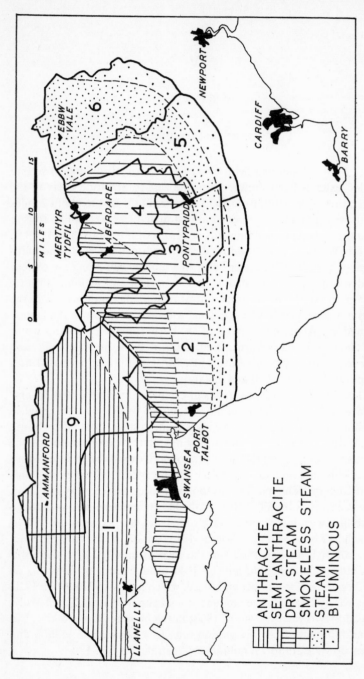

ANTHRACITE
SEMI-ANTHRACITE
DRY STEAM
SMOKELESS STEAM
STEAM
BITUMINOUS

Fig. 17. The South Wales coalfield.

1. *Nationalization*

In 1946 the mines were nationalized and the National Coal Board was given the task of '. . . . securing the efficient development of the coal-mining industry'. This inaugurated a new phase of planned reorganization and development. South Wales was grouped with the

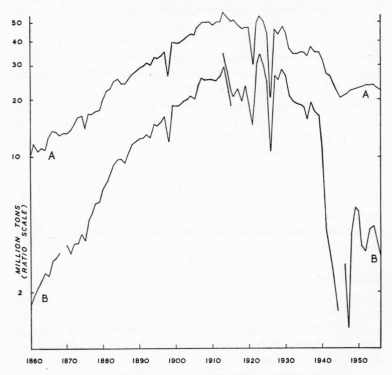

Fig. 18. South Wales: Coal production and exports, 1860–1957.

NOTE: A, output. B, exports. 1860–1913, exports only. 1913–57, exports and foreign bunkers.

Somerset and Forest of Dean coalfields to form the South Western Division, and more than 300 undertakings, ranging from some of the largest collieries in Britain to small hillside levels employing half a dozen or fewer men, were taken over. For administrative purposes the South Wales Coalfield was divided into seven areas.[1]

The industry in 1946 was in a very weak condition. It was threaded

[1] Originally the No. 1 (Swansea) Area covered the whole of the western sector of the coalfield and included 34 anthracite and 15 dry steam collieries. It proved too large and was later divided into the No. 1 (Swansea) Area and the No. 9 (Neath) Area.

through with old workings, and of the 155 pits employing more than 250 workers only 11 were less than 25 years old; the majority were over 40 and some were even a 100 years old. Most of the easily worked seams had been exhausted; few of the pits had been designed for mechanical coal-cutting. In 1944 only 32 per cent. of the output was cut by machines and only 54 per cent. mechanically conveyed. Power-supply, haulage, ventilation, and coal-preparation plant were inadequate, and the concentration of resources had been scarcely attempted. Thus, when the collieries were vested in the National Coal Board, there was ample scope for reconstruction. No less than 21 per cent. of the capital investment proposed in the *Plan for Coal* was to be devoted to the South Western Division.

The plan envisaged an expenditure of £97 million on capital investment in South Wales in the period 1950–65; by 1956 output was to increase to 32 million tons, of which 6 million tons would be anthracite. The reconstruction was to include four new pits and five reorganizations in the anthracite area, and three new pits and twenty-five reconstruction schemes in the steam and bituminous area. In the years 1947–55 actual capital expenditure on collieries and associated activities amounted to £51 million, and by 1955 several of the reconstruction schemes were well advanced and six new sinkings were in progress, but they were taking longer than was originally estimated.[1] Plans had to be revised, and the estimated output was reduced from 32 million to under 26 million tons. Nevertheless, to achieve this much-reduced output it was expected that capital expenditure in the South Western Division would have to be £148 million.[2] Thus, for the period 1950–65 the estimated expenditure of £191 million is £81 million greater than was forecast in the *Plan for Coal* for an increase in output of less than 3 million tons. The volume of investment is among the highest for any division and the expected rise in output is among the lowest; this emphasizes not only the difficult mining conditions but also the quality of coals required, which include the medium-volatile coking variety, the basic requirement of the rapidly expanding South Wales steel industry.

2. Developments since 1948

The war-time decline in production was arrested in the immediate post-war years, and since then the steps taken by the Coal Board to

---

[1] National Coal Board, *Investing in Coal*, London, 1956, p. 6.
[2] Ibid., ch. 3.

improve efficiency have raised output and increased productivity, but not to the extent expected. Table 40[1] shows the main trends in the coalfield since 1947. The gradual improvement has not been uniform throughout the coalfield, but this is not surprising when one realizes how widely the pits vary in age, natural conditions, and the type of coal mined. The main differences between areas are summarized in Tables 41 and 42.

TABLE 40
Trends in the South Wales coal-mining industry, 1948–59

Year	Number of mines	Output* (raised and weighed) (52 weeks)	Saleable output as a percentage of raised and weighed output	Percentage of raised and weighed output mechanically cut	Number of wage-earners†	Output per man-shift (overall)
		('000 tons)			('000)	(cwt.)
1948 .	203	26,500·1	83·9	n.a.‡	106·2	16·7
1949 .	173	27,286·8	82·6	41·3	102·6	17·8
1950 .	164	27,808·3	82·0	44·7	99·1	18·7
1951 .	163	28,541·3	81·0	46·6	100·3	18·4
1952 .	157	28,995·1	80·7	47·9	103·0	18·3
1953 .	155	29,115·1	81·5	50·7	101·5	18·5
1954 .	153	29,532·1	79·4	53·3	101·3	18·7
1955 .	149	28,704·9	78·9	59·3	98·2	18·7
1956 .	143	28,693·0	78·1	62·4	98·1	18·9
1957 .	141	29,256·9	76·8	63·6	98·6	19·1
1958 .	131	28,164·0	74·7	65·2	92·5	19·5
1959 .	118	26,346·7	73·7	65·4	88·2	20·3

* Output for 1948 relates to calendar years.
† At end of year.
‡ n.a. = not available.
Source: Statistical Section, South Western Division, National Coal Board.

(a) Output

Raised and weighed output increased by 3 million tons between 1948 and 1954; it declined slightly in 1955 but recovered again during the next two years only to fall rapidly after 1957: by 1959 output raised and weighed was less than it had been in 1948. It is not easy to compare the output performance of individual areas because of boundary changes in 1950 and 1953, but it is clear that there was a much bigger improvement in bituminous than in steam and anthracite districts. In 1959 the amount of coal raised and weighed in the No. 1 (Swansea) Area and the No. 9 (Neath) Area was less than it was twelve years earlier, whereas in the No. 4 (Aberdare) Area it was very much higher.

[1] Tables 40–42 follow the pattern adopted by Professor A. Beacham to show national trends and differences in regional characteristics. See Duncan Burn, ed., *The Structure of British Industry*, Cambridge University Press, 1958, vol. i, ch. 4.

TABLE 41

South Wales coal industry: Area analysis, 1948

Area	Number of mines	Output*		Percentage of raised and weighed output†		Number of wage-earners†		Output per man-shift	
		Raised and weighed	Saleable	Mechanically cut	Mechanically conveyed	Total	Face‡	Overall	Face
		('000 tons)	('000 tons)					(cwt.)	(cwt.)
No. 1 (Swansea) . .	66	4,467·6	3,891·4	27·0	51·5	22,156	7,817	14·2	40·1
No. 2 (Maesteg) . .	24	2,901·4	2,766·1	27·6	79·8	12,782	5,641	17·1	40·9
No. 3 (Rhondda) . .	32	4,547·7	3,856·3	23·8	94·0	18,110	8,521	16·7	36·7
No. 4 (Aberdare) . .	23	3,485·9	2,755·0	36·1	82·5	12,440	5,760	17·5	39·9
No. 5 (Rhymney) . .	18	5,147·7	3,893·7	59·7	92·5	16,129	7,340	19·6	46·4
No. 6 (Monmouthshire) .	40	5,999·9	5,111·8	59·4	81·6	24,570	11,106	16·3	34·8
South Wales .	203	26,550·2	22,274·3	41·3	81·0	106,187	46,185	16·7	39·1

NOTE: No. 9 (Neath) Area was not created until 1950. Prior to that the majority of anthracite collieries were part of the No. 1 (Swansea) Area.

* Calendar year.
† At end of year.
‡ Data not available for 1948; the figures given relate to 1949.
SOURCE: Statistical Section, South Western Division, National Coal Board.

TABLE 42

South Wales coal industry: Area analysis, 1959

Area	Number of mines	Output*		Percentage of raised and weighed output		Number of wage-earners†		Output per man-shift	
		Raised and weighed	Saleable	Mechanically cut	Mechanically conveyed	Total	Face	Overall	Face
		('000 tons)	('000 tons)					(cwt.)	(cwt.)
No. 1 (Swansea) .	15	1,777·0	1,448·8	45·5	79·6	6,987	2,636	19·6	52·9
No. 9 (Neath) .	21	2,340·0	1,695·6	55·8	88·4	10,342	3,679	15·2	44·1
No. 2 (Maesteg) .	18	3,198·4	2,813·6	66·8	98·8	11,950	5,243	21·5	50·2
No. 3 (Rhondda) .	15	4,038·9	2,868·6	42·5	98·2	13,703	5,958	19·8	47·2
No. 4 (Aberdare) .	15	4,499·2	3,144·3	66·3	95·4	12,734	5,063	22·8	59·3
No. 5 (Rhymney) .	12	4,640·1	3,129·9	75·3	99·9	13,819	5,871	20·8	51·5
No. 6 (Monmouthshire).	22	5,853·2	4,316·1	81·8	99·8	18,694	7,833	20·9	52·5
South Wales .	118	26,346·7	19,416·9	65·4	96·3	88,229	36,283	20·3	51·3

* 52-week year.
† At end of year.

SOURCE: Statistical Section, South Western Division, National Coal Board.

The amount of saleable coal produced, after reaching a peak of 23·6 million tons in 1952, has fallen steadily. As a proportion of the output raised and weighed it decreased from 84 per cent. in 1948 to 74 per cent. in 1959 when saleable output was approximately 3 million tons less than in 1948. This was due to two factors: an increase in the amount of dirt filled out with the coal, partly on account of the extended use of machines and partly through working a higher proportion of narrower and poorer seams, and secondly, the wider use of coal-cleaning plant. The contribution of the various areas to saleable output varied, but here again comparison is complicated by boundary changes. The combined output of the Rhymney, Aberdare, and Monmouthshire areas increased by over a quarter of a million tons; there was a slight improvement in Maesteg, but elsewhere output fell. This is a reversal of inter-war experience when output and employment were maintained much better in the west of the coalfield than in the east.

Before the war fluctuations in output reflected the demand for coal; a decline in demand was fairly quickly translated into falling output. Since 1939, however, demand has exceeded supply at ruling prices and the low level of production has been due to factors other than trade conditions.

(b) Manpower

The factors governing output are the number of workers, the average number of shifts worked per man-year, and the output per man-shift. Between 1900 and 1920 the number of miners in South Wales increased from 148,000 to 272,000: by 1936 the industry's labour force had contracted to 126,000. Early in the war there was some loss of manpower to the armaments industry, but the most serious drain followed the collapse of France in 1940 when many collieries were closed down and others worked part-time. Men left the industry in large numbers; in 1940 alone over 3,000 underground workers—about 50 per cent. of them from the coal face—left to join the services, and experienced workers were also leaving for other industries.[1] After 1941 the Essential Works (Coalmining Industry) Order, the steps taken to direct ex-miners back to the pits, and the drive to recruit men from other industries succeeded in checking the loss of manpower for a time, but towards the end of 1943 wastage again exceeded recruitment and continued to do so until the end of the war.

[1] Regional Survey Reports, *South Wales Coalfield*, H.M.S.O., 1946, p. 79.

When the war ended the most pressing need was to rebuild the coalfield's labour force. Juveniles and workers at the coal face were urgently required, and offers of underground employment were made even to men who had no previous experience. Recruitment at this time benefited from a steady inflow from three sources. Ex-miners were returning from the forces, over 4,500 in 1946. Between 1946 and 1948 about 17,000 ex-miners came back from other industries, and in 1948 2,000 foreign workers, mostly Poles, were placed in the mines of South Wales. By 1949, however, these sources had been exhausted. Meanwhile, the number of boys entering the industry fell off sharply when the school-leaving age was raised in 1948.

Yet even in this period recruitment was not enough to offset the heavy wastage. In South Wales pneumoconiosis is a major industrial problem; in the years 1945–7 nearly 12,000 miners were certified as suffering from this disease and were suspended from mining. After 1948 a man was no longer suspended unless the disease was accompanied by tuberculosis; those diagnosed as having pneumoconiosis were allowed to continue underground in 'approved conditions'. Arrangements were also made to assist men who had left the industry before July 1948 to return if they wished to do so. But, more important, since 1948 the number diagnosed has been falling and many found to be suffering from the disease are only slightly disabled, which shows that the campaign for dust suppression is having results. By 1953 all coal faces which were not naturally wet were receiving some form of treatment. The drain on manpower through other causes continued. After 1949 there was an abrupt change and, as Table 40 shows, a marked decline in the labour force in mining took place over the five years 1947–51.

In contrast to the preceding two or three years, 1952 was a much better year. The recession in trade eased the labour market, but the gain to mining was due to less wastage rather than to better recruitment. Fewer men left the industry and the decline in the number between 20 and 30 years of age was arrested. This good fortune proved to be temporary, and as industrial production expanded after 1953 there was a continued and severe shortage of mining labour in South Wales until the end of the decade.

Post-war fluctuations in manpower show that recruitment and wastage are greatly influenced by the level of industrial production. When output is high there is strong competition for mining labour in those areas of the coalfield where new industries have been

introduced.[1] Thus the Coal Board finds itself in an unenviable position.
When industry is booming it cannot find the men to mine sufficient
coal to meet the demand, and when manpower is available it is not
finding it easy to sell all the coal produced.

One of the effects of the loss of personnel over the years has been
to increase the average age of colliery workers. Table 43 shows that
in the period 1949–59 there was some increase in the number of

TABLE 43

Age distribution of wage-earners on colliery books, South Wales
National Coal Board mines only, 1949 and 1959*

Age-group	1949	1959
Under 16 . . .	765	741
16 and under 21 . . .	5,919	6,798
21 and under 26 . . .	11,728	7,764
26 and under 31 . . .	12,769	6,815
31 and under 41 . . .	24,531	19,298
41 and under 51 . . .	22,987	20,450
51 and under 65 . . .	20,513	23,938
65 and over	3,393	2,425
TOTAL	102,605	88,229

* At end of year.

SOURCE: Statistical Section, South Western Division, National Coal Board.

miners under 21; but the number between the ages of 21 and 41
fell by 15,000. Men in this age-group tend to be attracted to factory
employment. The biggest contraction, and it was very pronounced
after 1953, occurred in the age-group 26 to 31. Thus when wastage is
increasing the industry tends to lose young experienced workers, the
most active element in its labour force. This cannot fail to have an
adverse effect on productivity.

(c) Absenteeism

Absenteeism has an obvious bearing on output, and no aspect of
coal-mining has received more attention in recent years.[2] It is higher
in some years than in others but there has been a sharp increase since
1954. The average rate has gone up from 12·1 per cent. in 1948 to

[1] In 1955, for example, there was a severe shortage of labour in the Aberdare and
Rhymney areas. National Coal Board, *Annual Report, 1955*, p. 34.
[2] See William W. Haynes, *Nationalisation in Practice: the British Coal Industry*,
Bailey Brothers & Swinfen, London, 1953, pp. 161–4.

17·0 per cent. in 1959, and from 14 to 18 per cent. at the face. The rise in recent years has been more marked in South Wales than in the country as a whole. There is no simple explanation, but the fact that it tends to be heaviest in areas where productivity and earnings are highest supports the view that there is some connexion between the two. The figures themselves do not fully convey the effect on production and efficiency, since the incidence of absenteeism is not evenly

TABLE 44

Percentage absenteeism in the coal-mining industry, 1948 and 1959: South Wales, by area

Area	Overall		Face	
	1948	1959	1948	1959
No. 1 (Swansea)　.　.　.　.	9·8	14·4	11·5	16·1
No. 9 (Neath)　.　.　.　.　.	—	16·7	—	16·7
No. 2 (Maesteg)　.　.　.　.	9·0	16·2	10·3	16·9
No. 3 (Rhondda)　.　.　.　.	9·7	18·8	11·4	20·9
No. 4 (Aberdare)　.　.　.　.	10·7	18·5	13·3	20·1
No. 5 (Rhymney)　.　.　.　.	10·9	17·7	13·4	19·0
No. 6 (Monmouthshire)　.　.　.	9·6	15·4	10·7	16·2
South Wales　.　.　.　.　.	9·9	17·0	11·5	18·1

NOTE: No. 9 Neath Area was not created until 1950.

SOURCE: Statistical Section, South Western Division, National Coal Board.

distributed between various classes of wage-earners. It is more prevalent among underground workers, especially at the face, than among surface workers, and an undue proportion occurs among men under 30 years of age. The effect is to upset the balance of functions in the mine, which in turn disorganizes production; in mechanized pits there can be a loss of output out of all proportion to the absenteeism which caused it. But, irrespective of the method of working, the loss of output is much greater than the percentage of absenteeism suggest.

(d) Internal distribution of manpower

The internal distribution of manpower, especially the relative number employed at the face, has a considerable bearing on output. There is no information before 1949; but, after an initial drop in 1950, the number of face-workers increased up to 1953 and then declined by about 13,000 in six years. The number of surface workers fell by less than 7,000. Thus, while the proportion of face-workers to the total remained fairly constant up to 1955, it fell quite sharply in the following four years. Mechanization has the effect of disturbing the existing distribution; power-loading, for example, tends to reduce the number of men required at the face, but it may require extra men to deal with the more rapid flow of coal to the shaft bottom. The shift from face-work to work elsewhere underground in 1956–9 is partly explained by this fact. There has been a fairly steady reduction in the number of surface workers since 1951, but as a proportion of the labour force it has increased. In the post-war period it has averaged about 20 per cent. as against 17 per cent. in 1939. Mechanization is partly responsible, for it calls for more fitters and maintenance men, but the main reason is that the quality of coal is deteriorating and more men have to be employed on coal cleaning.

(e) Output per man-shift

It is customary to measure efficiency in terms of saleable output per man-shift (O.M.S.) and this has risen steadily in post-war years from 16·7 cwt. in 1948 to 20·3 cwt. in 1959. This compares favourably with the rise in the country generally. At the face O.M.S. has increased by 12·2 cwt. but it was still well below the national level in 1959.

The improvement in O.M.S. has been due to two main factors. First, there has been a contraction in the scale of mining with the closing of a number of the least productive pits. The extent to which output and employment are related to the number and size of collieries in production is shown in Table 45. The reduction was concentrated on mines employing less than 750 men. Of the pits closed, more than 40 per cent. were employing less than 250 and the very small ones had been virtually eliminated by 1959. In that year 18 collieries, employing between 1,000 and 1,500 men, accounted for almost one-quarter of the total labour force in National Coal Board mines, and they produced 22 per cent. of the total output. Usually the reserves of the mines which are closed are worked from neighbouring shafts with the result that a large proportion of the output of the coalfield is now obtained from relatively few collieries.[1] If we exclude mines employing less than 250 men, the average output per mine rose from 114,000 tons in 1948 to 175,000 in 1959; but this was well below the pre-war average of 209,000 tons in 1938 partly because of 'under capacity' working. One of the effects of the decline in manpower has

[1] By the end of 1959 only 118 mines were actually in production.

been a 'thinning out' of labour in collieries generally. Consequently, output per worker and the average output per mine have increased less than one would have expected.

The other factor in improving O.M.S. has been mechanized mining. There is no doubt that a key factor in raising productivity has been the increasing use of machinery for breaking down and transporting

TABLE 45

South Wales: Size distribution of collieries according to numbers employed, 1948 and 1959

Size range	Number of collieries		Number employed*		Saleable output '000 tons	
	1948	1959	1948	1959	1948	1959
Under 100	20	9	921	629	226·6	44·7
100–249	25	16	4,504	3,287	1,082·2	916·9
250–499	44	25	14,075	9,799	2,931·1	1,974·5
500–1,499	91	73	74,972	59,814	15,422·8	13,559·0
1,500–1,999	5	7	8,946	11,873	2,024·1	2,397·8
2,000–4,000	1	1	3,017	2,028	583·6	518·5
TOTAL	184	131†	107,435	87,430	22,270·4	19,411·4

* Weekly average.   † See footnote on p. 100.

SOURCE: Statistical Section, South Western Division, National Coal Board.

coal at the face. By 1959 there were over 700 machines and approximately 6,000 pneumatic picks in use and the proportion of coal mechanically cut had reached 65 per cent. of the total raised and weighed. Almost one-third of the machines were in the No. 6 (Monmouthshire) Area, and there were very few collieries producing steam and bituminous coal in which they were not being used. In the anthracite section there were fewer machines and fewer mines using them.

The other element in mechanization—the use of conveyors—had also made rapid strides and, in 1959, 96 per cent. of the raised and weighed output was mechanically conveyed. Power-loaders were also being introduced, but here again mechanization had proceeded much more rapidly in the eastern areas. In the west very little coal is power-loaded; the anthracite areas are less well-advanced because physical conditions are generally less favourable.

Large-scale mechanization has not resulted in any spectacular increase in O.M.S. and disappointment has been expressed on this account. However, the record must be viewed in the light of certain limiting factors. There was a steep rise in coal consumption after 1945, and so urgent was the need to increase output immediately that the attention of colliery officials was focused on short-term reorganization at the expense of long-term planning. Even short-term reorganization may interfere with production. The absolute priority given to current output impaired the Board's efforts to increase efficiency, and many pits with low productivity, which should have closed, have had to be kept going. Resources had also to be applied to maintaining existing capacity, and this added to the delay in completing major reconstruction schemes. The industry had lost much of its skilled labour and the training of new recruits takes time. Moreover, men under training and those engaged on development work are regarded as being fully productive but they normally produce less than half the amount of coal cut by skilled men.[1]

The point has now been reached when further mechanization, except for extension of power-loading and short-term reorganization, can add very little to productivity. In future, improvements in efficiency must be sought in large-scale reconstructions and new sinkings. At present most of the output from South Wales is obtained from collieries sunk before the beginning of the present century, and when a colliery reaches this age the task of getting coal usually becomes difficult and costly. The best and more productive seams have been exhausted and the industry is faced with deteriorating natural conditions. Thus a major effort is necessary even to maintain existing capacity.[2]

We have already referred to the National Coal Board's development plans for the South Wales coalfield. Table 46 gives the annual expenditure on major capital schemes[3] in the various areas. Since nationalization about £68 million, or just over 17 per cent. of the expenditure on major schemes in Britain as a whole, has been devoted to reconstruction in South Wales. Very little was done in the first two or three years, but after 1949 the rate of investment was accelerated; between 1954 and 1959 it more than doubled. It is too early to judge the effectiveness of what has already been done, for it takes years for such schemes to be completed; a new pit, for example, generally takes from five to ten years to come into full

---

[1] National Coal Board, *Annual Report, 1952*, p. 15.
[2] See Select Committee on Nationalized Industries, *Report*, H.M.S.O., 1958, p. 79.
[3] i.e. projects costing more than £250,000.

TABLE 46

Great Britain and South Wales areas: Annual capital expenditure (major schemes) in the coal-mining industry, (£'000) 1947–59

Year	Great Britain	South Wales	No. 1 (Swansea) Area	No. 9 (Neath) Area*	No. 2 (Maesteg) Area	No. 3 (Rhondda) Area	No. 4 (Aberdare) Area	No. 5 (Rhymney) Area	No. 6 (Monmouthshire) Area
1947	2,892·3	484·3	—	—	218·8	69·7	11·8	184·2	—
1948	5,241·5	857·3	31·0	—	259·2	110·5	44·7	411·8	—
1949	8,850·9	1,285·3	39·6	—	54·2	111·8	138·2	914·3	27·2
1950	10,612·7	1,929·0	24·7	—	56·3	59·0	494·9	1,254·0	39·9
1951	10,410·7	2,456·5	3·0	56·2	276·9	94·5	601·6	1,424·3	—
1952	16,612·3	3,056·6	20·4	100·2	358·3	390·7	851·4	1,305·4	30·2
1953	24,663·9	3,321·0	130·2	100·4	186·4	541·9	955·7	1,328·7	77·5
1954	38,228·5	5,306·6	744·7	444·2	245·4	1,144·3	1,816·6	777·3	133·7
1955	46,888·2	7,357·8	1,126·7	980·8	343·8	2,241·5	1,799·8	509·1	355·9
1956	52,806·1	9,036·0	1,342·2	1,052·4	721·1	3,703·3	1,217·8	273·3	725·9
1957	54,234·8	10,119·8	2,371·6	1,054·9	1,395·4	3,356·4	612·1	321·1	1,008·2
1958	59,132·9	10,699·9	3,082·3	1,160·8	980·9	1,211·3	622·4	919·2	2,722·7
1959	65,824·5	11,809·3	4,383·2	1,711·5	340·9	1,394·1	724·9	1,311·6	1,943·2
TOTAL	396,399·3	67,719·7	13,299·6	6,661·4	5,437·6	14,429·0	9,891·9	10,934·3	7,064·4

* Until 1950 the No. 9 (Neath) Area formed part of the No. 1 (Swansea) Area.

SOURCES: National Coal Board, *Reports and Accounts*, 1947–57.

production. However, something may be said about the allocation of resources between the different areas, for it gives some indication of the progress of reconstruction. In the first few years resources were concentrated on No. 4 (Aberdare) Area and No. 5 (Rhymney) Area, and in 1950 90 per cent. of the new investment was devoted to these areas because they were most likely to show fairly quick results. The reorganization included equipping some mines with the latest haulage and winning methods; and two of the biggest schemes were launched in these areas. The Nantgarw reorganization is one of the major horizon-mining projects undertaken by the National Coal Board. It is planned to work reserves of coking coal estimated to be 176 million tons; the coal is to be carbonized on the site, which includes coke ovens and a by-product plant. The other major scheme is at the Maerdy pit in the Rhondda Valley, which is being developed to work large reserves of sub-bituminous dry steam-coal. It is designed to have an output of 4,000 tons per day. These and other reconstructions are now nearing completion and expenditure is being tapered off as developments in other areas are speeded up.

In the last five years well over 26 per cent. of the total capital expenditure has been in the No. 3 (Rhondda) Area, where over £12 million has already been spent. At the Cwm colliery a major project is well-advanced to increase the output of high-grade metallurgical coal to over 5,000 tons per day, half of which will be treated at coke ovens situated near the colliery. The expansion of steel production in South Wales is a major factor inducing reorganization and development, as the region contains substantial reserves of high-quality coking coals which exist elsewhere in quantity only in Durham. Between 1946 and 1959 crude steel production increased from 2·6 million tons to over 5 million tons, and by 1970 it is expected to be half as much again. The expansion in output, coupled with the substitution of molten iron for scrap as the principal raw material,[1] requires increasing supplies of coke, and justifies the large sums spent on the reconstruction of pits producing metallurgical coal and new coke oven capacity by the National Coal Board. As Table 47 shows, the delivery of coals to coke ovens in South Wales from South Western Division collieries has more than doubled between 1948 and 1958.

The availability of suitable coals has become a factor influencing the location of new steel plants. The decision to site the new inte-

[1] See Chapter VI, p. 123.

grated steel works at Newport, rather than at Kidwelly, turned partly on the question of coal supplies and the overall development of the coalfield. For this reason, among others, the steel industry has tended to move eastwards, and when the new works come into production it is estimated that just over 90 per cent. of South Wales steel output will be concentrated in the coastal region east of Neath.[1]

TABLE 47

*Deliveries of South Western Division coking coals to
South Wales coke ovens (million tons)*

Year	N.C.B. coke ovens	Other coke ovens	Total
1948 . . .	0·5	1·6	2·1
1949 . . .	0·5	1·6	2·1
1950 . . .	0·5	1·7	2·2
1951 . . .	0·7	2·1	2·8
1952 . . .	1·0	2·3	3·3
1953 . . .	1·0	2·3	3·3
1954 . . .	1·1	2·4	3·5
1955 . . .	1·1	2·6	3·7
1956 . . .	1·1	3·8	4·9
1957 . . .	1·1	3·6	4·7
1958 . . .	1·2	3·4	4·6
1959 . . .	1·2	3·5	4·7

SOURCE: Statistical Section, South Western Division National Coal Board.

South Wales now accounts for about 25 per cent. of United Kingdom steel output and, as with iron in the 1850's, it is now the largest steel-producing area in Britain. In the early nineteenth century the expansion in the demand for iron was an important factor in the development of coal-mining on a large scale, but later coal displaced iron as the major expansive force. In the past decade, however, the process has been reversed. Steel is again exerting its influence on the pattern of mining development and has come to the fore as the most important determinant of Welsh economic growth.

The section most in need of rejuvenating was the anthracite district, where, despite steady progress in recent years, output in 1959 was just over $2\frac{1}{4}$ million tons, more than 50 per cent. lower than the peak of 1934: in addition, average costs in this district are far higher than anywhere else in the country. One new pit is situated at Cynheidre, about 5 miles north of Llanelly, and another at Aber-nant

[1] See Chapter VI, p. 137.

on the fringe of the Amman Valley; large-scale horizon mining will here be applied to exploit virgin seams of anthracite. Many of the present mines have been working for 50–75 years; most of them are 'drifts' which were highly productive in the early years but became uneconomic as operations extended deeper into the ground. Badly laid-out and ill-equipped, these undertakings employ a disproportionate number of men on tasks other than coal-getting; in some of them output is as low as 8 or 9 cwt. a man-shift.

Owing to delays in starting the major reconstruction, it became necessary to devote some resources to keep the old mines going until the new ones came into production. The colliery at Cynheidre is expected to produce a million tons of saleable coal a year—almost double the output of the six mines now working in the Gwendraeth Valley. At Aber-nant 2,000 men will be employed to produce 750,000 tons a year. When these and the other major projects come to fruition it is expected that the same number of men will be producing about 50 per cent. more coal.

(f) Earnings

Between 1948 and 1957 the average weekly earnings of all mine-workers increased by 86 per cent., but within the industry the rate of increase varied as between one group of workers and another. For example, the average weekly earnings of surface workers increased by 94 per cent. as compared with 85 per cent. for all underground workers. Nevertheless, surface workers were still the lowest paid mine workers in 1957. Their average weekly earnings at 268s. 4d. were 38s. 2d. less than the average paid to face-workers and 22s. less than the average for all mine workers. But these differences were much less than in 1952 when they were 45s. 11d. and 29s. 11d. respectively. Until 1957 the differential between various groups of workers tended to narrow because of the incidence of shiftwork and overtime. In addition to the Saturday shift, surface workers also worked additional shifts during the week and this led to a narrowing of the differential based on average weekly earnings.

On the other hand, while the differential based on earnings was narrowing as between different groups of workers in the coalfield, the difference in earnings between mine-workers in South Wales and all colliery workers in Great Britain tended to increase. In 1952 the overall average weekly earnings of colliery workers in South Wales were 12s. 3d. per week less than the average for Great Britain; in

1957, the difference was 14s. 7d., and by 1959 had further increased to 22s. 10d. Piece-work plays an important part in coal-mining, especially at the coal face, and whereas day-wage rates are negotiated nationally, piece-work rates are agreed to on a colliery basis, for regard must be had to the type of coal mined and working conditions generally. In South Wales, the proportion of the labour force engaged on piece-work is less than in Britain generally. In the last quarter of 1958, for example, the ratio of piece-workers to the total labour force was only 38·3 per cent. in South Wales as compared with 43·0 per cent. in Great Britain. In Britain 51·3 per cent. of the total wages earned in the period were paid to piece-workers, whereas in South Wales they received only 44·5 per cent. of the total. The lower ratio of piece-workers to the total labour force is, to some extent, a reflection of different mining conditions. In South Wales, where the pits are old, mining conditions are generally more difficult and this increases the proportion of day-wage men required for maintenance and other work. This, combined with a higher rate of absenteeism, especially among face-workers, was sufficient to depress average weekly earnings in South Wales as compared with Great Britain.

By using the Ministry of Labour Index of Retail Prices we can construct an index of real earnings. Whereas between 1948 and 1959 average money earnings increased by 78 per cent., average *real* earnings went up by only 16 per cent. Moreover, the rate of change in real earnings was not uniform throughout the period. Between 1948 and 1952 the advance in real earnings of all South Wales mineworkers was 7·8 per cent., an average of 2 per cent. per annum. In the period 1952–6 the movement was 12·2 per cent., an average of 3·0 per cent. per annum; finally, between 1956 and 1957 there was a slight decline in the rate of increase, which was 2·3 per cent. Thus, while the level of real earnings improved continuously between 1948 and 1957, the improvement was much more marked in the period 1952–6 than at any other time since the end of the war. Since 1957 real earnings have fallen and all colliery workers were worse off in 1959 than they had been in 1956.

The upward trend in money earnings was reversed during 1958. As the demand for coal declined, overtime was cut and the Saturday shift ceased to be worked. This had the effect of reducing the earnings of all workers, but, as one would expect, the restriction on overtime reduced the earnings of surface workers to a much greater extent than those of colliery workers in general. Compared with 1957, average weekly earnings of face-workers in 1959 had declined by 11s. 11d., whereas the earnings of surface workers fell by 18. 4d. The latter were receiving 44s. 7d. less than the average paid to face-workers, which was, approximately, the position in 1952.

Moreover, the restriction on overtime affected earnings in South Wales to a much greater extent than in the country generally and the earnings differential between South Wales and Britain widened still farther. This was because of the much higher proportion of day-wage men in South Wales and a continuing high rate of absenteeism. The earnings of piece-workers were not affected to the same extent as those of day-wage men, and it is this that accounts for the fact that the earnings of all mine-workers in South Wales declined by 4·5 per cent. between 1957 and 1959 compared with 1·5 per cent. in Britain.

3. *The North Wales coalfield*

Coal-mining in North Wales is on a much smaller scale than in the South; maximum output, approximately 3·5 million tons, was achieved in 1929 when just under 15,000 men were engaged in the industry. Output in 1958 was of the order of 2 million tons and the number of men on colliery books was under 8,000.

The coalfield lies along and under the Dee estuary and extends southwards in a narrow belt in Denbighshire and as far south as Oswestry. There are records of coal being worked in North Wales as early as 1410, but, as in South Wales, exploitation of the field did not really begin until the latter half of the eighteenth century, particularly around Brymbo and Ruabon. By 1914 most of the Flintshire workings had been abandoned because of lack of resources to cope with the danger of flooding; today there is only one colliery, Point of Ayr, operating in the region of the Dee estuary. In Denbighshire also a number of collieries were closed, especially in the inter-war period, because of difficult conditions, inflow of water and the exhaustion of seams. By 1946 the number of pits in production in North Wales had been reduced to sixteen but many of these were producing less than 50 tons per day.

The known reserves of the coalfield in workable seams of 2 ft. and over are in the region of 800 million tons. The coals are highly volatile and the output consists, in the main, of good-quality industrial gas and house coals, the Ruabon Yard seam, for example, being considered one of the finest house-coals. In the main Denbighshire field the area available for further development is fairly narrow, and within the proved area, the value of the field has been much reduced by the extensive mining of the better quality and easily mined seams, especially the main coal-seam. In Flintshire the greater part of the reserves lie to the east and north-east, and here the Point of Ayr colliery is working an unusually favourable field under the Dee estuary.

When the mines were taken into public ownership, the Coal Board was faced in North Wales,[1] as elsewhere, with the problem of arresting the decline in production and manpower, which had reduced output to 2 million tons in 1946. Output had been falling continuously since 1929 owing to the closure of mines and the loss of manpower; of the sixteen mines in operation in 1946, one-half of them were employing less than fifty men; their output was low and in the coalfield generally output per man-shift was below one ton. There was an urgent need to concentrate on the larger and more productive pits, and to increase productivity by reorganization and increased mechanization.

The first step was to reduce the number of pits. By 1948 only eight collieries were being operated by the Coal Board. That number was reduced to six in the course of the next six years and the process of reorganization was concentrated on these few units. Underground workings were reconstructed to permit greater mechanization and to give improved haulage and working conditions at Point of Ayr (where a new shaft was also sunk), Llay Main, and Gresford collieries. At Gresford an interesting development was the installation of equipment which breaks down the coal from the seam with compressed air, thus limiting the danger of working with explosives and at the same time producing more of the larger-size coal needed for domestic use.

Since 1954 the introduction of power-loaders has met with considerable success. At some collieries, Iftan for example, output per man-shift at the face has been more than doubled. In addition, colliery installations have been modernized and this has increased productivity.

The coalfield is noted for the large quantity of methane gas found underground, and Point of Ayr is believed to be the first in Great Britain to use gas direct from virgin seams to raise steam for power to serve the colliery, thus saving a large amount of saleable coal: in addition, a large power station, also operating on methane gas, has

[1] The North Wales coalfield was grouped with those of Lancashire and Cheshire to form the North Western Division of the Coal Board.

been constructed which provides the electricity needs of the colliery. In 1956 a new station built by the Wales Gas Board for the procuring and treatment of methane from the pit came into operation. From the Bershaw colliery methane is taken into the gas-works at Wrexham where it is refined into town gas and it is hoped to use substantial quantities of methane from the Gresford colliery for similar purposes.

The main trends in the coalfield since 1947 are given in Table 48, which shows that the reconstruction undertaken by the Coal Board has already produced some positive results. Output per man-shift has improved and some of the reconstructed collieries are now producing record outputs.

TABLE 48
North Wales coal industry, 1947–59

Year	Number of collieries	Saleable ouput	Wage-earners on colliery books	O.M.S. overall	Capital expenditure	Profit (+) or loss (−)
		('000 tons)	('000)	(tons)	(£'000)	(£'000)
1947	8	2,038	9·0	—	—	−291
1948	8	2,165	9·0	0·99	14·1	− 83
1949	8	2,120	8·8	1·02	164·7	+ 12
1950	7	2,188	8·5	1·08	101·5	+ 66
1951	7	2,338	8·9	1·05	104·4	− 58
1952	6	2,230	9·3	0·98	221·7	−398
1953	6	2,183	9·1	0·97	430·1	−396
1954	6	2,159	8·8	0·99	726·7	−547
1955	6	2,336	8·8	1·09	332·9	−329
1956	6	2,288	9·0	1·06	503·2	−234
1957	6	2,254	9·2	1·04	214·4	−729
1958	6	2,166	8·7	1·06	55·6	−611
1959	6	2,070	7·7	1·15	233·0	−301

SOURCES: National Coal Board, *Report and Accounts*, 1947–59.

4. Conclusion

Output performance of Welsh coalfields since the war is not impressive despite a substantial improvement in productivity; the results achieved are well below the expectations of the late forties. The financial record is set out in Table 49. Except for 1950 South Wales made losses every year since 1947. Only two areas—Aberdare and Rhymney—made consistent profits, with Rhondda a moderate

TABLE 49

Great Britain, and South Wales areas: Profit (+) or loss (−) per ton, saleable output of coal, 1947–59

Year	Great Britain		South Wales		No. 1 (Swansea) Area		No. 9 (Neath) Area*		No. 2 (Maesteg) Area		No. 3 (Rhondda) Area		No. 4 (Aberdare) Area		No. 5 (Rhymney) Area		No. 6 (Monmouthshire) Area	
	s.	d.	s.	d.	s.	d.	s.	d.	s.	d.	s.	d.	s.	d.	s.	d.	s.	d.
1947	−1	0	−9	8	−22	6	..	..	−10	6	−7	5	−5	1	−	10	−9	11
1948	+1	8	−4	7	−18	4	..	..	−7	1	−1	5	−2	6	+3	2	−2	3
1949	+2	11	−1	0·2	−12	1	..	..	−1	1	+3	3	+4	6	+5	11	−1	3
1950	+2	5	+1	10	−8	1	−18	0	−1	8	+3	0	+7	6	+5	9	−1	5
1951	+2	0	−2	4	−5	9	−23	5	−2	4	+1	3	+6	5	+2	10	−4	1
1952	+1	7	−1	8	−5	2	−25	4	−3	5	+1	11	+8	5	+3	9	−1	11
1953	+1	11	−1	10	−7	0	−3	6	−3	4	−1	3	+11	11	+3	10	+	4
1954	+1	7	−1	2	−9	1	−31	11	−3	9	−1	8	+14	1	+5	4	−1	3
1955	+1	9	−2	9	−8	4	−21	11	−5	7	−5	10	+11	8	+5	0	−2	1
1956	+2	7	−1	5	−4	11	−24	1	−4	5	+3	4	+10	11	+5	4	−1	4
1957	+1	7	−1	2	−2	9	−29	4	−1	9	+3	7	+8	4	+2	8	−3	2
1958	+1	1	−1	9	−9	7	−33	10	+4	3	+3	10	+11	7	+2	6	−2	3
1959	+1	0	−1	5	−13	5			+4	10	+1	4	+10	9	+2	7	+2	3

* See note to Table 46.

SOURCES: National Coal Board, *Report and Accounts*, 1947–59.

third: the average loss in the anthracite pits between 1951 and 1959 was as much as 25s. a ton. For the Coal Board it can be argued that it has been hampered by an unrealistic pricing policy and that the market value of coal has lagged behind other prices to the benefit, for example, of the steel industry. On the other hand, industrial disputes and restrictive practices have had a depressing effect on productivity. In 1955, the worst year, over half a million tons of coal were lost in the South Western Division because of stoppages and 'go slow' activities. In recent years the division has been responsible, on average, for nearly one-fifth of the output lost in the country as a whole through disputes.

TABLE 50

Great Britain and South Western Division: Output lost owing to disputes, 1947–59 ('000 tons)

Year	Great Britain	South Western	Division as a percentage of Great Britain
1947 . .	1,644	109	6·6
1948 . .	900	79	8·8
1949 . .	1,266	84	6·6
1950 . .	853	63	7·4
1951 . .	803	151	18·8
1952 . .	1,383	224	16·2
1953 . .	939	142	15·1
1954 . .	1,505	335	22·2
1955 . .	3,180	564	17·7
1956 . .	2,146	467	21·8
1957 . .	1,828	325	17·8
1958 . .	1,451	184	12·7
1959 . .	973	182	18·7

NOTE: The figures for the years 1954–9 include estimates of losses due to restrictions as well as to stoppages.

SOURCES: National Coal Board, *Report and Accounts*, 1947–59.

In some respects, however, there have been real gains. Technically the coalfield is already in much better shape. It is true that little new capacity has so far been brought into production and this explains why output has remained so consistently low. A great effort was required to maintain existing capacity and this will entail further heavy expenditure in the future. Nevertheless, now that arrears of maintenance have been made good there is reason to believe that the target set for 1965 will be achieved, but it will require very large capital expenditure. Productivity should increase, but any saving in operating costs will probably be more than offset by increased capital charges; the Board seems to have abandoned the idea that increased operating efficiency will lower costs.[1] Fortunately, the coalfield has solid advantages, particularly its range of special coals such as anthracite and high-quality coking coals.[2]

It is most unlikely that the industry will ever again experience the heavy unemployment of former years. We must recognize that the coalfield has a tradition of militancy and that there is still much suspicion and hostility. Nevertheless, there are signs of improvement in labour relations and the men are responding to the efforts to raise the efficiency of the pits. The hope is that new technical developments, active measures against pneumoconiosis, improved working conditions in new and reorganized pits, and generous welfare facilities will help to erase the legacy of the past and induce a greater spirit of co-operation in the future.

[1] *Investing in Coal*, p. 14.   [2] *Plan for Coal*, p. 4.

VI

STEEL

By JAMES DRISCOLL

IN recent years the South Wales steel industry has both grown faster and changed more in shape than at any time since the iron trade began to absorb the new steel-making processes in the 1860's and 1870's. The main purpose of this chapter is to outline this dual process of growth and structural change.

1. *The industry to 1935*

First it may be useful to sketch the historical background against which this recent resurgence must be viewed.

Although some iron had been made earlier, the South Wales iron trade really emerged in the latter part of the eighteenth century when charcoal was being replaced by coke in the smelting process. With ironstone and limestone easily available along the northern rim of the coalfield, the favourable supply of raw material led to a rapid development of iron-making at the heads of the valleys, along the Blaenavon–Dowlais–Merthyr–Hirwaun line. Iron output grew from 10,800 tons in 1788 to 200,000 tons in 1823, 453,000 tons in 1840, 720,000 tons in 1847, 871,000 tons in 1855, and 969,000 tons in 1860. Between 1820 and 1860 South Wales was Britain's largest iron-making district except for short intervals.

The technical developments in steel-making in the 1850's and 1860's checked the growth of iron-making. From the seventies onwards, steel-making was the main growth sector, while iron-making remained fairly stable at below the 1860 peak of 969,000 tons. Crude-steel production rose from 338,000 tons in 1879 to 811,000 tons in 1889, 988,000 tons in 1899, and 1,807,000 tons in 1913, at which date pig-iron output was 889,000 tons.

In product terms the area had a fairly wide range of output, with rails an important outlet, but sheets and tinplate emerged as a major speciality as the century progressed. The British tinplate trade came to be almost entirely concentrated around Swansea and Llanelly. Tinplate output rose from 0·75 million boxes in 1851 to 6·9 million boxes in 1881 and to 16·4 million boxes in 1913, of which over 60 per cent. went for export.

The inter-war years checked this upward trend in the South Wales steel industry. The general weakness of demand served to inhibit investment in additional capacity. Pig-iron production exceeded the 1913 level in only one year between 1919 and 1935; and although steel production was often above the 1913 level in that period, the gains were small and represented the use of capacity installed during the First World War. Moreover, even replacement investment was severely discouraged by the magnitude of fluctuations in demand. Between 1929 and 1931, iron output fell by two-thirds,—from 926,500 tons to 279,800 tons, and crude-steel production fell two-fifths—from 2·3 million tons to 1·3 million tons.

This check to investment would have weakened the position of the industry in any circumstances. In the conditions of the inter-war years, however, it was doubly unfortunate, since the check came just at a time when the need for new investment was growing. At the steel-making stage the tide of development clearly favoured large, integrated, hot-metal works rather than the small non-integrated cold-metal shops which accounted for much of the South Wales steel output.[1] At the finishing stage the introduction of wide continuous strip mills in the United States had set new standards for both costs and quality in the sheet and tinplate trades with which the Welsh hand mills could not long hope to compete. And over all, many of the South Wales finishing plants were not well-sited in relation to their supplying steelworks, which were themselves sometimes ill-located in the light of the progressive exhaustion of the Welsh ironstone deposits. By the early thirties the South Wales steel industry was showing many signs of ageing, the dangerous first symptoms of the vicious spiral of decay in an industry in which continuous and vigorous capital formation is a prerequisite for maintaining, let alone improving, its position. It was clear that a substantial commitment of new capital, put into different sorts of plant in different places, would soon be needed if the South Wales steel industry were not to pass into history.

[1] A 'cold-metal' works normally buys scrap and cold pig-iron, makes semi-finished steel, and sells this for further processing elsewhere. An integrated, hot-metal plant makes iron, uses this in molten form together with scrap thrown up internally, and then rolls the steel to the final product stage.

2. *Revival and growth*

It must be put to the credit of the Welsh steel-masters that, recognizing the necessity for change, they faced up to the implications of a massive modernization programme at a time when the outlook for the Welsh economy was exceptionally dark. The major revolution which has transformed the prospects for Welsh steel over recent years was conceived and begun in the depths of the depression of the early thirties. This renaissance turns principally on the creation of three new massive integrated works at Cardiff, Ebbw Vale, and Port Talbot—which now account for some three-quarters of South Wales steel output—and the gradual (and still only partial) withdrawal of smaller, older plants.

Cardiff

The transformation started with the development by Guest Keen Baldwins of the East Moors Works on a coastal site at Cardiff. Work on the plant began in 1934 and operations began in 1936. The works had an iron-making capacity of 500,000 tons a year; and although part was intended for the production of haematite iron for outside sale, most went for use in the adjacent steel furnaces, which had a capacity of 350,000 tons a year. The plant was designed to roll billets, sheet-bars, and small sections. Since 1936 substantial additional investment has been carried out, including a recent £3 million scheme to modernize imported ore-handling, and steel-making capacity is now appreciably more than double the plant's original 350,000 tons. The East Moors Works, owned since denationalization by Guest Keen Iron & Steel Co. Ltd.,[1] is immediately adjacent to and closely associated with the rolling mills of Guest Keen and Nettlefolds (South Wales) Ltd. which produce a wide range of re-rolled products from semi-finished steel supplied by the East Moors Works.

Ebbw Vale

There followed quickly the first major change in the sheet and tinplate trade. In 1935–8, on the cleared site of the old Ebbw Vale Steel Co., Richard Thomas & Co.[2] built a modern integrated wide strip-mill plant with a planned output of 400,000 tons a year of sheet and tinplate. The plant embodied two major technical innovations— it made use of the improved Bessemer process for steel-making and

---

[1] Now known as G.K.N. (Steel) Ltd.
[2] Richard Thomas & Co. and Baldwins Ltd. amalgamated in 1944–5.

it had Britain's first continuous wide-strip mills.[1] A third innovation followed in 1947: Britain's first electrolytic tinning plant—and substantial further improvements have been made. The works now has an ingot capacity of approximately 1 million tons a year.

The decision to build an integrated strip-mill plant at Ebbw Vale was criticized on locational grounds. The site involves transhipment of imported ores and a long haul for lean home ores, and has no easy access to its main markets. Richard Thomas & Co. originally wished the plant to be located on the Lincolnshire and Northamptonshire orefields and it was only after considerable political pressure that the plant was put down at Ebbw Vale on the ground of social necessity. Moreover, local site limitations have held iron- and steel-making capacity at Ebbw Vale below the capacity of the rolling mills and throughput has to be supplemented by the import of sheet slabs from Redbourn in Lincolnshire, involving costly freight movements. The Company's original plan for the new Newport plant envisaged reducing this long cross-haul by supplying slabs from Newport; but this, though an improvement, would still provide a less favourable cost position than would the development of a fully balanced integrated plant, had the site made that possible.

Port Talbot

In the late thirties another integrated wide-strip mill plant was under active consideration and certain preliminary work was done at Port Talbot. The war brought a ban on new investment in steel but the scheme was revived on a larger scale afterwards when four companies—Guest Keen Baldwins, Richard Thomas & Baldwins, John Lysaght, and Llanelly Associated Tinplate—set up the Steel Company of Wales. Three new plants were envisaged: an integrated iron- and steelworks with a hot wide-strip mill and associated cold reduction mills at Port Talbot; and two other works for the cold reduction of Port Talbot strip into tinplate.

The centre of this complex is the Port Talbot works, the largest steelworks in Britain. This plant takes in the modernized Port Talbot and Margam melting shops, as well as the main melting shop at the Abbey Works, newly built on adjoining land. The steel from all three shops goes to feed the primary mill and the 80-in. continuous hot-strip

---

[1] The Ebbw Vale plant included three continuous strip mills, a 56-in. hot mill and two (56-in. and 42-in.) cold reduction mills. The 42-in. cold reduction mill was replaced by a new 5-stand 42-in. mill with an additional 150,000 tons of capacity in 1955.

mill at the Abbey Works which produces hot-rolled wide-strip and plate.

This hot-rolled strip then forms the raw material for four major finishing units. Much of it goes for further processing in the 80-in. cold reduction mill at the Abbey Works, to be turned into sheets for motor bodies and similar uses. Another part goes to the 48-in. reversing mill at the Orb Works, Newport, to produce electrical sheet. The rest goes westwards to the two new tinplate works at Trostre and Velindre, each centred around a wide continuous cold reduction mill,[1] there to be converted into cold reduced tinplate. The Trostre plant came into operation in 1953 and the Velindre plant in 1956.

The Port Talbot works has been continuously expanding since operations began there in 1951. The steel industry's 1953-8 development programme embodied plans to increase its crude-steel capacity to 2·4 million tons, almost as much as the whole of the South Wales steel industry produced in 1945. The steel industry's 1957-62 programme included a further £50 million scheme which has now brought capacity up to 3 million tons. The new scheme includes another 30-ft. blast furnace with ancillary plant and an oxygen-enriched Bessemer shop with an annual capacity of 600,000 tons of steel. The additional 600,000 tons throughput can be dealt with by the existing hot mills, with modifications, but a new 56-in. cold reduction mill was added to increase sheet production.

The Port Talbot complex, like the Ebbw Vale scheme, has suffered to some extent from political interventions. The siting of the two tinplate plants at Trostre and Velindre, in the Swansea–Llanelly area, was dictated by social rather than economic considerations. The hot coil from Abbey Works could well have been made into tinplate in adjacent plants, thus avoiding the cost and difficulty of moving the coil westwards over inadequate and congested roads.

Closure of old plants

The development of new plants has necessarily involved the closing of obsolete or badly-sited works producing similar products. The plants affected fall into two groups: the sheet and tinplate hand mills, and the non-integrated cold-metal steelworks supplying them.

The sheet and tinplate hand mills were doomed once the new con-

---

[1] 48-in. at Trostre and 42-in. at Velindre.

tinuous wide-strip mill emerged between the wars. But they have been a very long time a-dying, first because of the check to steel investment imposed during the war and then because of the exceptionally rapid growth of demand for sheet and tinplate since the war which has outstripped the growth of strip-mill output until recently. A first group of hand-mill plants were put out of operation in 1953–4 when the opening of production at Trostre coincided with a temporary check to demand, but the main closures came in 1958 when the balance of supply and demand again eased and consumers felt more free to express their preference for the better-quality—and cheaper—strip-mill products. Of the twenty-two tinplate hand-mill plants operating at the beginning of 1957 only two remained open at the end of 1959, 250,000 tons of annual capacity having been withdrawn. Of the nine hand-mill sheet plants operating at the beginning of 1957, only three remained open at the end of 1959, 120,000 tons of annual capacity having been withdrawn. It must be expected that the remaining 20,000 tons of hand-mill tinplate capacity and 120,000 tons of hand-mill sheet capacity will also be withdrawn before long.

The closure of these hand mills reduced the demand on the cold-metal steelworks in the western part of South Wales. Although both the companies concerned and the British Iron and Steel Federation arranged for production to continue at a loss for a while, in order to ease the social problems of closures, alternative outlets could not be found, and four of these works closed in 1958—all obsolete high-cost plants. In all, about 360,000 tons of steel-making capacity was thus withdrawn.

Other plants

The developments at Port Talbot, Ebbw Vale, and Cardiff so fill the eye that there is some danger that the very considerable progress being made elsewhere may be given less than adequate attention. The Steel Company of Wales's Orb Works at Newport, Britain's major producer of electrical sheets; Richard Thomas & Baldwins' Panteg Works, an expanding alloy steel producer; Whitehead's at Newport, a major re-rolling unit and Britain's leading producer of narrow cold-rolled strip; Stewarts & Lloyds at Newport, an important tube works: these and other South Wales plants have made marked advances in recent years and form an important and vigorous part of the South Wales steel industry, helping to diversify the output of an over-specialized industry.

3. The scale and causes of growth

The reconstruction of the South Wales steel industry in recent years is reflected clearly in the vigorous upward trend of output. Between 1946 and 1957[1] crude-steel production in South Wales and Monmouthshire increased by 90·6 per cent., from 2·65 million tons to 5·05 million tons, an advance of 2·4 million tons.

TABLE 51

South Wales: Crude-steel production, 1946–59

Year	'000 tons	Year	'000 tons
1946 .	2,651	1953 .	4,050
1947 .	2,668	1954 .	4,323
1948 .	3,098	1955 .	4,607
1949 .	3,219	1956 .	4,706
1950 .	3,407	1957 .	5,056
1951 .	3,475	1958 .	4,479
1952 .	3,720	1959 .	5,025

The fundamental cause of this upsurge must be sought outside Wales. The Welsh economy is not sufficiently highly developed to generate a demand for steel of anything like 5 million tons a year, nor has its rate of expansion been adequate to generate an additional demand of 2½ million tons over the post-war period. Table 52 seeks to illustrate this imbalance between local demand and local supply. These consumption estimates should be treated with very considerable caution. Nevertheless, the broad picture of an 'exporting' area dependent on demand from other parts of Britain and overseas is clear enough. Moreover, the changes over 1951–9, which should be less distorted by statistical deficiencies, reinforce this view. In that period, the increase of 260,000 tons in local consumption was completely inadequate to generate the increase of over 1·4 million tons in local production.

[1] Because of the shape which the 1958–9 recession took in the South Wales steel industry, the choice of a best recent year for the purposes of comparison is difficult. Neither 1959 (the most recent year for which figures are available) nor 1957 (the year of record crude-steel output) is wholly satisfactory. On balance, 1957 probably reflects more accurately both overall growth rates and the normal product pattern and so has been used in many instances in this chapter. However, it remains open to the objection that it understates the growth and relative current importance of the strip-mill plants and 1959 figures have been used instead where these factors are particularly relevant.

The fundamental cause of the growth of the South Wales steel industry lies then in the general expansion of the British economy as a whole since the war and in the shift in the pattern of that economy

TABLE 52

South Wales: Estimated consumption and production of steel ('000 tons, ingot equivalent), 1951 and 1959

	1951	1959
Apparent consumption of finished steel*	660	920
Production†	3,624	5,025
Excess of local production . .	2,964	4,105

* Ingot equivalent of estimated total finished steel consumed.
† Actual tonnage of ingots and castings produced.

towards more steel-intensive forms of expenditure, such as investment, consumer durables, and steel-containing exports. Its progress has basically been dependent on influences outside Wales.

The relative advance

The South Wales steel industry has not only grown in absolute terms along with the rest of Britain's steel industry; it has also advanced relatively as against other steel-making districts. Between 1946 and 1957 South Wales crude-steel output rose by 90·6 per cent., whereas production in the rest of Britain rose by 65·7 per cent. Accordingly, the South Wales share of total United Kingdom steel production expanded from 20·9 per cent. to 24·4 per cent. From being the second-largest steel-making district before the war, South Wales has now moved into the leading place. The industry's dependence on non-Welsh demand has certainly not operated to check its growth.

Indeed, the factors which have given South Wales a more-than-proportionate share in the overall growth of steel production in Britain are again to be found outside Wales. The South Wales steel industry has been fortunately placed to benefit from the operation of two of the main determinants of the pattern of growth for the British steel industry as a whole. These have been: on the demand side, an exceptionally fast rate of increase in demand for thin, flat products—sheets, tinplate, and light plates; and on the supply side, a growing reliance on pig-iron made from imported ore as the major steel-making raw material. As regards the former, thin, flat products have long been a South Wales speciality, so the region has been exceptionally favoured by this particular emphasis within the overall fast-growing demand. As regards the latter, greater reliance on ore imports has naturally meant a tendency for expansion to be fostered on coastal sites, and so South Wales' long coastline and good harbours have made it a favoured area. Other districts were, of course, helped by one or other of these or similar growth factors: but South Wales has reaped the benefit of both.

TABLE 53

Iron and steel industry, 1953–9: Capital expenditure* by district

District	£'000
1. Derbyshire, Leicestershire, Nottinghamshire, Northamptonshire, and Essex	29,367
2. Lancashire (other than 10), Denbighshire, Flintshire, and Cheshire	48,934
3. Yorkshire (other than 5 and 9)	None
4. Lincolnshire	54,010
5. North-east coast	111,224
6. Scotland	54,369
7. Staffordshire, Shropshire, Worcestershire, and Warwickshire	32,767
8. South Wales and Monmouthshire	156,506
9. Sheffield	40,114
10. North-west coast	5,180
TOTAL	532,471

* The figures relate to production facilities for iron and steel activities as defined in the Iron and Steel Act, 1953, and do not include development schemes costing £100,000 or less, or expenditure on ironfounding and steelfounding.

SOURCES: Iron and Steel Board *Annual Reports*, 1958 and 1959.

This favourable position in terms both of demand and location has attracted to South Wales a high proportion of the total investment in the British steel industry. Table 53 shows the division of steel investment by district since 1953, a period which post-dates the heavy initial expenditure at Port Talbot. Over this period, South Wales took just short of one-third of the total investment in steel, although it accounted for only between one-fifth and one-quarter of crude-steel output.

4. *The changing structure*

Since 1935 the South Wales steel industry has experienced not only rapid growth but also major changes in its structure. Four changes, in particular, stand out. Firstly, the industry has carried through a major revolution in the techniques of producing thin, flat products, its major speciality, which has led to the displacement of a number of small hand-mill plants by a few large continuous strip-mill plants. Secondly, this move to larger units at the finishing end has reinforced the technical factors encouraging the displacement of the small cold-metal steelworks by the large integrated hot-metal steelworks. Thirdly, as a result of this, the region has moved away from reliance on scrap as its major steel-making raw material to reliance on molten iron, involving the development of a blast-furnace sector more than three times the pre-war size. And finally, since much of this blast-furnace capacity is dependent on supplies of imported ore, there has been a strong tendency for the industry to abandon scattered inland centres, many of them in the west, and to move to ports of entry for, foreign ore in the centre and east of the region.

The pre-steel-making sectors

The most striking structural changes have occurred in the 'pre-steel-making' sectors of the South Wales industry, i.e. in the blast furnaces designed to make iron, and in the complex of plant servicing the blast furnaces.

Before the war, South Wales relied heavily on scrap as its major steel-making raw material. Since the war, however, the British steel industry has based its development planning on the encouragement of an increasing use of iron rather than scrap in the steel furnaces and expansion in South Wales has conformed to this pattern. Given both the absolute growth in steel production and this relatively greater usage of iron as against scrap per ton of steel, total iron requirements have increased sharply.

As a result, there has been a marked expansion of iron production in recent years. Over the years 1946–59 the output of iron increased 165·3 per cent. as against an 89·6 per cent. rise in steel output. Of the 1959 production of 2,682,000 tons, 2,516,900 tons was basic iron and only 134,000 tons haematite iron. This stands in sharp contrast to the position as late as 1929 when over three-quarters of South Wales iron production was of haematite quality.

This increase in iron production has not been due to an increase in the number of blast furnaces. There were eleven in South Wales at the end of 1946 and twelve at the end of 1959.[1] It has been due, rather,

[1] Five at Port Talbot, three at Ebbw Vale, and four at Cardiff.

to three other factors. Firstly, and most important, there has been a marked growth in the size of the blast furnaces: whereas only two of the furnaces had a hearth diameter of over 20 ft. and none was

TABLE 54

South Wales: Iron production, 1946–59

Year	'000 tons	Year	'000 tons
1946 .	1,011	1953 .	1,653
1947 .	1,024	1954 .	1,894
1948 .	1,173	1955 .	1,975
1949 .	1,203	1956 .	2,195
1950 .	1,232	1957 .	2,525
1951 .	1,351	1958 .	2,511
1952 .	1,545	1959 .	2,682

above 22 ft. in 1946, seven were over 20 ft. and four over 25 ft. in 1959, the largest having a hearth diameter of 31 ft. Secondly, advances in operating techniques have led to a more intensive utilization of capacity: as the number of furnaces went up by one over 1946–59, the average number actually in blast per week rose from 6·85 in 1946 to nearly ten in 1959. Thirdly, the striking development of ore-preparation processes has reduced the work which has to be done in the furnaces and has thus increased their output.

Taken together, these factors have led to a sharp increase in blast-furnace productivity, i.e. in the output per furnace.

TABLE 55

South Wales: Annual output per furnace in blast, 1938–59

Year	'000 tons of iron
1938 . .	128·1
1946 . .	147·8
1955 . .	209·6
1957 . .	235·8
1959 . .	271·5

The South Wales output per furnace, at 271,500 tons a year, is much above the United Kingdom average of 160,600 tons a year.

Equally striking advances in operating efficiency are recorded by the figures of coke consumption per ton of iron produced. This has fallen steadily, from 20·45 cwt. in 1946, to 18·35 cwt. in 1955, and to

16·10 cwt. in 1959, indicating rising fuel efficiency. In all, the industry used 3·7 million tons of coal in 1959, of which 3·2 million tons went to coke ovens. Considerable quantities of coke-oven gas are fed into the South Wales gas grid.

Most of South Wales' pig-iron is made from imported iron ore, although continuing use is made of such local ore as remains available and of Midlands (especially Oxfordshire) ores. Most of the imported ore comes from French North Africa, Sweden, northern France, northern Spain, and Newfoundland, and the circle of supply is widening further.

TABLE 56

South Wales: Sources of iron ore consumed, 1937 1954, and 1959

		1937		1954		1959	
Source	Iron content	'000 tons	%	'000 tons	%	'000 tons	%
	(%)						
Imports	55	1,021	61·1	2,670	72·3	3,917	81·4
Wales	50	226	13·5	114	3·1	129	2·7
Midlands	25–32	425	25·4	907	24·6	766	15·9
TOTAL	—	1,672	100·0	3,691	100·0	4,812	100·0

More and more of the ore now undergoes some form of treatment before being charged to the blast furnaces. Ore preparation, including sintering, has become a new link in the production chain in recent years. In 1959 the region used 1,702,000 tons of sinter in its blast furnaces as against only 158,000 tons in 1948.

The increase in ore imports has required substantial investment in ore-handling facilities. The dock facilities at Port Talbot have been extensively modernized and extended, and a £3 million scheme to modernize the Guest Keen Iron & Steel Co.'s wharf and raw materials handling plant at Cardiff has recently been completed.

The steel-making sector

The upward trend of steel output over the post-war years has been set out in Table 51 on p.120. Over the years 1946–57, crude-steel output rose by 2·4 million tons, or 90·6 per cent., from 2·65 million tons to 5·05 million tons.

The balance of steel-making processes has moved sharply in favour of basic open-hearth steel in recent years. The basic open-hearth process accounted for nearly 90 per cent. of South Wales steel output in 1959.

TABLE 57

South Wales: Crude-steel production, by process ('000 tons), 1918–59

Year	Open hearth		Bessemer		Electric	Other
	Acid	Basic	Acid	Basic		
1918	950·3	708·2	399·4	—	—	—
1929	947·3	992·1	394·9	0·1	0·4	1·3
1937	822·0	1,800·1	—	—	4·0	2·7
1951	436·5	2,690·5	—	295·6	47·0	5·6
1957	233·6	4,739·0	—	377·7	56·7	9·2
1959	92·4	4,439·4	—	446·7	41·3	5·5

Bessemer production, which revived with the opening of the new Bessemer shop at Ebbw Vale in 1938, is now increasing in importance and with recent developments at Port Talbot may soon exceed 1 million tons a year.

Although South Wales remains almost entirely concentrated on common steels, alloy steel production is growing. Between 1955 and 1957, it nearly trebled, rising from 30,769 tons to 85,400 tons.[1] The Steel Company of Wales rolls low-alloy, high-strength plates at Port Talbot, and Richard Thomas & Baldwins produces similar plates at Panteg, for which important expansion plans have recently been announced.

As in the case of iron production, the expansion of steel production since the later thirties has resulted from an increase in output per furnace rather than from any increase in the number of furnaces. Counting open-hearth furnaces only, the total declined from 119 in 1937 to 97 in 1959. The growth in the size of furnaces, however, is marked, as Table 58 on p. 127 shows. The increased size of furnace, together with such other factors as the change to hot-metal practice, the introduction of the continuous working week, and the newly developed use of oxygen in steel-making, has led to present output per furnace being 140 per cent. greater than 1938.

The increased size and productivity of furnaces is closely associated with the shift from cold-metal to hot-metal practice. Although there

[1] There was some falling away during the recession, and 1959 output was 53,200 tons.

were still eight cold-metal works as against three hot-metal works at
the end of 1959, the hot-metal works account for three-quarters of

TABLE 58

South Wales: Number of open-hearth furnaces, 1937 and 1959

Furnace capacity per heat (tons)	No. of open-hearth furnaces	
	1937	1959
Under 60	86	41
60–99	30	18
100–199	3	21
200–299	—	17
TOTAL	119	97

TABLE 59

South Wales: Annual output per open-hearth furnace, 1938–59

Year	1938	1946	1955	1959
'000 tons .	29·1	29·2	51·5	70·4

South Wales steel output and the proportion will tend to grow. The
shift from cold- to hot-metal practice is reflected in the very sharp
change in the pig-iron and scrap ratios[1] in recent years.

TABLE 60

South Wales: Pig-iron and scrap consumed in steel-making, 1937–59

Year	Pig-iron consumed	Scrap consumed	Pig-iron: scrap ratio
	('000 tons)	('000 tons)	('000 tons)
1937 . . .	948·5	1,886·6	36:72
1951 . . .	1,678·6	2,172·9	48:63
1959 . . .	2,872·6	2,797·5	56:56

Whereas South Wales was very heavily dependent on scrap as its
principal steel-making raw material before the war, rather more pig-
iron than scrap is now consumed. For many years South Wales has
been an importing area for scrap, drawing heavily on London and

[1] i.e. the consumption of pig-iron (or scrap) expressed as a percentage of crude-steel
production.

south-east England, but despite the closure of so many of the cold-metal shops in the west of South Wales this 'import' requirement seems likely to continue.

The finishing sector

At the finishing end of the South Wales steel industry, the emphasis is heavily on thin, flat products—sheets, tinplate, and light plates. Sheets (1,401,700 tons) and tinplate (1,121,800 tons) together accounted for over 67 per cent.[1] of the total output of finished steel (3,750,100 tons) in 1959.[2] In turn, South Wales accounted for more than half of all United Kingdom deliveries of sheets and for virtually all United Kingdom deliveries of tinplate.

The production of sheet and tinplate is increasingly concentrated in the strip-mill plants. The 80-in. and 56-in. continuous mills at Port Talbot, the 56-in. continuous mill at Ebbw Vale,[3] and the 48-in. reversing mill at Orb Works, Newport, account for over 95 per cent. of present sheet output, the Newport works concentrating on electrical sheet. The remainder comes from mechanized and hand mills at Panteg, Neath, Llanelly, and Pontnewynydd. The two 48-in. and 42-in. continuous mills at Trostre and Velindre and the 42-in. continuous mill at Ebbw Vale account for all but 1 per cent. or so of present tinplate output, the only remaining tinplate hand mills being at Webb, Shakespeare, & Williams's works at Pontardulais and at the Redbrook Tinplate Company's works near Monmouth.

As well as sheet, the Port Talbot and Ebbw Vale mills roll plate, the balance shifting with demand fluctuations. In 1957 South Wales producers' deliveries of non-alloy plates totalled 384,000 tons, nearly all from the strip mills, of which 293,000 tons was light plate and 91,000 tons medium and heavy plate.

The general pattern of specialization in the area is shown in Table 61, which sets out deliveries by product of non-alloy finished steel. The 1957 figures are again used, as they give a more accurate picture of the normal production pattern.

Apart from sheet, tinplate and plate, light rolled sections and bars form the most important product group. Deliveries amounted to

[1] The 1959 share (67 per cent.) is probably exaggerated somewhat, since the recession affected strip-mill products less than other products. In 1957, sheets and tinplates accounted for 60 per cent. of total South Wales finished sheet production.

[2] All figures in this section relate to tonnages of finished steel. Total output in finished tons is lower than total crude-steel output in ingot tons by a ratio of approximately 1:1¼ overall.

[3] There is some flexibility in the division of sheet and tinplate rolling as between the two Ebbw Vale mills.

TABLE 61

South Wales: Steel deliveries by product ('000 tons), 1957

Product	Home	Export	Total
Ingots, billets, &c., for outside use . .	12·9	4·3	17·2
Plates	370·5	13·3	383·8
Other heavy rolled products* . . .	60·2	2·3	62·5
Wire rods, &c.	175·0	18·2	193·2
Bright bars	0·4	..	0·4
Light rolled sections and other bars . .	468·6	39·6	508·2
Hot-rolled strip	30·6	10·9	41·5
Cold-rolled strip	101·3	13·0	114·3
Sheets	896·2	292·2	1,188·4
Tubes and pipes	39·1	57·2	96·3
Steel forgings†	0·3	..	0·3
Steel castings	..	..	..
Tinplate, &c.	607·9	413·9	1,021·8
Total, non-alloy	2,763·0	864·9	3,627·9
Total, alloy	46·4	4·0	50·4
GRAND TOTAL	2,809·4	868·9	3,678·3

* Including heavy rails.   † Including tyres, wheels, and axles.

508,200 tons in 1957. These products come mainly from Guest Keen Iron & Steel Co. and Guest Keen & Nettlefolds, both at Cardiff, and Whitehead's at Newport. Then follow wire rods (193,200 tons), from Guest Keen & Nettlefolds; cold rolled strip (114,300 tons), mainly from Whitehead's and Guest Keen & Nettlefolds; tubes and pipes (96,300 tons) from Stewarts & Lloyds at Newport; and other heavy rolled products (62,500 tons) from Guest Keen Iron & Steel Co.

Given the existence of a number of non-integrated steelworks and non-integrated re-rolling mills, an important part of the South Wales steel trade is taken up with intra-industry transfers of semi-finished steel for further conversion, particularly of re-rolling billets and sheet and tinplate bars. In 1957 the position was as follows:

Intra-industry movements of semis, 1959* (tons)

	Re-rolling billets, &c.	Sheet bars
From South Wales steelworks to South Wales mills .	591,500	64,300
From South Wales steelworks to other mills . .	442,900	49,600
From other steelworks to South Wales mills . .	158,400	80,900

* Re-rolling billets and sheet bars only, excluding transfers to own works.

The closure of four non-integrated steelworks, twenty hand-mill tinplate plants, and six hand-mill sheet plants in 1958 has reduced the importance of this trade in semis and a further decline is to be expected. Nevertheless, it is likely to remain of significance, since some of the West Wales steel plants remain in operation as billet producers and Whitehead's and Guest Keen & Nettlefolds remain as major re-rolling units.

Table 62 shows the destination of South Wales steel deliveries, by consuming industries. To avoid distortions introduced by the relative shifts between industries in the 1958-9 recession, the 1957 pattern is again used.

TABLE 62

South Wales: Steel deliveries by consuming industries, 1957
('000 tons)

	Non-alloy	Alloy*	Total	%
Home deliveries				
Coal-mining	97·7	0·2	97·9	2·7
Iron and steel	188·9	0·4	189·3	5·1
Agricultural machinery . .	21·6	0·3	21·9	0·6
Machine tools . . .	3·5	. . *	3·5	0·1
Constructional engineering .	87·9	0·3	88·2	2·4
Other non-electrical engineering	110·9	8·3	119·2	3·2
Electrical machinery and apparatus	138·9	1·9	140·8	3·8
Motor vehicles, cycles, and aircraft	452·6	0·3	452·9	12·3
Railway rolling stock† . .	65·6	24·7	90·3	2·4
Bolts, nuts, nails, &c. . .	64·7	. .	64·7	1·8
Drop forgings, &c. . . .	33·1	6·9	40·0	1·1
Wire drawing and wire manufactures	39·4	. .	39·4	1·1
Hollow-ware	550·4	. .	550·4	15·0
Metal furniture, &c. . . .	119·1	0·6	119·7	3·3
Building and contracting . .	177·8	0·2	178·0	4·8
Other uses and unallocated .	192·2	1·2	193·4	5·3
Stockholding merchants . .	418·7	1·1	419·8	11·4
Total, home	2,763·0	46·4	2,809·4	76·4
Exports by producers . .	864·9	4·0	868·9	23·6
TOTAL DELIVERIES . . .	3,627·9	50·4	3,678·3	100·0

* . . = under 100 tons.
† Includes both British Railways and private firms.

The hollow-ware industry is the largest customer of the South Wales steel industry. In 1957 it took 550,400 tons of steel, almost all of it tinplate, or 15 per cent. of total South Wales deliveries.[1] The hollow-ware industry includes not only domestic hollow-ware producers, but also manufacturers of food containers, non-food containers, and of industrial hollow-ware (such as kegs and drums). Of these four groups, the manufacturers of food containers form the largest consuming group.

Almost as important a consumer is the motor-vehicle, cycles, and aircraft group. The 1957 figures shown in Table 62 above—452,900 tons, or 12·3 per cent. of all deliveries—tend to understate the importance of this group, being depressed by the recession in the motor industry in 1957. Deliveries in 1959 rose to 595,300 tons, making it the largest consuming industry in that year. Some three-quarters of direct sales to this group consist of sheet.

Together, the hollow-ware and motor industries account for about one-third of all home sales by South Wales steel-producers, a high degree of dependence on a few market outlets.

Other important consuming industries include the iron and steel industry itself (5·1 per cent. of 1957 deliveries); building and contracting (4·8 per cent.); electrical machinery and apparatus (3·8 per cent.); metal furniture, &c. (3·3 per cent.); general engineering (3·2 per cent.); and coal-mining (2·7 per cent.). About one-ninth of all sales are made through stockholding merchants.

South Wales exports nearly a quarter of its finished steel. In 1957 exports totalled 868,900 tons, or 23·6 per cent. of all deliveries.[2] Tin-plate is the main export. In 1957 exports took 413,900 tons out of total tinplate deliveries of 1,021,800 tons, involving a high degree of concentration on exports sales. Australia, New Zealand, South Africa, Malaya, Argentina, Denmark, Hong Kong, and Spain were the main markets for tinplate in 1957. Other important exports are of sheets (292,000 tons in 1957), tubes and pipes (57,000 tons), light rolled products (39,600 tons), hot- and cold-rolled strip (23,900 tons), wire rods (18,200 tons), and plates (13,300 tons).

5. *The future*

The picture presented of the South Wales steel industry since 1935 has been one of rejuvenation, of growth, and of structural change.

[1] In 1959 it fell to second place behind motors, but actual receipts rose to 588,300 tons (15·7 per cent.).

[2] In 1959 exports fell slightly to 834,100 tons or 22·2 per cent.

Looking ahead into the sixties, the same three features are likely to appear.

The Newport scheme

The main feature of the next decade will be the development by Richard Thomas & Baldwins of a new integrated strip-mill plant at Llanwern, near Newport. This plant was first projected as early as 1954. Considerable differences of view appeared, however, first as to the timing of construction in relation to the growth of demand for thin, flat products and then as to the nature of the products to be made at the plant in its early stages and finally as to its location. These differences caused considerable delay in reaching final conclusions on the desirability and nature of the plant. Eventually, however, on 16 November 1958, the Prime Minister told the House of Commons that the Government had decided in favour of two strip-mill projects, at Newport and at Ravenscraig in Scotland, each of which was to have an initial capacity of 500,000 tons a year of thin, flat products, but both of which were to be capable of considerable further expansion.

The Government's announcement met with some criticism. It was widely held that sociological and political factors had been allowed to override technical and economic ones in the choice of the Scottish site. In particular, technical opinion opposed the splitting of the project since the mention of half a million tons of thin, flat products as the initial output at Newport was thought to involve either the installation of uneconomically small units of plant or else the underemployment of the large units technically desirable.

The Company have overcome this obstacle by providing for a substantial production of semi-finished steel for further processing at Ebbw Vale in addition to the half-million tons of finished products, thus providing a more adequate load for the high-capacity blast furnaces and rolling mills; it quickly secured Government approval for a quarter-million-ton increase in finished output; and it consistently shaped its development planning in the light of the technical needs of the massive outputs envisaged for the future. Its early decision to install a fully-continuous hot strip mill at once rather than to begin with a semi-continuous mill and to convert it to fully-continuous operation later quietened technical doubts about the viability of the new plant.

The Stage I plans for the Spencer Works at Newport provide for the building on a greenfield site of an integrated iron and steel works capable of producing about 1·4 million tons of crude steel a year, together with hot and cold mill capacity for rolling thin, flat products. The works will rely mainly on imported iron ore brought in through new ore-unloading faculties at the adjacent Newport docks, but will also use considerable quantities of home ore from Oxfordshire. All ore will be sintered before going to the two 30-ft. blast furnaces, which should produce about 1·3 million tons a year of basic iron. In turn, all of this iron, together with scrap arising in the works, will be fed into three 100-ton L.D. oxygen-blown converters with an annual output of 1·4 million tons of crude steel. The Spencer Works will thus be the first British works to rely entirely on this new pneumatic process in place of the traditional open-hearth furnaces and Bessemer converters.

The initial output of finished products at Newport will be of the order of 850,000 tons a year, of which the greater part will be cold reduced sheet and the remainder hot-rolled coil, sheet, and plate. In addition, semi-finished steel (slabs and hot-rolled coil) will be supplied to Ebbw Vale for further processing there. The plant will employ about 5,000–6,000 men and is planned to start producing cold-reduced sheets in the first half of 1962. The cost of these Stage I developments is variously estimated at £100 million–£125 million.

The next stage will be to balance up the plant, which involves expanding iron-making and steel-making capacity at one end and cold-rolling and finishing capacity at the other sufficiently to provide a full load for the very high-capacity units in the middle of the production chain. The ultimate capacity of these hot mills when fully stretched cannot yet be estimated, but it may be that Stage II developments may proceed as far as an output of 3–4 million ingot tons a year. This development should proceed at a reasonably low capital cost, so growth up to the 3–4-million-ton level should make Newport increasingly competitive.

Port Talbot

Whatever the potentialities at Newport, the Steel Company of Wales's complex centred on Port Talbot remains at present the biggest unit in the South Wales steel industry and it must be expected that an attempt will be made to maintain this position.

Development at Port Talbot has just about reached the crucial point at which the rest of the plant has expanded far enough to generate a throughput which strains the highest-capacity units, the slabbing mill and the hot strip mill, a point at which basic questions arise as regards the duplication of these heavy units of plant. The scheme to duplicate strip-mill capacity by installing a new 48-in. hot strip mill alongside the existing 80-in. mill indicates clearly that the Company intends to expand further at the Port Talbot site. This project, though geared initially to a comparatively limited expansion of output from 3 million to 3·6 million ingot tons, would not be economic unless conceived in the context of an ultimate expansion of all iron-making to something of the order of 5–6 million ingot tons. This plan for a second hot strip mill at Port Talbot was not approved by the Iron and Steel Board, who feared that the addition of this mill to those envisaged at Newport and Ravenscraig would create wasteful excess capacity. The Company, therefore, proceeded to relieve the strain on the slabbing mill and the hot strip mill by more modest adjustments—in the former case, by the conversion of the original slabbing mill to a higher-capacity universal mill and the projected installation of a newly developed continuous slab-casting plant; and in the latter case, by an agreement providing for slabs from Port Talbot to be rolled-down on the new hot strip mill at Newport and then returned as hot-rolled coil for further processing at Port Talbot, Trostre, or Velindre. Further expansion, however, will clearly necessitate much more radical extensions and it seems likely that these will come in the near future.

An important element in any large-scale expansion at Port Talbot concerns additional ore-unloading facilities, as the present docks provide only limited access for smaller ore-carriers. An increase in ore imports must involve either a substantial redevelopment of Port Talbot docks or else a more radical decision to develop at Milford Haven.

West South Wales

Even if the market for South Wales steel continues to grow at the pace envisaged by the main producers, some parts of the region must decline in face of the impact of the massive expansion planned at Newport and Port Talbot. In particular, this must affect the position in West South Wales, where the remaining obsolete hand mills and the older cold-metal steelworks are concentrated.

The hand mills cannot expect to continue in production much longer in view of their high production costs, the less attractive quality of their product, and their labour difficulties. The prospects for the cold-metal steelworks, however, are less clear-cut. In the short run, the loss of hand-mill outlets and the planned replacement of ingot sales to Ebbw Vale by slabs from Newport must increase the pressure for their closure. In the longer run, the introduction of high-efficiency continuous billet mills in integrated plants, and the 'backward integration' of re-rollers into billet production by the use of comparatively cheap electric arc furnaces and continuous-casting plants, are bound to be unfavourable to independent billet makers; and among the remaining producers of sale billets the West South Wales cold-metal shops must be handicapped by their location in a scrap-deficit area a long way from the main re-rolling centres of the Midlands.

There is no doubt that the main steel plants in the Swansea–Llanelly area will be the two cold reduction tinplate mills of the Steel Company of Wales at Trostre and Velindre. Further growth seems likely at both plants. The trend of the long-term demand for tinplate is regarded as very favourable; and the Company's decision to include in its development plan a new strip mill of a width especially suited to rolling hot strip for tinplate is a fair indication of its determination to provide facilities to meet a considerable part of that demand.

Ebbw Vale

It is an open question whether the growth at Newport may adversely affect the strip-mill plant at Ebbw Vale as well as the older plants in West South Wales. Richard Thomas & Baldwins already have considerable development under way at Ebbw Vale, involving an increase from 700,000 tons to 850,000 tons in ingot output and including the installation of Britain's first L.D. converter. This certainly implies that the Company anticipates a bright future for Ebbw Vale.

Nevertheless, the development at Newport can hardly fail to have an important influence on the pace and possibly on the shape of development at Ebbw Vale. At the very least, the likely rate of expansion at Ebbw Vale will probably be slower than might otherwise have been expected, as any growth of orders will be met by utilizing the latent capacity at Newport in the first instance. To put the impact higher, any severe weakening of the market for thin, flat products might face the Company with the problem of allocating an inadequate total volume of orders between its two hot strip mills; in such circumstances, there might be a tendency to keep the new mill at

Newport reasonably fully loaded in order to spread its heavier over-heads. One suggestion which has been made is that, bearing in mind the comparatively narrow width of the hot strip mill, Ebbw Vale might gradually become a specialized plant, concentrating on certain sizes and types of product, instead of seeking to produce the whole of its present range of thin, flat products.

Other developments

In looking ahead the massive scale of events in the strip-mill field tends to overshadow developments elsewhere. Yet in fact, nearly all the other South Wales plants are closely examining possible expansion or modernization plans.

For example, at Cardiff, G.K.N. (Steel) Ltd., the biggest non-strip-mill plant in South Wales, plans to increase crude-steel production by a third by 1963, from 750,000 tons to 1 million tons a year. The keynote of its programme is the use of new technical advances to secure still greater output from existing heavy units of plant, a method which, by offering substantial increases in output at a com-paratively low cost per ton, is particularly well-adapted to a decade in which the emphasis in the steel industry may be rather more on improving efficiency and rather less on increasing production.

The overall picture

The three threads of rejuvenation, growth, and structural change stand out clearly in this survey of future prospects. As regards re-juvenation, the decade ahead will see the completion of the process begun in the depths of the depression of the thirties, with the final replacement of all the obsolete hand mills by major integrated strip-mill plants. By the mid-sixties the South Wales sheet and tinplate trade should be well able to meet competition from any part of the world.

In assessing growth, allowance must be made for the withdrawal of a considerable amount of cold-metal capacity in West South Wales. Even so, the district may reasonably look forward to a net increase of almost a half over its present steel capacity by (say) 1970, by which date it should be approaching a level of steel output three times as high as at the end of the war. Pig-iron production, moreover, should show a still faster rate of growth.

Finally, as regards structural change, there should be much to record. As the sixties progress, South Wales steel production is likely to become increasingly concentrated in the four main plants at

Port Talbot, Newport, Ebbw Vale, and Cardiff. The cold-metal sector may shrink to three or possibly even fewer works, responsible for a declining share of total output. This shift should be accompanied by a further movement of the pig-iron–scrap balance towards greater reliance on molten iron in steel-making, with a consequent further enlargement of blast-furnace, ore-preparation, sintering, and coke-oven capacity and of ore-unloading facilities. At the finishing end, though the degree of specialization on thin, flat products will increase with developments at Newport and Port Talbot, the district may see a vigorous growth of capacity in other trades, which will help reduce its vulnerability to set-backs in the consumer durables industries and canning. Finally, geographically the twin shifts noted earlier—the move to the coast and the trend to the east—will continue. Over 90 per cent. of South Wales steel production may arise in the area east of Neath by the late sixties, with the Swansea–Llanelly region suffering a major decline as a crude-steel-making area, and the Newport–Cardiff area emerging as one of Britain's major steel concentrations.

This prosperous future, however, depends on three major factors outside the control of the industry. Firstly, of course, it depends above all on the continued expansion of the British economy as a whole. Secondly, it will be much affected by the pattern of that expanding economy and the broad division of national expenditure between investment (which would favour other heavier steel-making districts more) and consumption (which would favour South Wales, with its emphasis on thin, flat products for consumer durables). Thirdly, it will also be influenced by the development of national policy towards reliance on home or foreign ore, the former policy weakening and the latter strengthening the growth prospects of the South Wales industry with its basic dependence on imported ores. Provided no unforeseen turn in these three fields disturbs the picture, however, the prospects of the South Wales steel industry are bright. If there were to emerge a larger and more widely based circle of steel-using industries in South Wales, its prospects would be brighter still.

VII

TRANSPORT

By J. HAMISH RICHARDS

INVESTMENT in transport facilities in the second half of the nineteenth century had fully kept pace with the needs of the expanding South Wales coalfield. Canals, railways, and roads ran down the valleys, linking iron- and steelworks and collieries with the ports, and the east–west main lines in North and South Wales were more than adequate, partly as a by-product of the system of communication established between England and Ireland.

1. *The South Wales ports*

The Second World War caused a sudden shift in the direction of traffic and in the use of ports. It became necessary to transport Welsh coal and metal products on a large scale into England by rail and to import through the South Wales ports, and distribute throughout the country, food and raw materials from abroad. Meanwhile the export trade in coal became negligible. When the war ended the old pattern of trade was not restored. The primacy of coal exports disappeared, and oil became increasingly important both as an import and as an export. Much of the port equipment which had been built for a flourishing coal trade became redundant. The magnitude of this change can be seen if we consider the figures in Tables 63–65 showing the volume of activity since 1913 in the South Wales ports— Newport, Cardiff, Penarth, Barry, Port Talbot, and Swansea—taken as a group.

In 1913 these ports handled 47·2 million tons of inward and outward cargo: by 1959 the total was down to 16·6 million tons. In this period the tonnage exported fell from 42·1 million to 6·2 million, and the tonnage imported rose from 5·1 million to 10·4 million. Overshadowing everything else is the drastic decline in coal shipments from the peak of 37 million tons in 1913 to less than 3 million tons in 1959; the only redeeming feature has been the emergence of an export trade in oil products amounting to just over 2 million tons. On the import side the elements of growth in the period 1913–59

TABLE 63

Trade at the South Wales ports—Newport, Cardiff, Penarth, Barry Port Talbot, and Swansea, 1913–59

Year	Total trade ('000 tons)	Inward traffic ('000 tons)	Inward traffic (% of total)	Outward traffic ('000 tons)	Outward traffic (% of total)
1913 . . .	47,233	5,133	11	42,100	89
1938 . . .	24,528	3,909	16	20,619	84
1947 . . .	10,245	4,382	43	5,863	57
1948 . . .	13,651	5,091	37	8,560	63
1950 . . .	18,586	7,154	38	11,432	62
1952 . . .	22,583	10,008	44	12,575	56
1954 . . .	21,438	9,811	46	11,626	54
1956 . . .	18,838	9,951	53	8,887	47
1959 . . .	16,529	10,356	63	6,173	37

SOURCES: Council for Wales and Monmouthshire, *Report on the South Wales Ports*, Cmd. 9359. British Transport Commission, *Statements of Trade at the South Wales Docks.*

TABLE 64

Inward shipments at the South Wales ports ('000 tons), 1913–59

	1913	1938	1947	1954	1956	1959
Total . . .	5,133	3,909	4,382	9,811	9,951	10,356
Coal and coke .	. .	. .	91	87	308	. .
Iron and other ores .	1,700	990	1,621	3,080	3,683	4,327
Iron and steel .	695	392	140	458	421	155
Oil and spirit .	. .	559	675	4,450	3,532	4,108
Building and road-making materials .	n.a.*	159	195	566	703	707
Pitwood and mining timber . .	n.a.	645	490	335	286	193

SOURCES: As Table 63, with additional data from the *Annual Statement of Trade of the United Kingdom*, 1913, vol. ii.

* n.a. = not available.

were in iron and other ores (1·7 million to 4·3 million tons) and oil (from zero to 4·1 million tons). Thus, the total volume of trade is now less than 35 per cent. of what it was on the eve of the First World War; and exports account for only 37 per cent. of this reduced flow of traffic.

The main reasons for this reversal of fortunes are to be found in the factors which have determined the progress of the British economy since the war. Like rural depopulation, the decline of the ports is part of the price of economic growth. There is a conflict between the new and the old, and the enrichment of the wider community made possible by technical advance necessarily implies the extinction of obsolete ways of doing things. Without losing sight of this funda- mental truth, we must be careful to ask whether some of the equip- ment which seems to be permanently redundant is the victim of

TABLE 65

Outward shipments at the South Wales ports ('000 tons), 1913–59

	1913	1938	1947	1954	1956	1959
Total . . .	42,100	20,619	5,863	11,626	8,887	6,173
Coal, coke, and patent fuel . . .	37,036	19,562	4,545	7,032	5,580	2,747
Oil and spirit . .	..	206	431	3,269	2,153	2,154
Tinplates .	695	349	157	314	311	475
Iron and steel goods		228	215	442	388	563

SOURCES: British Transport Commission, *Statements of Trade at the South Wales Docks*. Finlay Gibson, *A Statistical Account of the Coal Mining Industry*, Cardiff, 1922. *Annual Statement of Trade of the United Kingdom*, 1913, vol. ii.

discriminatory practices. Is it possible that, if certain changes were made in the structure of railway rates, some of the port facilities of South Wales would prove economic? Is the volume of surplus capacity excessive as a result of rigidities in the price mechanism which are themselves an inheritance from the past?

One cannot say that Newport and Cardiff are remote from the west Midlands; from Birmingham the distance by rail to Liverpool is 89 miles, to Newport 96 miles, to Cardiff 107 miles, and to London 110 miles. Certain features of the rail and dock charges now in exis- tence can be explained only in the light of the past. At the beginning of the century London and Liverpool bargained with the railway companies for special rates for transporting various commodities from the Midlands; the Welsh ports at that time were far too pre- occupied with coal to be interested in demanding similar concessions on general merchandise. The British Transport Commission thus in- herited a complex system of preferential rates. This legacy makes transport to Cardiff much more expensive than transport to London. For example, in 1954 the rail rate for motor-cycles from Birmingham to London (110 miles) was 89s. 9d. a ton, whereas from Birmingham to Cardiff (107 miles) it was 126s. 1d. a ton.[1] This handicap is felt mainly by the eastern ports of Newport, Cardiff, and Barry, for Swansea and Port Talbot have reaped the benefit of the traffic in oil and iron ore. We saw in Chapter VI that there has been appreciable investment in ore-handling facilities and that the docks at Port Talbot have been modernized and extended.

The analysis of post-war structure in Chapter II brought out a marked shift towards manufacturing and light engineering, and one might expect a proportion of this new output to be shipped abroad from Welsh ports. There are no comprehensive statistics to draw on, but the evidence which does exist is significant. According to a return made to the Cargo Clearing House of the Industrial Association of Wales and Monmouthshire, eighty firms in South Wales exported over 11,000 tons of miscellaneous manufactured goods in May 1954, and less than 5,000 tons went through local ports. A survey of firms outside Cardiff but within a 30-mile radius of the city was made by the Cardiff Junior Chamber of Commerce in 1957; it found that, whereas exports from this area in 1956 totalled 29,500 tons a month, only 4,900 tons a month went through the port of Cardiff. The other outlets were Swansea, Newport, London, Southampton, Mersey, Avonmouth, and the east coast ports. The most frequently used port was London. Of the 61 categories of exported goods covered by the inquiry, 50 were recorded as going through London, compared with only 30 using South Wales ports. Even the dominating exports, i.e. iron and steel products (67 per cent. of the total) and heavy chemicals (14 per cent. of the total) were to some extent being shipped from Merseyside, London, and other English ports. It is noteworthy that where the quantity sold abroad is very small, e.g. in a number of the products of the trading estate firms, the goods tend to be shipped through an English port and not from South Wales. This is true of such items as valves, rubber products, toys, flooring material, window castings, photographic accessories, and hardware.

How are these facts to be interpreted? Some of the plants located in Wales are branches or subsidiaries of firms whose headquarters are in England, usually in London or the Midlands; it is only natural that the choice of export outlet should depend on considerations affecting the whole and not just the part which happens to be in South Wales. Other factories make semi-finished products which are

[1] For other examples see Council for Wales and Monmouthshire, *Report on the South Wales Ports*, Cmd. 9359, 1955, p. 24.

sent to England for the final stage, or they manufacture component parts which are assembled and exported outside Wales. Small firms producing goods of very high value in small bulk find it economic to send their output by post. The absence of regular cargo liner sailings from South Wales to various destinations means that a ship may have to go to other British ports in order to have a full cargo.[1]

Those whose livelihood depends on the South Wales ports speak in terms of a 'fight for survival' and urge that measures should be adopted to deflect traffic in their favour. One can understand this point of view. It is justified in so far as these ports are handicapped by discriminatory practices serving the interests of other ports, and these should not be tolerated any more than other restrictive practices. However, any reform likely to take place in the near future will have only a minor effect. The plight of the South Wales ports is mainly due to a permanent shift in effective demand; their huge capacity was brought into existence to serve needs which are no longer present.

2. *The Railways*

During the Second World War the Great Western Railway was called upon to transport a greatly increased volume of imports from the South Wales ports and to take large quantities of coal and steel through the Severn Tunnel. By the end of 1940 for every extra coal train passing through the tunnel three passenger trains had to be taken off or diverted; it was kept open on Sundays for these coal trains even though this meant postponing normal maintenance and improvements. The task of 'quadrupling'[2] the line between Newport and Severn Tunnel Junction was completed during 1941 at a cost of £250,000. The extent of the adjustment is shown by the following figures. In September 1939 the railways carried on an average each week 350,000 tons of coal from Welsh pits to the ports, 183,000 tons to inland destinations in South Wales, and 88,000 tons to inland destinations outside South Wales. In September 1941 the ports received only 146,000 tons a week, while inland destinations in South Wales took 201,000 tons and other inland destinations 155,000 tons. During October and November 1941 over 700 trains (including 300

---

[1] See Cardiff Junior Chamber of Commerce, *Report on a Survey of Local Trade and Industry Imports and Exports, 1956/7* (mimeographed).

[2] 'Quadrupling' means converting a line into four tracks. See C. I. Savage, *Inland Transport*, History of the Second World War, United Kingdom Civil Series, London, 1957.

coal trains) were using the Severn Tunnel, Gloucester, and Hereford routes. Traffic through the Welsh ports had to be curtailed, not because they were over-worked but because the railways had reached their limit. The provision of loops and more quadrupling eased the strain during 1942, but the demands for rail transport still exceeded available capacity.

After the war, when the railways were nationalized, the problem of arrears of maintenance loomed large. The need was less pressing in South Wales, for substantial capital outlays had had to be incurred to meet exceptional war-time demands. It soon became evident that the new pattern of coal consumption which had emerged during the war was going to last. In 1938 63 per cent. of the coal produced in South Wales passed through the ports, 21 per cent. was used locally, and 16 per cent. was sent by rail to England: fifteen years later only 30 per cent. went through the ports, whereas local consumption absorbed 46 per cent. and 24 per cent. went to England.[1] Extra lines have been provided to cater for new collieries and coke ovens, and changes have been made in wagon construction to increase the load per vehicle.

The analysis of the post-war expansion of the steel industry in Chapter VI showed that South Wales now imports almost 4 million tons of iron ore and produces a quarter of the crude-steel output of the United Kingdom. An important part of the operations consists of intra-industry transfers of semi-finished steel for further conversion, particularly of re-rolling billets and sheet and tinplate bars. Of the total deliveries of 3,678,000 tons of steel in 1957, 15 per cent. were taken by the hollow-ware industries and 4 per cent. by the electrical machinery and apparatus trades. This has entailed a greatly increased demand for rail transport and for investment in supplementary sidings and marshalling yards. 'Metal trains' run daily to the Midlands and London, specially built wagons take hot strip coil from the Abbey Works to Trostre, and others carry pickled coil to Velindre. The Welsh railway network, originally brought into being by the needs of a coal-exporting economy, is now becoming increasingly the servant of a dynamic steel industry. But the valley network, linking the collieries to the ports, lies in a north–south direction. Despite the decline in exports, the direction of coal-haulage has not changed; much of the coal is still taken down the valley to the coke ovens

[1] See H. H. Swift, 'The Importance of the South Wales Area to the Western Region', a lecture to the British Railways Debating Society, Jan. 1954.

situated on the edge of the coalfield, and coke is then taken to the steel-works which are found along the coast. Apart from the extra sidings and lines needed at new collieries and coke ovens, this railway net-work of 1914 adequately caters for the traffic of 1960. The steel industry requires an east–west rather than a north–south axis to link the steelworks with one another and with the English markets. To meet the needs of the growing steel industry it is vital that east–west traffic is speeded up both by the introduction of improved methods of signalling and the laying of new tracks.

3. Road and air transport

The annual censuses of mechanically propelled vehicles show that motor-traffic in Wales has been expanding far more rapidly than in other parts of Britain. The indexes given in Table 66 (the latest available) indicate that the number of goods vehicles using Welsh main roads more than doubled between 1938 and 1953, whereas the increase in the country as a whole was 88 per cent. Since 1953 this trend has continued at an even greater rate. The total number of licensed vehicles in Wales in 1959 (415,000) was 66 per cent. higher than in 1953, while the number of goods vehicles increased by 42 per cent. in the same period. This has caused serious congestion in the industrial areas and the approaches to them. During one week in August 1954 the average number of vehicles passing over Newport bridge (a major link between South Wales and England, taking only two streams of traffic) was nearly 1,000 an hour; by 1960 this figure had more than doubled. Another much-used bridge over the River Wye at Chepstow is limited to single-line working and to vehicles under 24 tons.

TABLE 66

Great Britain, England, Scotland, and Wales: Indexes of traffic on Trunk and Class I roads, 1953 (1938 = 100)

Area	Total me-chanically propelled vehicles	Cars	Motor-cycles	Omni-buses	Goods vehicles	Pedal-cycles
Great Britain . .	124	104	146	140	188	64
England . . .	123	103	146	137	183	62
Scotland . . .	123	99	150	144	197	77
Wales	136	113	147	171	237	126

SOURCE: *Report on the Administration of the Road Fund*, H.M.S.O., 1953.

Between March 1949 and March 1959 over £78 million was spent on Welsh roads, of which over £14 million was devoted to the new construction and major improvements of the 937 miles of trunk road. The main projects of this period are to be found on the Newport–Swansea section of the A 48 and include both the Briton Ferry by-pass and the Neath by-pass. In addition, the new Conway bridge was opened, while a 2-mile stretch of dual carriageway on the Cardiff–Merthyr Tydfil road merely points to the better conditions that will eventually be found throughout the Taff Valley. It is possible that construction outside Wales will have an even greater influence on the Principality than internal improvements. The Ross Spur motorway was opened in 1960 and the Birmingham–Bristol motorway, when extended to the South Wales ports in the form of a dual carriageway, should result in increased activity at the ports, even though Bristol is likely to reap the greater advantage.

Four features of the Ministry of Transport's plan for the future are worthy of note.

In North Wales the A 55 coastal route is to be improved, thus strengthening the link between the main centres in the north of the Principality and the industrial areas of Lancashire and the Midlands, from whence come the majority of the visitors to the northern holiday resorts. In addition to the new bridge at Conway, work has begun on the Queensferry viaduct and by-pass.[1]

Another important feature is the continuation of the Ross Spur to Newport via Raglan, where it will join up with the Heads of the Valleys road. The completion of this three-lane route will provide modern communications between Swansea, the industrial valleys, and the Midlands.

Thirdly, the construction of a dual carriageway from Newport to Swansea (the Welsh section of the London–South Wales motorway) with by-passes at Newport, Cardiff, Cowbridge, and Port Talbot, will bring considerable benefit to West Wales. The much-needed Port Talbot by-pass is an ambitious scheme involving complex engineering problems, as a big part of it will be on a viaduct. There is a plan to relieve the notorious traffic congestion at Newport by taking the London–South Wales motorway north of the town. This will entail a new bridge over the Usk. A second river-crossing in the town centre will also be constructed during the decade.

[1] For a detailed account of these schemes, see A. G. Curtis and J. J. Liptrott, 'Three Big Projects put Wales on the Road Map', *Western Mail, Transport Review*, June 1960.

Ironically, the most important Welsh feature of the Ministry of Transport plans is outside Wales, namely, the long-awaited Severn Bridge, which, along with the new Wye Bridge, is to be completed by 1965–6. The Severn Bridge is essential to any plan to improve communications. At present traffic has to make a detour through Gloucester; the road between Newport and Gloucester, a distance of 44 miles, is winding and undulating. South of Gloucester the only means of crossing the Severn, apart from the railway tunnel, is an old motor-ferry at Beachley–Aust capable of carrying about 400 vehicles a day.

The economies to be expected from the Severn Bridge were illustrated by Sir David Llewellyn (M.P. for Cardiff North, 1950–9) in the debate in the House of Commons on 29 April 1955.[1] First, a South Wales steel firm would save about 9s. 2d. a ton on a journey from Cardiff to south-west England and about 3s. 8d. a ton on a journey from South Wales to London. Secondly, a large transport organization, operating an average of thirty-six vehicles a day between South Wales and south-west England and 190 vehicles a day from South Wales to London, has estimated that, given an actual operating cost of 1s. per mile, there would be a net saving of £62,500 a year on operating costs alone, quite apart from the time saved. An expert has forecast the economies in transport operating costs at £4 million per annum, compared with an estimated cost of the whole South Wales–West Midland motorway scheme of £37,400,000 including £10,600,000 for the Severn bridge.[2]

The construction of a new trunk road linking North and South Wales has been under discussion since 1931. Arguments that such a road would open up North Wales as a tourist centre, facilitate the transport of agricultural products of mid-Wales to urban markets, diminish the remoteness of central Wales, and foster the growth of industry in rural areas have been dismissed by the Ministry of Transport. The tourist industry of North Wales is best provided for by the improvement of east–west routes, while the existing roads through Wales only require relatively minor alterations to make them capable of carrying the limited volume of traffic which goes that way.

Instead of a new trunk road, the Ministry propose to use existing roads on a route from Pentrefoelas to Builth Wells. Under these

[1] *Hansard*, vol. 540, 29 Apr. 1955, cols. 1301–10.
[2] C. T. Brunner, Past President of the Institute of Highway Engineers, in a paper read before the National Conference of the Town and Country Planning Association, Dec. 1955. A more recent estimate of the cost of the bridge is £16 million.

proposals only 3 miles of new road will have to be built, but 57 miles of Class I road have already been added to the trunk road system. Already numerous sections of this roadway have been improved. Although political dreams will not come true, Wales will be provided with an adequate link between north and south.

Many of the minor roads in rural Wales are unfortunately below standard. The burden of maintenance and improvement has exceeded the resources of many local authorities; the Council for Wales and Monmouthshire has more than once emphasized the seriousness of the problem,[1] and the need has also been recognized in a Government White Paper.[2]

In June 1955 the Government introduced the Agricultural (Improvement of Roads) Bill,[3] to enable the Minister of Agriculture and the Secretary of State for Scotland to make grants to highway authorities for improvements to unclassified and unadopted roads serving livestock-rearing areas. The Bill provided for grants amounting to £4 million. It has been criticized on the grounds that when it was originally planned the Minister of Agriculture intended to spend £4 million in Wales alone. That sum, however, had to be shared between Wales and certain areas in England and Scotland.

Access to the ports is inadequate, both from the Midlands and from the valleys. Narrow, old-fashioned highways are hampering industrial development and adding to costs. Congestion at Newport, Chepstow, and the Severn Tunnel will be aggravated as motor-car manufacturing and steel production increase in the Cardiff and Newport areas. The present picture, dominated by bottlenecks and holdups, is depressing, but the future is bright. In the late 1960's the Severn Bridge, the Birmingham–Ross Spur–Cardiff highway, the Heads of the Valleys road, the Newport by-pass, and the Port Talbot by-pass are likely to be completed; the North Wales coast route will be nearing completion and the Cardiff–Merthyr Tydfil and Newport–Swansea dual carriageways will come at a later stage. This major investment, along with numerous minor improvements being carried out each year, will give Wales a system of highways capable of meeting all the demands placed upon it by a constantly growing economy. With the construction of new highways Wales will benefit from closer integration with the rest of the kingdom.

[1] The Council for Wales and Monmouthshire, *A Memorandum by the Council on its Activities*, 1950, and *Second Memorandum by the Council on its Activities*, 1953.
[2] White Paper on Rural Wales, Cmd. 9014, 1953.
[3] *Hansard*, vol. 542, 10 June 1955, col. 142.

It is unlikely that air transport in Wales will ever become a major means of communication; the volume of traffic is shown in Table 67. The number of passengers using Cardiff Airport rose from 10,200 in 1952 to 46,400 in 1958 but declined to 41,200 in 1959. The volume of freight carried is small. There are hardly any export products of high value in small bulk which would be suited for shipment by air. Internationally, Wales is well served by London Airport—less than 150 miles from Cardiff; and internally the difficulty in getting from north to south cannot be compared with the problems facing anyone who has to travel from central Scotland to either the Highlands or the Islands by any means other than by air.

TABLE 67

Activity at Cardiff airports* (Pengam Moors and Rhoose), 1950–9

	Unit	1950	1952	1954†	1955	1958	1959
Passengers handled .	Number	5,780	10,232	23,932	33,144	46,357	41,220
Terminal . .	,,	5,779	8,054	18,072	22.857	35,179	28,213
Transit . . .	,,	1	2,178	5,860	10,287	11,178	13,007
Scheduled . . .	,,	4,924	9,920	21,791	30,917	38,160	39,904
Terminal . .	,,	4,924	7,750	15,957	20,677	27,081	26,932
Transit . . .	,,	—	2,170	5,834	10,240	11,079	12,972
Charter . . .	,,	856	312	2,141	2,227	8,197	1,316
Terminal . .	,,	855	404	2,115	2,180	8,098	1,281
Transit . . .	,,	1	8	26	47	99	35
Freight handled . .	short tons	0·9	6·0	369·0	428·0	222·2	367·9
Set down . . .	,,	0·1	2·0	351·0	398·0	13·8	16·8
Picked up . .	,,	0·8	4·0	18·0	30·0	208·4	351·1

* Figures for 1950 relate to Pengam Moors Airport only; figures for 1952, and 1954 include traffic at Rhoose Airport.

† Pengam Moors did not operate after Mar. 1954.

SOURCE: *Digest of Welsh Statistics.*

Rhoose Airport is used mainly by Cambrian Airways and Aer Lingus, and the main routes are to Dublin, Liverpool, the Channel Islands, and France. The volume of tourist traffic has been increasing rapidly and there is every prospect that this will continue in the future.

4. *Summary*

The picture emerging from this chapter is one of surplus capacity in some forms of transport co-existing with crippling deficiencies in others. When an area experiences simultaneously a wave of technical innovations in its major industries and a profound shift in consumer demand, it is impossible in the short run for the media of transport to adapt themselves. The transition is marked by painful frictions. With only a small windfall of investment in railways made under the exigencies of war, South Wales in the 1950's had to face a radically new pattern of demand with a transport system geared to the needs of forty years before. However, there are now signs that the fundamental adjustment is taking place and that the Welsh economy of the 1960's will have a network of communications very different from what it inherited at the end of the Second World War.

VIII

INCOME AND CONSUMERS' EXPENDITURE

By J. PARRY LEWIS

SOME progress has been made in recent years in overcoming the difficulties involved in measuring income regionally. In this chapter we present an estimate of the national product of Wales and compare it with the results obtained by Dr. Edward Nevin. A fairly complete account of personal incomes can be given on the basis of statistics published by the Commissioners of Inland Revenue. Finally, we shall indicate the pattern of household expenditure and the main features of wholesale and retail trade as revealed by the Census of Distribution.

1. *The national product*

We define the Welsh national product as the total amount that is added to the value of goods and services as the result of work performed in Wales. It is equivalent to the sum of all incomes (earned and unearned) accruing to persons in Wales, after making appropriate allowances for income from abroad (which in this context includes England).

Everyone who has used the National Income and Expenditure figures for the United Kingdom is aware of the difficulties surrounding these estimates. Even when primary data are plentiful, there is still much uncertainty. The Central Statistical Office considers that its estimates of the gross national product of the United Kingdom are unlikely to be wrong by more than 3 per cent. (some £600 million), but it is less sanguine about the reliability of some of the component parts. It feels, for example, that probably the error in its estimate of gross domestic fixed capital formation lies between 3 per cent. and 10 per cent.; while stock appreciation and net income from abroad are subject to an error which is quite likely to be greater than 10 per cent. Even estimates of consumers' expenditures on such items as furniture, private motoring, and cycling have this unknown error, quite probably exceeding 10 per cent.[1]

[1] See Central Statistical Office, *National Income Statistics, Sources and Methods*, London, 1956.

If estimates for the United Kingdom have errors such as these, it is not surprising that until recently the fragmentary data available for Wales deterred statisticians from attempting similar calculations on a regional basis. Since the Second World War, however, the various censuses of production and the 1950 Census of Distribution have made the outlook more promising.

The foundation of our analysis is the Census of Production, 1948, the results of which were published in great detail for regions. It covered industrial undertakings, including public utilities, mines, and quarries. Private firms, nationalized industries, and government establishments were all included. Firms were required to supply information about the calendar year; but, where the firm's business year differed from the calendar year, a return for the appropriate business year was accepted. Firms employing ten people or fewer were usually asked to state only the nature of their business and the number of persons employed. Larger establishments had to supply more detailed information, including the value of gross and net output and the amount paid in wages and salaries.

The censuses of 1949 and 1950 were rather less detailed than that of 1948, but still contain a great deal of valuable regional information. The 1950 census omitted the building and contracting trades and made only limited inquiries of those firms which were also being asked to supply information for the Census of Distribution. The 1951 census had a wider scope and was similar to that of 1948. Before referring to the later censuses we shall take a look at the estimates based on those already mentioned.

Miss Phyllis Deane's estimates of annual earnings in 1948, summarized in Table 68, show that the average annual earnings in Wales are almost identical with the United Kingdom average. Although the proportion of employees engaged in manufacturing industries was low compared with the United Kingdom, the average wage was high. Agriculture showed a very poor return. In mining and quarrying the average earnings were lower than elsewhere but still considerably above the average for all industries; it is because almost a sixth of the employed population was engaged in this industry that the average earnings were so high. Except in manufacturing industries, Welsh average earnings were always lower than the United Kingdom average and usually lower than the Scottish; but a greater proportion of Welsh workers were to be found in the well-paid industries.

The aggregate annual earnings of £275·5 million estimated for

TABLE 68

United Kingdom, Wales, and Scotland: Average numbers employed, average annual earnings, and aggregate earnings, by industry group, 1948

	Estimated average numbers employed ('000)			Average annual earnings (£)			Aggregate earnings (£m.)		
	United Kingdom	Wales	Scotland	United Kingdom	Wales	Scotland	United Kingdom	Wales	Scotland
Agriculture, forestry, and fishing	966·7	42·7	127·6	279	222	255	270·2	9·5	32·6
Mining and quarrying	876·7	140·8	98·5	385	366	392	338·0	51·6	38·6
Manufacture	8,098·4	243·0	756·0	310	321	289	2,514·4	77·9	218·6
Building and contracting	1,323·7	59·8	146·7	317	305	320	419·1	18·2	47·0
Gas, electricity, and water	318·3	13·1	23·8	344	320	323	109·5	4·2	7·7
Transport and communication	1,778·0	90·0	191·7	370	363	356	657·3	32·7	68·3
Distributive trades	2,077·2	80·7	229·9	278	257	256	577·0	20·7	58·9
Insurance, banking, and finance	431·6	10·2	31·1	457	421	421	197·4	4·3	13·1
Public administration	1,463·0	69·9	122·2	348	310	330	509·2	21·7	40·3
Professional services	1,320·9	57·9	144·4	345	344	348	455·3	19·9	50·3
Miscellaneous services	1,805·8	70·3	160·7	223	211	212	402·4	14·8	34·1
TOTAL, ALL INDUSTRIES	20,460·3	878·2	2,032·6	315	314	300	6,449·8	275·5	609·5

SOURCE: Phyllis Deane, 'Regional Variations in United Kingdom Incomes from Employment', *J.R.S.S. (A)*, vol. cxvi, Part II, 1953.

1948 by Miss Deane arose from all industries. The total wages and salaries of people working in larger establishments covered by the 1948 Census of Production came to only £148 million. This sum was shared between about 444,000 employees. Smaller firms in the same industries employed a further 26,000 people. It is clear that the Census of Production covers only about half of Welsh industry, and we shall have to try to supplement its information from other sources. First, however, we must note two problems raised by regional analysis of Census of Production data. One is that of estimating how much is earned by employees in small establishments employing not more than ten people, about which little information is published. The second is more difficult, arising out of the confidential nature of returns made by firms to the Board of Trade. Where publication of regional information about a certain trade would disclose facts about a particular firm, it was withheld. Of the 150 trade groups for which some data were published, 60 were such that the publication of complete figures for Wales would have involved breach of confidence. The Summary Tables published by the Board of Trade say nothing about the output or earnings of small firms, but do contain totals for large firms covering all trades including those for which separate information has been withheld.[1]

By making reasonable inferences from figures of output per head and regional employment, it is possible to estimate the output and earnings of small firms and of trades for which Welsh figures are not given. The results are set out in Table 69. It is not easy to check the plausibility of individual items. However, it is encouraging to note that, according to the Summary Tables,[2] total wages and salaries of persons employed in large firms amounted to £147·7 million and that, if we assume that the 26,000 people employed in small firms received the same average pay as the 444,000 in larger firms, we obtain a total of wages and salaries of £156·5 million for all firms covered by the census, which happens to be identical with the total presented in Table 69.

These calculations cover only about half of the Welsh wage and salary bill. For the other half we may turn, for 1950, to the Census of Distribution and other sources and use heroic assumptions to extract estimates, which in some cases are of doubtful validity.

[1] Board of Trade, *Censuses of Production for 1950, 1949 and 1948, Summary Tables*, Part I, 1953, Table 3.
[2] Ibid., Table 3.

Similarly, it is possible to estimate the Welsh gross domestic product, which may be defined as the value of goods and services being made available for consumption or added to wealth as the result of work performed in Wales. By making some arbitrary allowances for smaller establishments and for trades for which Welsh information is not given, we can calculate fairly accurately the total

TABLE 69

Wales: Estimated remuneration of workers in certain industries, 1948 (including employers' National Insurance contributions)

	£m.	£m.
Mining and quarrying		49·5
Manufacturing industries		
Treatment of non-metalliferous mining products other than coal	3·6	
Chemical and allied trades	5·2	
Metal manufacture	28·9	
Engineering, shipbuilding, and electrical goods .	11·2	
Vehicles	4·7	
Metal goods not elsewhere specified . . .	4·8	
Precision instruments, jewellery, &c. . . .	0·8	
Textiles	3·5	
Leather, leather goods, and fur	0·4	
Clothing	1·8	
Food, drink, and tobacco	6·2	
Manufactures of wood and cork	1·8	
Paper and printing	1·6	
Other manufacturing industries	1·2	
Total manufacturing industries		75·6
Building and contracting		27·0
Gas, electricity, and water-supply		4·4
TOTAL FOR ABOVE INDUSTRIES		156·5

addition to output by the industries covered by the census, but it is much more difficult when we come to the total product of such industries as agriculture and banking, insurance, and finance.

Table 70 compares our estimates with those reached by Dr. Edward Nevin.[1] It will be seen that Dr. Nevin's original estimate of £483·75 million for the gross domestic product of Wales compares very closely with our own preliminary estimate of £486·9 million, although the

---

[1] Edward Nevin, *The Social Accounts of the Welsh Economy, 1948 to 1952*, University of Wales Press, Cardiff, 1956, and *The Social Accounts of the Welsh Economy, 1948 to 1956*, University of Wales Press, Cardiff, 1957.

component figures show some variation. The revised total of £506 million is much larger than ours, but since the latter was never intended to be more than a rough indication (relying, as it did, on some doubtful assumptions about the industries in the lower half of the table), it is probable that Dr. Nevin's revised estimate of the gross domestic product is nearer the mark than our preliminary one. It will

TABLE 70

Wales: Gross domestic product by industry of origin, 1950 (£m.)

	Income from employment		Total product		
	Nevin's first estimate	Nevin's revised estimate	Nevin's first estimate	Nevin's revised estimate	Lewis's estimate
Agriculture	12	13	26	34	29
Mining and quarrying . . .	52	53	57	57	56
Manufacturing industries . .	91	94	151	151	151
Building and contracting . .	26	31	32	36	36
Gas, electricity, and water . .	6	7	8	12	12
Transport and communications .	31	32	46	44	47
Distribution	24	28	48	52	49
Banking, insurance, and finance .	6	5	9	8	7
Other services	23	13	43	44	42
Public administration and defence .	29	24	29	24	23
Public health and education . .	16	21	15	21	16
Dwellings	..	4	15	16	15
Domestic services	3	4	3	4	4
Services to private non-profit-making bodies	..	..	..	4	..
Gross domestic product excluding stock appreciation . . .	..	..	483	507	487
Less Stock appreciation . .	..	..	27	25	..
Residual error	..	..	1	..	..
Gross domestic product at factor cost	..	..	458	482	..

SOURCES: Nevin, *The Social Accounts of the Welsh Economy 1950*, Department of Economics, University College of Wales, Aberystwyth, 1955. Nevin, ed., *The Social Accounts of the Welsh Economy 1948 to 1956*, Welsh Economic Studies No. 2, University of Wales Press, Cardiff, 1957.

be noticed that in most cases Dr. Nevin's corrections are in the same direction as the differences between his own preliminary estimates and ours, although in many cases they are greater in magnitude.

Table 71 compares our preliminary estimates and Dr. Nevin's final estimates of the net output of manufacturing industries. Once again, while the totals agree, there are disparities in the component parts, notably in the food, drink, and tobacco group. In so far as these estimates rely on the Censuses of Production for the years before 1952, they are reasonably reliable. The same cannot be said for industries not covered by the census. Despite the results of the

1950 Census of Distribution, the Central Statistical Office considers that even its United Kingdom estimates of wages in the distributive trades may have errors exceeding 10 per cent. The wage bill in insurance, banking, and finance has a similar possible error, as have a number of other items in the lower half of Table 71. One has only to note the methods used by the Central Statistical Office to see the impossibility of obtaining regional estimates for many of these items with margins of error that are at all reasonable. It is even more difficult to use the data collected since 1952.

TABLE 71

Wales: Net output of manufacturing industries, 1950

	£m.	£m.
Treatment of non-metalliferous mining products other than coal	6·1	7
Chemical and allied trades	14·0	12
Metal manufacture	58·7	57
Engineering, shipbuilding, and electrical goods . .	15·7	16
Vehicles	10·5	12
Metal goods not elsewhere specified	8·5	8
Precision instruments, jewellery, &c.	2·1	2
Textiles, leather, leather goods, fur, and clothing . .	16·2	14
Food, drink, and tobacco	7·6	14
Manufactures of wood and cork	3·2	3
Paper and printing	3·3	3
Other manufacturing industries	4·0	3
Error	1·2	
TOTAL	151·1	151

Column 1 shows our own estimates and column 2 Dr. Nevin's.

The Censuses of Production for 1948–51 sought information for all establishments within their scope. The 1952 Census, however, relied on a sample of about one establishment in six, and that of 1953 on only one in seven. The 1954 Census was similar to those taken in 1948 and 1951 but the presentation of results is inferior. For the first time the Board of Trade calculates the principal aggregates for the whole of an industry, estimating the output of smaller establishments by assuming that output per head is the same in smaller establishments as in the larger ones. The only Welsh information published is of this kind. In some cases it does not matter, but in other industries common experience and analyses of output by size of establishment suggest that error may be introduced in this way; and in our estimates for 1950 adjustments for this factor had often to be made. This is now impossible. The other point is that sometimes the data are published to a very inadequate number of figures. For instance, the net output of brass manufactures in Wales is given as '£0·35 million', while employment is given as '0·57 thousands', but for the gas-supply industry we are given a net output of simply '£4 million' and an employment of '5 thousands'. Quite apart from the fact that the error of rounding in one case may exceed the published data in another, and so make addition rather difficult, this device removes all meaning from a number of calculations. The 1954 Census of Production is of much less use to regional statisticians than it could have been.

As we have already shown, except for those industries covered by the Census of Production, and even for these except in the earlier years, the calculation of net output entails wide margins of error. A further source of error is introduced when we attempt to allow for stock appreciation, and any estimate of the gross domestic product must suffer accordingly. To turn this estimate of gross domestic product into the gross national product, we have the awkward problem of allowing for net income from abroad. In the present state of our knowledge this is virtually impossible. An alternative approach is to build up the account from the expenditure side. It is tempting to rely heavily on the Census of Distribution for this, but it is rather risky. Even apart from this, the expenditure approach to the national product can be completed only if we have enough information about Welsh imports and exports. As for net income from abroad, our present state of knowledge makes this impossible.[1]

We conclude that with the primary statistics at present available it is too much to expect an accurate estimate of the national product of Wales. The margin of error in the only published estimates of net income from abroad cannot be overlooked; it is dangerous to use estimates which may be not only of the wrong magnitude but also of the wrong sign. We must, instead, be content with an estimate of gross domestic product which ignores income from abroad.

2. *Personal incomes*

Inland Revenue reports contain information about incomes *assessed* in a particular year and not *received* in that year. The

---

[1] This matter is discussed more fully in the *Bulletin of the Oxford University Institute of Statistics*, vol. xix, No. 3, Aug. 1957, in two papers, one by myself and one by Dr. Nevin.

statistics used in this section are based on assessments made in 1949/50 and 1954/5. But an assessment may be made at any time within six years of the end of the financial year in which it is earned. In addition, a real difficulty arises out of Schedule D incomes, since the assessment of trading profits and professional earnings is based on the profit made in the taxpayer's accounting year ending in the preceding year of assessment. Hence it is possible for the 'assessed income' of a given year to include sums earned some time during the previous six years. Bearing these complications in mind, we follow the Inland Revenue Commissioners in assuming that the assessments for, say, 1949/50 relate to wages, salaries, and dividends arising in that year and to profits and professional earnings made in the preceding year.

Another source of trouble is not so complicated but may cause rather more uncertainty. Usually a Schedule E assessment is made in the area of employment rather than in the place of residence, although there are important exceptions to this rule. On the other hand, Schedule D assessments normally depend on the location of the head office of the business concerned. Consequently a person with incomes from more than one source may have assessments made in more than one place. For the years 1949/50 and 1954/5 the Inland Revenue Commissioners conducted sample censuses of the returns in order to obtain information about the total incomes of people with more than one source of income. The first census was a 10 per cent. sample and the second a 5 per cent. The results were published in full for the whole of the United Kingdom, Wales, Scotland, and Northern Ireland, and (to a lesser extent) for counties.[1] In this geographical break-down the income census allocated the whole of a person's income to the county in which the major segment of income was assessed, and this would not always be the county of residence or even of employment. For example, the great majority of non-industrial civil servants and members of the armed forces and the merchant navy were treated centrally, and appear in the United Kingdom analysis but not in the Welsh figures. These factors are bound to introduce uncertainty into the regional figures. It would therefore be unwise to attempt any refined calculations or ambitious estimates.

Two other points may be made about discrepancies between the

---

[1] *94th, 95th, 99th, and 100th Reports of the Commissioners of Her Majesty's Inland Revenue*, Cmd. 8436, Cmd. 8726, Cmnd. 54, Cmnd. 341.

results of the income censuses and independent statistics. First, there is a deficiency in the income reported as arising from interest and dividends taxed at source. The *94th Inland Revenue Report* tells us that it seemed to affect mainly the income ranges below £2,000 and resulted in many people with incomes below that figure appearing in a bracket lower than the correct one. Secondly, National Insurance statistics reveal that in 1949/50 there were over a million married women in employment in the United Kingdom of whom the Inland Revenue had no trace and 'a large number' five years subsequently. Many of these women were probably not earning enough to be taxed.

Having indicated the pitfalls, we shall now compare incomes assessed in Wales with those in the United Kingdom and examine their distribution by type between 1949/50 and 1954/5, the regional and local differences and the distribution by type of income are summarized in Table 72.

During the five years, 1949/50 and 1954/5, the number of assessments of earned income made in Wales rose from 865,615 to 875,900, an increase of 1·2 per cent. compared with 1·5 per cent. in the United Kingdom. The people concerned earned £307·2 million in 1949/50 and £439·7 million five years later. The average earned income in Wales thus rose from £355 to £502, and in the United Kingdom from £383 to £531.

When we look at the components of earned income we notice some interesting differences between Wales and the United Kingdom. The number of profit and professional earning assessments made in Wales increased in the five years by 17 per cent. (from 79,889 to 93,618) compared with only 6 per cent. in the United Kingdom, and the average assessment rose by 20 per cent. from £462 to £552 as against 11 per cent. from £595 to £659 in the United Kingdom. While these Schedule D incomes are much lower in Wales and their rate of increase was only half that of earned incomes generally, they nevertheless went up more in Wales than in the United Kingdom both absolutely and relatively.

Earned incomes are divided into three categories, the first of which is wages and salaries, the main source of income. The number of assessments made in Wales was virtually the same in 1954/5 as five years earlier, while there was an increase of nearly 3 per cent. in the United Kingdom. The amount of money assessed under this heading rose by over £100 million, which raised the average ('principal source') wage and salary by 40 per cent. from £331 to £462. In the

United Kingdom the corresponding rate of increase was 38 per cent., from £344 to £475.

TABLE 72

Wales and the United Kingdom: Classification of incomes (before tax) by type of income, 1949/50 and 1954/5

Type of income	Year	Wales			United Kingdom		
		Number of cases	Amount	Average	Number of cases	Amount	Average
		('000)	(£m.)	(£)	('000)	(£m.)	(£)
1. *Earned income*							
(a) Profits and professional	1949/50	80	36·9	462	1,454	865·5	595
Earnings (Schedule D)	1954/5	94	51·7	552	1,547	1,019·6	659
(b) Wages and salaries, &c. (Schedule E)							
(i) Principal source .	1949/50	777	257·3	331	17,657	6,065·3	344
	1954/5	777	359·3	462	18,155	8,628·2	475
(ii) Wife's earnings .	1949/50	30	4·5	154	1,412	225·0	159
	1954/5	78	17·0	217	2,562	559·7	218
(iii) Other . . .	1949/50	..	5·9	..	..	290·1	..
	1954/5	..	6·9	..	..	227·7	..
(c) Family allowances .	1949/50	130	2·6	20	2,735	52·2	19
	1954/5	150	4·8	32	3,282	102·7	31
TOTAL EARNED INCOME .	1949/50	866	307·2	355	19,552	7,498·2	383
	1954/5	876	439·7	502	19,847	10,537·8	531
2. *Investment income*							
(a) Property (A and B) .	1949/50	182	8·3	45	3,761	189·8	50
	1954/5	240	8·2	34	5,005	210·6	42
(b) Investments and dividends . . .	1949/50	..	17·0	..	..	684·8	..
	1954/5	..	20·4	..	..	850·8	..
TOTAL INVESTMENT INCOME	1949/50	224	25·3	113	5,255	874·6	166
	1954/5	253	28·6	113	5,445	1,061·4	195
TOTAL GROSS INCOME .	1949/50	..	332·6	375	..	8,372·8	418
	1954/5	..	468·3	525	..	11,599·2	572
Deductions							
(a) Expenses . . .	1949/50	..	14·8	..	..	314·7	..
	1954/5	..	18·5	..	..	422·2	..
(b) Interest, &c. . .	1949/50	..	2·1	..	..	79·6	..
	1954/5	..	2·9	..	..	103·5	..
TOTAL NET INCOME . .	1949/50	887	315·7	356	20,040	7,978·5	398
	1954/5	891	446·8	501	20,280	11,073·6	546

NOTE: The U.K. figures include non-industrial civil servants, and members of the armed forces and merchant navy. The Welsh figures do not.

SOURCES: *94th Inland Revenue Report*, Tables 90 and 98, corrected from notes on p. 94 of the *95th Report*; and *99th Report*, Tables 55 and 63.

The most significant change was in the amount of wives' earnings. The number of these assessments rose by no less than 165 per cent. (from under 30,000 to 78,000) compared with 81 per cent. in the United Kingdom. This is far more than the increase in employment of married women during this period and may be attributed to wage increases which brought many into the taxpaying categories for the first time. Average earnings rose from £154 to £217 (by 41 per cent.) and the total amount under this heading moved from £4·5 million to £17 million. Wives' earnings were still less than 4 per cent. of total earned income in Wales, compared with over 5 per cent. in the United Kingdom.

It seems that the relative growth in average earned income in Wales was due partly to the spectacular but misleading increase in the assessed income of wives and partly to the rise in the number of assessments and average income of professional people and traders. The overall expansion of about 40 per cent. in wages and salaries conceals wide variations between industries.

The number of people assessed for property income rose by 31 per cent. from 182,000 to 240,000, but total income from this source stayed at just over £8 million, the average falling from £45 to £34. In the United Kingdom the rate of growth in the number of property incomes was a little higher at 33 per cent. and the sum went up from £190 million to £211 million, bringing the average from £50 to £42. Over a quarter of the people paying tax in Wales had some income from property or land. The proportion in the United Kingdom was slightly lower, but this may be due to the presentation of the data which excludes the non-property-owning members of the armed forces from the regional figures.

The total of those receiving income from interest, dividends, and/or property increased by 13 per cent. from 224,000 to 253,000. The corresponding rate of increase in the United Kingdom was only a third of the Welsh rate but the income received in the United Kingdom rose by over 25 per cent., 12 per cent. greater than the Welsh rate of increase. In 1954/5 the average income from this source in Wales was £113, £82 less than the United Kingdom average.

The conclusion so far is that average income from all sources is lower in Wales than in the United Kingdom; but during the period under review the gap in earned income tended to narrow while the disparity in investment income considerably widened. We must remember, however, that these aggregates conceal a number of significant differences in the distribution of individual incomes.

Before considering the spread of individual incomes we may note some comparisons drawn by Miss Phyllis Deane between Wales and the other eleven standard regions of the United Kingdom.[1] Miss

[1] Phyllis Deane, 'The Geographical Distribution of Assessed Incomes', *Economic Journal*, June 1953, pp. 477–82, and 'A Correction', id., ibid., Dec. 1953, p. 920.

Deane calculated the average total income assessed before tax for each of the twelve standard regions in 1949/50. For Northern Ireland the average was £348 as compared with £356 for Wales. All the other ten regions had higher averages, ranging from £369 for the Northern to £395 for the Midland, which had the highest except for London and the South-East at £442. The figure for Scotland was £380. This analysis, however, suffers from the fact that civil servants and members of the armed forces and merchant navy are assessed centrally. Miss Deane adjusted the published figures for counties by distributing the wages and salaries of these people according to regional employment figures. This adjustment brought average assessed wages and salaries 'from principal sources' for Wales to £333, seventh down the list of the twelve regions; profits and professional earnings, at £462, were lowest of all, and the average of £46 for income from property was eighth.

When we look at the uncorrected county figures we find that the average assessed income is high in the counties of Glamorgan (£507 in 1954/5) and Monmouthshire (£514), where in 1949/50 seven-eighths of the total assessed income was 'principal source' Schedule E income, and only 2 per cent. came from property, although much income from property in these counties accrues to persons whose main place of assessment is elsewhere. Radnorshire, which had the highest average assessed income in 1949/50 (£365 compared with £363 for Glamorgan) also had the highest average income from property in that year. Just as Schedule E incomes are highest in the industrial counties, so those under Schedule D arising from profits and professional earnings tend to be high in agricultural counties, although the distinction here is not as clear-cut, partly because of the non-agricultural earnings in this schedule and the varying fortunes of agriculture itself.

In Table 73 the distribution of individual incomes is given in the form of cumulative percentages. The kind of fact that can be gleaned is, for example, that in 1954/5 69 per cent. of the people assessed in Wales had incomes of £350 and over, and between them they received 84 per cent. of the total net income assessed. We find that in 1949/50 50 per cent. of the people in Wales were getting £300 a year or more and it was about the same in the country as a whole; five years later 50 per cent. in both countries were receiving £450 or more a year. An interesting change occurred during the period. By 1954/5 a marked bunching of Welsh incomes in the range £300–£599 had appeared, as shown in the following summary:

Year 1954/5

Range of net income	Percentage of cases within the range	
	Wales	United Kingdom
(£)		
155–299	22·5	23·4
300–599	53·4	49·3
600–999	20·3	21·5
1,000 and over . . .	3·8	5·8

Table 73 shows that half the British net income in 1954/5 went to people with incomes of £600 and over; in Wales people in this upper range received only 42 per cent. of total income. Indeed, five years previously only 20 per cent. of Welsh income went to those getting

TABLE 73

Wales and the United Kingdom: Cumulative percentage distribution of net income, 1949/50 and 1954/5

Annual net income over	Percentage of cases				Percentage of net income			
	Wales		U.K.		Wales		U.K.	
	1949/50	1954/5	1949/50	1954/5	1949/50	1954/5	1949/50	1954/5
135	100·0	..	100·0	..	100·0	..	100·0	..
150	96·1	..	96·3	..	98·5	..	98·7	..
155	..	100·0	..	100·0	..	100·0	..	100·0
200	81·6	92·8	81·7	92·4	91·4	97·4	92·3	97·5
250	66·7	85·0	67·4	84·5	81·9	94·0	84·2	94·2
300	49·7	77·5	52·0	76·6	68·8	89·8	73·6	90·3
350	35·7	69·0	39·0	68·2	56·1	84·3	63·0	85·3
400	25·0	59·5	28·6	59·2	44·9	77·2	53·2	79·1
450	17·3	49·5	21·0	50·0	35·6	68·8	45·1	72·0
500	12·0	39·8	15·6	41·4	28·6	59·6	38·8	64·5
600	6·4	24·1	9·3	27·3	20·1	42·4	30·2	50·4
700	4·1	14·4	6·4	17·3	15·9	29·9	25·4	38·9
800	2·9	8·4	4·8	11·3	13·5	21·0	22·5	30·3
900	2·4	5·3	3·9	7·8	12·1	15·9	20·5	24·8
1,000	1·9	3·8	3·3	5·8	11·1	12·9	19·1	21·3
1,250	..	2·1	..	3·5	..	9·4	..	16·8
1,500	1·0	1·5	1·8	2·5	8·0	7·6	14·7	14·4
1,750	..	1·1	..	1·9	..	6·4	..	12·6
2,000	0·7	0·8	1·2	1·6	6·1	5·5	12·0	11·3
2,500	0·4	0·5	0·8	1·0	4·5	4·0	9·9	9·3
3,000	0·3	0·3	0·6	0·8	3·5	3·0	8·3	7·8
4,000	0·1	0·2	0·3	0·4	2·2	2·6	6·3	5·8

SOURCES: Based on *94th Inland Revenue Report*, Tables 90 and 98, and *99th Report* Tables 55 and 63.

£600 or more a year. Of the taxpayers of the United Kingdom 1·6 per cent. had incomes of £2,000 or over: in Wales only 0·8 per cent. were in this group.

Recent trends in industry have had effects on the distribution of income by sex and marital status, details of which are shown in Table 74. The share of wages and salaries going to married persons tended to increase during the period under review. Single females and widows received about a third of the investment income. It is possible to analyse the distribution of investment incomes by considering the amounts accruing to persons in different income groups. Nearly 93 per cent. of the net income in Wales in 1949/50 was earned compared with 90 per cent. in the United Kingdom. The situation was about the same five years later.

If we take all the people in Wales who had net incomes (from whatever source) of £200–£249 in 1949/50, we find that earned incomes (net of expenses and other deductions) accounted for 94·3 per cent. of the total net income, leaving 5·7 per cent. as investment income. In 1949/50 net earned income exceeded 90 per cent. for all brackets below £700, but by 1954/5 this was true of all below £1,000. In the bracket £800–£900 the proportion coming from earned income in 1949/50 was 85 per cent. in Wales and 88 per cent. in the United Kingdom; five years later the rise in earned incomes had brought these percentages to 96 and 95 respectively. Again, in the bracket £2,000–£2,500 in 1949/50 earned income comprised 73 per cent. in Wales and 71 per cent. in the United Kingdom; by 1954/5 these proportions had become 80 per cent. and 75 per cent.

It is clear that income from investment is less important in Wales than in the United Kingdom; so, too, is the eking out of low earned incomes by investment, investment being most prevalent in the middle-income groups. The comparison of 1949/50 and 1954/5 figures show how much greater was the growth in earned incomes as compared with investment incomes during the period.

3. Consumers' expenditure

Interesting information on the pattern of consumers' expenditure may be obtained from the *Report of an Enquiry into Household Expenditure in 1953–54*, published in 1957 by the Ministry of Labour and National Service. Nearly 13,000 households supplied detailed accounts of their income and expenditure over a period of four weeks and 688 of them were in Wales. The inquiry shows the average weekly

TABLE 74

Wales and the United Kingdom: Percentage distribution of income by marital status, 1949/50 and 1954/5

	Profits and professional earnings		Wages and salaries: principal source (Schedule E)		Total earned income		Property (Schedules A and B)		Interest and dividends		Total investment income	
	1949/50	1954/5	1949/50	1954/5	1949/50	1954/5	1949/50	1954/5	1949/50	1954/5	1949/50	1954/5
United Kingdom:												
All persons	100·0	100·0	100·0	100·0	100·0	100·0	100·0	100·0	100·0	100·0	100·0	100·0
Single males	12·5	12·7	20·3	18·1	18·6	16·3	10·3	9·1	12·8	12·8	12·8	12·1
Single females	6·3	6·0	13·7	11·9	12·3	10·8	20·8	19·4	35·1	37·9	33·5	34·2
Married persons	81·2	81·3	66·0	70·0	69·2	72·8	68·9	71·5	52·1	49·3	58·2	53·7
Wales:												
All persons	100·0	100·0	100·0	100·0	100·0	100·0	100·0	100·0	100·0	100·0	100·0	100·0
Single males	14·2	15·0	22·8	19·0	21·1	17·6	11·8	10·4	14·4	9·5	13·5	9·7
Single females	7·8	7·3	9·6	9·3	9·2	8·8	20·2	18·8	36·6	44·8	31·2	37·4
Married persons	78·0	77·7	67·6	71·7	69·7	73·6	68·0	70·7	49·1	45·8	55·3	52·9

SOURCE: See Table 73, p. 163.

expenditure, on various goods and services, of households in seven income groups. It is necessarily a very small sample, so that a large single outlay by one family can have a disproportionate effect on the average for a group.

The average weekly expenditure of Welsh households with incomes of under £3 a week was £3. 10s. 5d. compared with £3. 7s. 9d. in the United Kingdom. Thus, the members of the poorest section of the Welsh community were either dis-saving or accumulating debt at a faster rate than their United Kingdom counterparts or they were receiving greater unrecorded financial assistance from relatives. Welsh households receiving between £3 and £6 a week were also spending each week a sum greater than their incomes (5s. 3d. a week in excess of the highest income in the group) but this was nothing like the excessive spending recorded for the £6–£8 a week group, where the average expenditure was £9. 3s. 9d. The corresponding groups in the United Kingdom were, on average, spending *less* than the *highest* income in the group. But in Scotland and Northern Ireland, the £6–£8 groups were following the Welsh example of over-spending but to a smaller degree—1s. per week greater than the highest group income in Scotland and £1. 2s. 2½d. in Northern Ireland. It thus appears that in the poorer households, the propensity to get into debt is higher in Wales than elsewhere. The explanation may be that the survey was taken at a time when the television habit was spreading rapidly in Wales.

Although the average total expenditure of the 688 Welsh households is virtually the same as that of the 12,911 United Kingdom households—£12 a week—the patterns are by no means the same. The average Welsh household spent more on food and durable household goods, considerably more on clothing and footwear, and less on fuel, housing, transport, and services than its British counterpart. Differences in socio-economic structure and the fact that television did not reach Wales until 1952 may account for these regional variations.

The most interesting feature of the analysis by income group is the proportion of outlay on three basic things—housing, fuel, and food. The lowest income group spent, on average, 61 per cent. on these necessities as against 39 per cent. by the wealthiest members of the community. The proportion spent on housing and fuel declined progressively as income increased but that on food followed a different pattern. Within the £3–£6 group 37 per cent. of total outlay went on food; and about the same was true of the £8–£10 group. For each succeeding income range the proportion spent on these commodities progressively declined. The £8–£10 families appear to be able to buy relatively more semi-luxuries, such as biscuits, frozen vegetables, fruit, and eggs, which are outside the range of the lower income groups; but once the initial demand has been satisfied there is no significant increase in the quantity required as income rises.

The families in the £3–£6 group spent more on housing than those receiving between £6 and £10 a week, the excess being mainly outlay on decoration and repairs. For all households with a weekly income of less than £20 there is only a difference of a few pence in the expenditure on fuel. This may be attributed to the fairly uniform standard of housing found in Wales. The weekly expenditure on alcoholic drink increases both absolutely and relatively as income goes up; in the case of tobacco there is a relative decline in the upper income groups.

Expenditure on durable household goods varied a great deal from one group to another. The poorest families only devoted 2 per cent. of total expenditure to these commodities. Those in the £3–£6 bracket spent 10s. a week or 8 per cent. of total expenditure; those with the highest incomes spent 7 per cent. or 31s. 8d. per week, but the £10–£14 group spent 10 per cent. (over 27s. 1d.) on household goods. The two lowest and the highest group spent very little on television; all others devoted about a third of durable household funds to the purchase of a set. For those receiving less than £10 per week, transport is relatively unimportant, but once the car-owning class is reached there is a sharp rise in both actual and relative expenditure on this item.

Because of the size of the sample no really satisfactory pattern of 'service' expenditure can be obtained: where commodity prices are high and purchases are spasmodic, the patterns revealed by the available data can so easily differ from the norm. It is only in commodity groups where prices are relatively low and fairly standardized that reasonable patterns may be observed. This is illustrated by the expenditure on clothing, where wide variations from one group to another are observed. The poorest families devoted 8·8 per cent. to clothing, but the wealthiest spent 17·5 per cent. in this way. The £14–£20 families devoted 11·9 per cent. of total expenditure to clothing but the figures for the other three groups were much higher—between 13·5 and 14·7 per cent. Much of this expenditure was on outer

TABLE 75

Wales: Household expenditure by income group, 1953–4

Commodity or service	Under £3 s. d.	£3– s. d.	£6– s. d.	£8– s. d.	£10– s. d.	£14– s. d.	£20 and over s. d.	Wales average s. d.	United Kingdom average s. d.
Housing . . .	10 0	15 3	14 0	14 8	18 6	27 1	27 10	18 8	21 3
Fuel, light, and power	7 8	9 10	11 9	11 2	11 4	12 11	15 1	11 8	12 4
Food . . .	25 7	45 11	63 8	76 1	89 0	105 6	129 5	81 5	79 10
Alcoholic drink . .	1 3	2 1	3 8	5 11	6 8	12 10	21 9	7 10	8 2
Tobacco . . .	2 2	5 11	12 4	13 1	16 7	26 11	29 4	16 5	15 11
Clothing and footwear .	6 3	11 6	27 0	26 11	35 7	37 6	76 11	32 11	28 3
Durable household goods .	1 4	10 3	18 7	14 10	27 1	22 9	31 8	20 0	16 4
Other goods . .	4 9	8 10	13 0	13 11	15 4	20 10	28 5	15 8	16 10
Transport and vehicles .	1 5	6 2	7 4	9 7	19 5	18 4	30 11	14 4	16 9
Services . . .	9 11	9 3	11 6	12 9	21 9	29 6	45 9	20 4	22 10
TOTAL (including miscellaneous expenditure on pocket money for children, &c.). .	70 5	125 3	183 9	200 0	263 2	316 3	439 9	240 6	240 2

SOURCE: Ministry of Labour and National Service, *Report of an Enquiry into Household Expenditure in 1953-4*, H.M.S.O., 1957, Tables 35 and 45.

clothing—expensive articles which in a small group can result in an average far removed from reality.

While average incomes in Wales were below those for the United Kingdom in both 1949/50 and 1954/5, average expenditure in 1954 was about the same in both areas. It is possible to explain this apparent inconsistency. We have already seen that the poorer families in Wales are more prone to get into debt than their English and Scottish counterparts (though this may, of course, be the result of sampling errors). However, when we look at gross savings in Wales and the rest of the kingdom, we find that *per capita* saving in Wales was much lower than that in the rest of the kingdom both in 1948/9 and 1958/9. The Welsh figure of £23·3 per head in 1958/9 is only 70 per cent. of the *per capita* figure for the United Kingdom as a whole and ten years earlier, when *per capita* saving in Wales was £11·6, was only 65 per cent.

Actual and *per capita* saving has been increasing both in the United Kingdom and Wales. The absolute increase between 1948/9 and 1958/9 in Wales was 104 per cent., while in the rest of the kingdom it was 106 per cent. On a *per capita* basis the rise in Wales was 101 per cent. as against 90 per cent. elsewhere.

4. *Distribution*

A study of the mechanism by which goods are distributed from the producer to the final consumer is based on the results of the *Census of Distribution and Other Services* published in several volumes between 1950 and 1955.[1] There is not as much detail for Wales as for Great Britain as a whole, and there is nothing about profit margins in Wales. Fortunately, however, the Board of Trade has published regional data wherever practicable, and there is interesting information even for small towns. We have also had access to some unpublished figures obtained during the course of the inquiry. In taking the census the authorities had to overcome a number of technical difficulties; in using the results and drawing conclusions, particularly for separate regions, one must never lose sight of the limitations of the data.[2]

[1] Board of Trade, *Census of Distribution and Other Services, 1950*. The separate volumes have the sub-titles: *Retail Trade, Short Report* (1952), vol. i; *Retail and Service Trades, Area Tables* (1953), vol. ii; *Retail and Service Trades, General Tables* (1954); and vol. iii, *Wholesale Trade* (1955).

[2] The major difficulties are as follows: allowance had to be made for differing business years; hence all data do not relate to exactly the same period. The response to the inquiry was a little over 90 per cent. Some establishments carry on several

In 1950, when the census was taken, there were in Wales nearly 100,000 full-time employees engaged in distribution and about 14,000 working part-time; between them they received wages and salaries amounting to £26 million. There were, in addition, 35,000 engaged full-time on their own account and 10,000 part-time unpaid workers. Full particulars are set out in Table 76. We cannot trace changes in the structure of this industry over time, although Chapter II showed that in the insured labour force the number of women per 100 men increased from 90 to 118 between 1948 and 1958. However, the wealth of information in the census enables us to give a fairly complete cross-section for the year 1950. It is a unique opportunity to throw light on a sector of the economy about which little has hitherto been known.

The information about retail and service trades is limited by the lack of regional analyses of the data for organization. On the other hand, we know a great deal about establishments. Not only are there detailed figures for Wales showing the number of them, their sales, employment, and outlays on wages and salaries for each type of business, but there are also data for the twenty Welsh towns with populations exceeding 25,000. Figures are given separately for each county and for each of the sixty-three towns with populations between 2,500 and 25,000. Separate statistics about twenty of these smaller towns have been supplied by the Board of Trade.

We shall first glance at the broad picture. In 1950 some 105,000 people were engaged in retail trade in Wales. This represents 4 per cent. of the population, which is only slightly smaller than the corresponding percentages of 4·6 for Great Britain. In Wales over a quarter of the people working in retail trades were full-time unpaid workers (being proprietors or their families and friends), compared with under a fifth in the rest of the country. Three-fifths of these full-time unpaid workers were males. Full-time paid workers totalled 58,000, of whom 27,000 were males. About 18,000 of the employees in retail trade were part-time workers. The service trades employed another 30,000 people, of whom 26,000 were full-time. Taking the retail and service trades together, we find that there were 133,000 workers, of whom 111,000 were full-time, with an equal number of men and women. If we ignore working proprietors and unpaid workers, we find that there were 77,000 full-time and 13,000 part-time

activities and the census attempts to identify shops with their principal sales but this need not always present a satisfactory result.

TABLE 76

Wales: Employment, in distribution and service trades, 1950 ('000)

	Working proprietors, unpaid helpers				Paid employees						Full-time workers			Total (all workers)
	Full-time		Part-time		Full-time				Part-time		Proprietors and unpaid	Paid employees	Total	
					Male		Female							
	Male	Female	Male	Female	All ages	Under 18	All ages	Under 18	Total	Male only				
Total retail .	15·9	10·8	2·3	5·5	27	4	31	7	10	4	27	58	85	103
Total wholesale .	1·3	0·1	0·2	0·2	16	1	5	1	1	1	1	21	23	24
Total distribution .	17·1	11·0	2·4	5·7	43	5	36	8	11	5	28	80	108	127
Service trades .	4·9	2·2	0·7	1·2	8	1	10	1	3	..	7	18	26	30
TOTAL .	22·0	13·2	3·2	6·9	51	6	47	9	14	5	35	98	133	157

NOTE: These data show the numbers engaged during the week ending 24 June 1950. Except for the first four columns, data are given correct to the nearest thousand. . . . = fewer than 500.

SOURCE: Based on *Census of Distribution and Other Services, 1950*, vol. ii, Table 3 and vol. iii, Table 5A.

employees, receiving between them nearly £19 million in wages, salaries, and bonuses.

The 29,000 retail establishments had average sales of £7,200 compared with £9,300 in Great Britain as a whole. There were nearly 5,000 establishments with sales of less than £1,000, the average for these being only £490 during the year. Further detail is given in Table 77, which shows that 4 per cent. of the establishments accounted for a third of the sales.

TABLE 77

Wales and Great Britain: Retail establishments by size of sales, 1950

	Wales			Great Britain
	Estab- lishments	Sales	Sales per estab- lishment	Sales per estab- lishment
		(£'000)	(£)	(£)
Total Retail	29,143	209,535	7,190	9,268
Sales of up to £1,000 . .	4,801	2,397	493	488
£1,000– . . .	6,172	10,551	1,709	1,736
£2,500–	6,963	25,340	3,639	3,674
£5,000–	6,106	43,134	7,064	7,103
£10,000–	3,831	57,194	14,920	15,004
£25,000–	826	27,790	33,644	33,843
£50,000 or more . . .	384	43,129	112,315	139,041

SOURCE: *Census of Distribution, 1950*, vol. ii, Table 6.

There were great variations between different kinds of shops. General stores (which included department stores) topped the list with average sales of £126,000. Second highest came furniture stores, with an average of £17,700. Some of these had a very large turnover, 47 of them over £50,000. On the other hand, 98 of the 576 establishments were under £1,000. Shops dealing in clothes, with an average of £8,700, tied with those selling chemists' and photographers' goods. Of the 4,778 clothing establishments, 1,070 sold less than £1,000; but there were 1,052 above £10,000, 97 of these over £50,000. The only remaining kind of retail business with sales above the overall average of £7,200 was the grocery group, in which shops tended to be rather larger. Catering establishments had average sales of £3,700, one-third of them under £1,000 and nearly as many between £1,000 and £2,500.[1]

[1] For further detail see *Census of Distribution, 1950*, vol. i, Table 5.

Over three-quarters of the retailers in Wales were 'one-shop firms', a higher proportion than in the rest of the country. For these the average sales were only £4,900, compared with the British figure of £6,300. The sales of co-operative societies tend to be around £20,000 per establishment. One of the significant findings was that 11·3 per cent. of all the retail trade in Wales was made in co-operatives; in the rest of Great Britain the proportion was 11·9 per cent. In certain lines the co-operatives have a very large share: they account for over one-fifth of all the groceries sold in Wales; in the rest of the country the fraction is as high as one-quarter. It is surprising to find that, whereas in the rest of Great Britain 13 per cent. of the total retail sales of coal, builders' materials, and corn are made in the co-operative stores, in Wales the fraction is only 5 per cent. And again, in the rest of the country 25 per cent. of undertakers' business is in the hands of co-operatives and only 14 per cent. in Wales.

We shall now examine some of the differences between various towns in Wales. Table 78 gives the average sales per establishment

TABLE 78

Wales and Great Britain: Average retail and service sales by size of town, 1950

Town size (*population*)	Wales			Great Britain
	Sales	Establish-ments	Sales per establish-ment	Sales per establish-ment
	(£'000)		(£)	(£)
Under 2,500	38,449	8,943	4,299	5,760
2,500–10,000 . . .	32,085	5,428	5,911	6,950
10,000–25,000 . . .	39,160	5,266	7,436	7,147
25,000–50,000 . . .	53,489	7,507	7,125	7,933
50,000–100,000 . . .	4,929	828	5,942	8,902
100,000–250,000 . . .	75,645	8,772	8,623	8,663

SOURCE: Board of Trade, *Census of Distribution, 1950*, vol. i, Tables 1 and 8.

according to size of town in Wales and in Great Britain; for this purpose we have had to combine the retail and service trades since there are no separate figures for the smallest towns. We find that in the four large towns of Cardiff, Swansea, Newport, and Rhondda, average sales per establishment were very close to those for the rest of the country. In the next group there is only one

Welsh town—Merthyr Tydfil. In the third group there are fifteen with an average rather lower than that in the rest of the country. Towns with a population between 10,000 and 25,000 have higher average sales per establishment than elsewhere; but for the smaller towns, and especially for towns and villages with fewer than 2,500 inhabitants, average sales are much lower than in the rest of Great Britain. This analysis does not reveal the differences that almost certainly exist between one kind of business and another, although the census does provide the material for such an inquiry. To some extent the differences are explained by the existence of a larger number of shops than one would expect, especially in the rural areas. In the whole of Wales there are 14·1 establishments per thousand population, which does not diverge much from the position in the rest of the country, but in districts with fewer than 2,500 people the number of establishments per 1,000 was 11 in Wales compared with only 9 in the country as a whole.

There is surprisingly little wholesale trading in Wales. The 2,290 establishments (8·8 per 10,000 persons compared with 11·4 in Great Britain) had sales totalling £214 million during 1950. This was equivalent to £82 *per capita*, which is much lower than the average of £287 for Great Britain. Wales not only has fewer wholesale establishments in relation to population, but the average turnover is also comparatively low. Bristol, with a population one-sixth that of Wales, has one-third as many wholesale establishments and these have total sales almost as great as those for the whole of Wales.

Tables 79 and 80 show how the small size of the establishment is reflected in the numbers employed and in the average earnings. The number of wholesalers dealing in food is what one would expect from the size of the population; on the other hand, their sales, though over a third of the Welsh total, are low compared with the British figures. The high proportion of wholesalers dealing in agricultural goods, coal, and petroleum products reflects the industrial structure of the country, but coal is the only commodity in which Welsh sales form a greater proportion of the British sales in relation to population.

To some extent these differences may be more apparent than real. Wholesalers sometimes had difficulty in giving details of sales and receipts in their separate establishments, and in these cases the totals were entered in the area containing the head office. Probably a number of establishments in Wales are in this category and so the sales are understated.

TABLE 79

Wales and Great Britain: Receipts, sales, employment, and wages in wholesale trades, 1950

	Wholesale establishments	Receipts		Sales		Persons engaged (total)		Wages and salaries (year)	
Wales	2,290	£156,297,000		£213,770,000		24,015		£7,399,000	
	per 100 population	per capita	per establishment	per capita	per establishment	per 100 population	per establishment	per paid employee	per establishment
		(£)	(£'000)	(£)	(£'00)			(£)	(£)
Wales	8·8	60·1	68·2	82·2	93·3	0·92	10·49	332	323·1
Great Britain	11·4	192·1	169·1	286·7	234·3	1·61	14·19	399	534·4

SOURCE: Based on *Census of Distribution, 1950,* vol. iii, Tables 1 and 5A.

TABLE 80

Wales: Wholesale distribution by industry group, 1950

	Establishments	Receipts per establishment	Sales per establishment	Total engaged	Wages and salaries	Percentage distribution of establishments		Welsh establishments as % of Great Britain	Welsh sales as % of Great Britain
		(£'000)	(£'000)	('00)	(£'00,000)	Wales	Great Britain		
Agricultural products, supplies	231	48·9	63·2	19	5	10·1	6·6	6·3	1·7
Builders' materials, hardware	130	63·9	80·6	17	6	5·7	6·8	3·4	3·7
Coal	111	208·3	348·3	8	3	4·8	2·5	8·0	9·8
Metals, metal products	33	..	224·1	7	3	1·4	2·2	2·7	1·1
Timber	51	84·8	93·1	9	3	2·2	2·7	3·4	1·3
Scrap and waste material	80	29·8	37·1	9	3	3·5	3·6	4·0	3·0
Other industrial materials	30	7·8	50·2	2	1	1·3	4·7	1·2	0·1
Machinery and vehicles*	150	36·9	36·3	17	5	6·6	6·2	4·4	1·3
Electrical goods	55	35·5	36·9	6	2	2·4	2·3	4·3	1·5
Groceries, confectionery, drinks	363	96·3	115·5	54	15	15·9	12·5	5·2	1·6
Other food	395	43·2	100·4	34	10	17·2	12·4	5·7	2·7
Clothing, footwear, textiles	145	41·3	47·0	12	4	6·3	1·3	2·1	0·8
Chemicals, oils, drugs	18	..	39·5	2	1	0·8	2·3	1·3	0·1
Furniture, musical instruments	26	11·3	12·8	2	1	1·1	1·1	4·1	..
Glass, china, earthenware	11	30·1	..	2	..	0·5	0·9	2·1	..
Paper, stationery, books	79	33·3	33·4	7	2	3·4	4·2	3·4	2·2
Petroleum products	102	124·2	124·1	11	4	4·5	2·5	7·4	2·9
Tobacco	103	..	104·7	6	1	4·5	3·7	5·0	..
Other manufactured goods	25	..	14·4	1	..	1·1	3·1	1·5	..
Secondhand goods	18	..	102·3	1	..	0·8	1·4	2·3	..
General	122	64·1	64·5	11	3	5·3	5·2	4·2	..
Warehousing	12	12·3	..	2	1	0·5	0·4	5·1	..
TOTAL	2,290	68·2	93·3	240	74	100·0	100·0	5·4	1·6

SOURCE: Board of Trade, *Census of Distribution, 1950,* vol. iii, Tables 4 and 5B.
* Excluding electrical machinery.

One reason for the shortage of wholesalers is suggested by the census statistics and seems to be confirmed by general observation. In the whole of Great Britain only about a quarter of the sales of wholesalers were direct to home retailers, about a third were to industrial users and the Government, and about a sixth to other wholesalers (who, in turn, might sell either to retailers or to other wholesalers, or to some other body). Retailers buying from wholesalers would, of course, sell their goods for more than they paid for them. Despite this, total wholesale sales in Great Britain amounted to just over £13,000 million, while retail sales came to only £5,000 million. The difference is explained mainly by sales to industry and to the Government, exports and sales of the same goods several times by successive wholesalers. On the other hand, in Wales the turnover of wholesalers was £214 million while that of retailers was £210 million. Welsh retailers undoubtedly make large purchases from wholesalers in England, and this is probably the key to the statistics just quoted. But another reason is that Welsh *industry* is more inclined to buy from English wholesalers. Moreover, a high proportion of the Welsh firms are ultimate wholesalers, selling direct to the retailer; and if this is so it would encourage industry to sidestep the local source in the hope of obtaining speedier service or a larger discount by buying from somebody nearer the original source.

The geographical factor is more obvious. It is profitable for wholesalers to be in densely populated centres or where they have easy access to suppliers, on the one hand, and to markets, on the other. Some South Wales towns fulfil these requirements reasonably well, but North and central Wales have no suitable centres. On the average, wholesalers in North Wales had sales of about £50,000 and each employed about eight persons. Sales per establishment were highest in Caernarvon, which is well situated for markets. On the other hand, there was greater activity in Wrexham, which is also conveniently located for suppliers. The North relies chiefly on firms in Shrewsbury, Chester, Birkenhead, and Liverpool.

In the South, there are thirteen towns with twenty or more wholesalers, the principal ones being Cardiff (with nearly 600), Swansea (with nearly 300), Newport (with over 150), and Milford Haven (with over 100). Between them these four towns have almost half the total number of wholesale firms in Wales and over half the total sales, but Cardiff is the only centre which can claim to have a comprehensive wholesale trade on any scale. It is noteworthy that two-thirds of the

Welsh clothing and textile businesses and over half of the furniture and musical-instrument dealers are to be found in the capital. On an average, Cardiff wholesalers had sales of about £130,000 and employed about 14 people per establishment.[1]

5. *Summary*

The main conclusion is that the gross domestic product per head of the working population in Wales is about 8 per cent. below the corresponding figure for the United Kingdom. Wales appears to be below the British level roughly to the same extent as Scotland. Average earned income in Wales in 1954/5 was £502 as against £500 in Scotland. These generalizations must, however, be read in the light of what has been said about the quality of the data available. In personal incomes we found in Wales a marked 'bunching' in the middle range (£6–£12 a week) and a smaller proportion of total income derived from investment and property as compared with the United Kingdom. No significant differentials were revealed by the survey of family budgets; there is a tendency in Wales for the outlay on housing and fuel to be relatively less than in the country as a whole.

[1] Further detail for individual towns is obtainable from the *Census of Production, 1950*, vol. iii, especially Tables 4–6.

IX

POPULATION

By J. PARRY LEWIS

ONE of the indicators used in Chapter I to trace the outlines of Welsh economic development since 1850 was the rate of increase of population particularly as affected by the balance of external migration. There were wide fluctuations over the century and some of their demographic effects can be seen at the present time. In this chapter we shall analyse some aspects of the structure of population since the Second World War.

The rapid increase of population in England and Scotland, which was a feature of the nineteenth century, had reached its zenith by the seventies, but in Wales it continued until the first decade of this century, as shown in Chapter I. Even in the decade 1911–21 the increase of 10 per cent. in Wales was double the English rate and treble the Scottish. The figures are set out in Table 81. The expansion of the South Wales coalfield, with its high rate of natural increase and induced immigration, gave the two counties of Glamorgan and Monmouthshire a population which was two-thirds of the total for the Principality.

Between 1921 and 1931 there was a sharp reaction; the Welsh population actually fell by 2 per cent., while that of England rose by 6 per cent. Most of the outflow was from the coalfields; the population of the Rhondda valleys fell from 163,000 in 1921 to 111,000 thirty years later. The effect on age and sex composition reflects the severity of the contraction. In 1931 the proportion in the age-group 5–19 was 27·3 per cent. in Wales and 24·9 per cent. in England and Wales: in 1951 the proportions in the 25–39 age-group were 21·7 per cent. in Wales and 22·1 per cent. in England and Wales. This shrinkage in the youthful element in Wales was most evident among males. Both in 1931 and in 1951 there were about 108 women to every 100 men in England and Wales. In Wales, however, the female: male ratio changed from 100:100 in 1931 to 104:100 in 1951; the incidence of migration had been heaviest among men born between 1905 and 1925.

It was not until the eve of the Second World War that the flood of emigration caused by the depression began to subside. As a result of rearmament and measures to aid depressed areas, the population of Wales fell by only 600 between June 1938 and June 1939 as compared with a decline of 13,000 in the previous twelve months. Soon, war-time evacuation from England made itself felt, and in 1941 the civilian population of 2,626,000 was the highest since 1930. This artificial influence, affecting mainly the rural areas and more remote towns, was on the wane between 1941 and 1945.

TABLE 81

England, Scotland, and Wales: Enumerated population, decennially, 1851–1951

Year	England		Scotland		Wales	
	Population	% increase	Population	% increase	Population	% increase
	('000,000)		('000,000)		('000)	
1851	16·8	..	2·9	..	1,163	..
61	18·8	12·0	3·1	6·0	1,286	10·6
71	21·3	13·4	3·4	9·7	1,412	9·8
81	24·4	14·6	3·7	11·2	1,572	11·3
91	27·2	11·6	4·0	7·8	1,771	12·7
1901	30·5	12·0	4·5	11·1	2,019	14·0
11	33·7	10·3	4·8	6·5	2,421	19·9
21	35·2	4·7	4·9	2·6	2,656	9·7
31	37·4	6·0	4·8	−0·8	2,593	−2·4
39*	39·0	..	5·0	..	2,567	..
51	41·1	..	5·1	..	2,597	..

* Mid-year estimate.

SOURCES: *Census 1951, Preliminary Report*, Table VII; *Annual Abstract of Statistics*, 1939.

The early post-war years saw an increase in numbers as people returned from the forces and settled down in civilian jobs, often in industries which had not existed before the war. Since then there has been a fairly steady increase. Radnorshire, the county with the smallest population, continued to lose people to the industrial areas, while Caernarvonshire, after a phase of expansion in the thirties (largely through evacuation in 1939), recorded a loss after the war. Until 1957 (when unemployment rose) Pembrokeshire saw a rapid post-war growth, while increasing industrialization caused the population of Flintshire to be 40 per cent. higher than in 1921. The counties of Glamorgan and Monmouthshire have substantially increased their population since 1939, but they are still below the 1931

level. In the years 1931–51 Wales lost 6·7 per cent. of its population
through migration, which was almost equal to the natural increase
of 6·9 per cent. In England and Wales together, natural increase in
the same period added 8·2 per cent. and migration another 1·3 per
cent. These trends are illustrated in Table 82.

TABLE 82

Wales: Population of counties, 1921–57 (thousands)

County	1921	1931	1939	1951	1957	Percentage change 1931–51	
						Natural increase	*Other*
Anglesey . .	51·2	48·9	51·3	50·7	52·0	1·8	1·5
Brecknock .	61·1	57·3	54·4	55·9	56·3	5·0	−7·2
Caernarvon .	119·3	119·4	135·0	123·1	122·1	−1·2	3·9
Cardigan . .	57·7	55·1	58·0	54·1	53·4	−5·5	2·0
Carmarthen .	176·7	179·1	174·9	170·6	170·3	4·3	−8·2
Denbigh . .	154·4	157·0	171·8	170·0	169·5	5·4	2·9
Flint . .	102·0	112·3	135·8	144·8	147·2	10·2	18·5
Glamorgan .	1,271·8	1,227·2	1,173·9	1,196·0	1,213·5	8·2	−10·4
Merioneth .	41·8	42·6	45·2	40·5	39·1	−1·6	−2·4
Monmouth .	457·7	435·9	411·9	422·5	429·9	10·3	−11·8
Montgomery .	50·9	48·1	49·1	45·5	44·9	3·6	−8·7
Pembroke .	91·5	86·4	85·4	90·4	93·7	6·3	−2·1
Radnor . .	21·7	21·0	20·8	19·9	19·1	4·5	−10·7
Wales . .	2,658	2,590	2,567	2,584	2,611	6·9	−6·7

SOURCES: 1921, 1931: Resident Population at mid-year. *Census 1931, General Table*,
Table 9B. 1939, *National Register*, Civilians only. Considerable evacuation had already occurred. Other years: Home population (including armed forces stationed in
area and merchant seamen), *Registrar-General's Mid-year Estimates*. Percentage
change: *Census 1951, General Tables*, Table 8.

Despite the vast emigration, the number of households in Wales
increased between 1931 and 1951 from 638,000 to 751,000. This
addition of 113,000 households during a period when the population
was practically stationary was due to a falling birth-rate and an ageing
population. In 1931 the average size of the private household was
just under four persons: twenty years later it was less than three and
a half. In these twenty years, the proportion of households with one
or two persons rose from one-quarter to one-third, while the proportion with six or more persons fell from almost one-fifth to one-
tenth.

The decline in the birth-rate which began in the 1870's was inter-
rupted by the First World War and then continued until the eve of
the Second World War. In England the birth-rate began to rise

slightly in 1935, but in Wales the effect of the prolonged depression was to postpone any increase until 1938, even though the marriage rate had gone up from 14·4 in 1931 to 16·4 in 1934. As a result of the war the marriage rate went up to nearly 21 per 1,000 in 1940, but the birth-rate did not reach a peak until four years later, when it was over 19 per 1,000. In 1944 the marriage rate was as low as 15, and in the following year the birth-rate was barely 17. With the end of the war and the restoration of normal family relations, the marriage rate rose again to nearly 20, and in 1947 births were at the peak rate of over 20.

There is much variation in birth-rates as between different counties. Between 1949 and 1956, the average birth-rate in Pembrokeshire was as high as 17·1. In the two industrial counties of Glamorgan and Monmouthshire, it was 16·8 and 16·4 respectively. It was also 16·4 in Anglesey. In Wales as a whole it was 16·0, and the lowest counties, with rates of under 14·0, were Cardiganshire, Caernarvonshire, Merioneth, Radnorshire, and Carmarthenshire. To some extent these rates reflect differences in age and sex structure. If we make allowance for this, by adjusting the local birth-rates for age and sex differences and then comparing these with the national birth-rate, we find that the adjusted birth-rate was about 5 per cent. higher in Wales than in England. The counties with the highest standardized rates are Anglesey and Montgomeryshire, where the birth-rate is 15 per cent. higher than one would expect. It is only a trifle lower in Pembrokeshire. In Merioneth and Radnorshire, where the actual birth-rates are low, the standardized rates are high, indicating that the low birth-rates are entirely due to the age and sex composition of the populations. Glamorgan, which has the fourth highest birth-rate, is only ninth in the list of standardized rates; its actual birth-rate is high largely because of its favourable age and sex structure. In the counties of Cardigan, Caernarvon, and Carmarthen the actual and standardized birth-rates are low, but the relative positions of these three counties are reversed, the lowest standardized rate belonging to Carmarthen, where even after allowing for its peculiar age and sex structure, the birth-rate is almost 10 per cent. lower than one would expect.

The illegitimacy rate in England is higher than in Wales (5·0 per cent. in 1949–50 as compared with 3·9 per cent.). There is a tendency to infer from these figures that chastity is more prevalent in Wales than in England, but this is a false inference for two reasons. First, statistics of births cannot be relied upon as indicators of departure from chastity, as this need not result in conception. Apart from this, illegitimacy figures do not provide the whole story as the earlier legitimate births, occurring in the first nine months of marriage, also have to be considered. For this reason we must remember that the relative number of legitimate first babies conceived before marriage is greater in Wales than in England.

During the period 1949–51 20·2 per cent. of legitimate first babies in England and Wales were born in the first nine months of marriage: in Wales the proportion was as high as 23·7 per cent. In the Registration Division of Wales I (the counties of Brecknock, Carmarthen, Glamorgan, and Monmouth) the percentage was 23·1, while in Wales II (the rest of Wales) it was 25·2. The relative number of legitimate first babies conceived before marriage was greater in Wales than in England in every age-group, and the relative disparity increases with the age of the mother, as is shown in Table 83.

TABLE 83

Wales, and England and Wales: Legitimate first maternities, 1949–51; percentage occurring in 0–8 months after marriage

Age of mother	Wales I	Wales II	Wales	England and Wales
Under 20	68·5	73·1	69·2	67·2
20–24	25·8	30·0	26·8	23·2
25–29	11·4	14·7	12·3	9·7
30–34	10·4	12·5	11·0	8·7
35–39	11·4	12·2	11·7	9·3
40–44	13·1	11·7	12·6	10·2
All ages	23·1	25·2	23·7	20·2

SOURCE: Based on *Registrar-General's Statistical Review of England and Wales*, Part II, Civil Tables QQ and RR.

Considering both illegitimacy and early first maternities, in England and Wales, we find that the extent of pre-marital conception was about the same in both countries, one conception in eight taking place before marriage, but the chance of the parents marrying before the arrival of the baby was greater in Wales. This may be attributed to the settlement pattern in rural Wales, coupled with its Nonconformist background.

Analysis of the ages of persons married in 1951–3[1] shows two main

[1] Based on the Registrar-General's Statistical Reviews for 1951–3, Table M.

differences between Wales and England, which are borne out by
Table 84, giving the marital condition of people enumerated in Wales
in 1951. In every age-group between 15 and 64 the proportion of
married men was lower in Wales than in any other region. On the
other hand, the proportion of married women in Wales is higher than
in England only for those over 35 years of age (i.e. roughly for people
married before the war). This means that even though they married
rather later in life, the same proportion of women ultimately married

TABLE 84

Wales, and England and Wales: Marital condition by age, 1951 (proportion per 1,000 in each age-group shown by marital state)

	Males						Females					
	England and Wales			Wales			England and Wales			Wales		
Age	S	M	W	S	M	W	S	M	W	S	M	W
All ages 15 and over	438	523	39	457	500	43	405	487	108	409	483	108
	265	684	51	288	656	56	248	616	136	244	618	138
15–19	995	5	0	996	4*	0	956	44	0	956	44	0
20–24	762	237	1	785	214*	1	518	480	2	529	469	2
25–34	272	720	8	310	682*	8	182	798	20	184	798	18
35–44	120	862	18	146	836*	18	137	821	42	132	826	42
45–54	92	877	31	114	853*	33	151	759	90	138	766	96
55–64	78	850	72	101	818*	81	155	624	221	136	628	236
65–74	84	773	183	108	692	200	156	428	416	134	430	436
75–84	79	530	391	99	494	407	164	222	614	139	226	635
85+	65	311	624	83	278	639	172	77	751	135	80	785

S = Single, M = Married, W = Widowed or Divorced.
* indicates that no region has a lower figure.
SOURCE: *Census 1951, General Tables*, Table 29.

in Wales as in England; but men not only got married later but
more were likely to remain bachelors. To some extent this reflects
the comparative shortage of women in Wales at an earlier period.
The most usual age of marriage is in the range 20–24 years, but in
Wales the proportions of both males and females who are married are
lower in this age-range than in England. This may be due partly to
a tendency to prolong full-time education. There is also the fact that,
at all ages above 45, Wales has a higher proportion of widowed
people, and it is possible that their children are inclined to postpone
marriage in order to look after them: but this cannot be the whole
of the cause.

The falling birth-rate before the war was accompanied by a
generally falling death-rate, punctuated by a number of sharp fluctuations. During the whole period under review, the birth-rate in Wales

always exceeded the death-rate, as it also did in the counties of
Glamorgan, Monmouth, Brecknock, and Flint. In Carmarthenshire
the death-rate was higher only in 1951 and 1954–6; in Pembrokeshire
only in 1937 and in Denbighshire only in 1940. Radnorshire showed
a natural increase in every year except 1937, 1941, and 1956, while in
Montgomeryshire there was a natural decrease only in 1937 and 1940.
In Cardiganshire there was a natural decrease every year except in
1947 and 1948. In Caernarvonshire there was a natural decrease
except in 1943–4 and 1946–9. Merioneth had a more variable
pattern in the later years, with natural increase in 1931, 1944–5, 1947–
9, 1953, and 1956. Only Anglesey has firmly reversed the pre-war
trend, and since 1942 there has been natural increase in that county.

In post-war years the maximum number of deaths occurred in 1951
and 1955. The death-rate has been substantially higher than in England and Wales as a whole, and even when we allow for differences in
age-structure, the Welsh death-rate every year since 1949 has been
between 6 per cent. and 11 per cent. higher than would be expected
from English experience. Taking the average death-rates between
1949 and 1956, we find that Cardiganshire had the highest, with
Caernarvonshire a distant second, closely followed by Merioneth and
Anglesey. Carmarthenshire and Denbighshire were also above average
while Flintshire and Monmouthshire were lowest. These death-rates,
however, are affected by age-structure. One expects the death-rate in
Cardiganshire, where there is an unusually large proportion of elderly
people, to be higher than in Glamorgan. Allowing for this factor, we
find that the county in which the adjusted death-rate most exceeds the
national death-rate is Carmarthenshire, where the disparity is 15 per
cent. The second highest ratio is shown by Glamorgan, where it is
14 per cent. higher. Third highest is Monmouthshire and fourth Caernarvonshire. These four counties contain heavy industries. In only two
counties—Montgomeryshire and Radnorshire, the least industrialized
of all—is the adjusted death-rate lower than the national rate.

Death-rates are higher in Wales than in England for both men and
women. In the *Decennial Supplement* for 1951 the Registrar-General
calculates standardized mortality rates (S.M.R.s) for various groups.
These rates are for people aged between 20 and 64 and are based on
deaths registered in 1949–53. For example, the index shows how
mortality among, say, teachers compares with the mortality in other
occupations; the S.M.R. for male teachers is the number of deaths of
male teachers aged 20–64 registered during 1949–53 expressed as a

percentage of the number of such deaths which would have occurred if the death-rates in each separate age-group within the teaching profession had been the same as in the standard population consisting of all the males in England and Wales. Calculations of this kind have been made for different areas and occupations, and the results are summarized by dividing the occupations into five groups. These are:

Class I Professional, &c.
  II Intermediate
  III Skilled (including some mine-workers, transport workers, clerical workers, and armed forces)
  IV Partly skilled (including some agricultural workers)
  V Unskilled

Table 85 shows the S.M.R.s for males in each of these five groups. In each group the Welsh S.M.R. exceeds that for England and Wales together. Whereas in England and Wales together the S.M.R. for

TABLE 85

Wales, and England and Wales: Standardized mortality rates, males, 1949–53

		Social class						
Region	Cause	I	II	III	IV	V	Unemployed	All classes
Wales . . .	All causes . .	103	95	123	101	121	136	113
	Cardiovascular .	134	108	120	88	110	99	109
	Respiratory .	57	69	133	107	131	124	113
	Remainder .	109	102	117	110	123	181	115
England and Wales	All causes	97	86	101	94	118	124	100
	Cardiovascular .	121	102	102	86	103	87	100
	Respiratory .	57	66	102	97	142	128	100
	Remainder .	105	87	98	99	114	158	100
Wales I, urban areas .	All causes . .	103	105	127	107	125	..	119
	Cardiovascular .	129	129	123	91	112	..	114
	Respiratory .	70	87	139	121	146	..	129
Wales I, rural districts .	All causes . .	113	86	121	95	108	..	106
	Cardiovascular .	156	99	113	87	93	..	103
	Respiratory .	37	55	148	87	118	..	106
Wales II, urban areas .	All causes . .	101	101	111	101	117	..	108
	Cardiovascular .	154	115	107	98	112	..	110
	Respiratory .	53	65	111	94	107	..	95
Wales II, rural districts .	All causes . .	94	81	113	87	115	..	99
	Cardiovascular .	105	78	129	72	112	..	98
	Respiratory .	42	54	101	81	90	..	80

SOURCE: Registrar-General's *Decennial Supplement, 1951, Occupational Mortality*, Part II, vol. i, Tables DT, DV, and DX, and vol, ii, Table 9A.

the unskilled (Class V) is much higher than for any other, this is not true of Wales, where the S.M.R. is at a maximum in Class III which includes a large proportion of mine-workers. A similar but less pronounced pattern is to be seen in the S.M.R.s of married women grouped according to their husband's occupation, and this probably reflects the tendency of a wage-earner's illness to strain the health of the family and sometimes to transmit disease.

Table 85 also shows the S.M.R.s arising from two important causes—respiratory and cardiovascular diseases. In Wales the first of these is particularly prevalent in Class III owing to the incidence of pneumoconiosis. As one would expect, the distribution of S.M.R.s by area and occupation[1] shows that the highest rate is in coal-mining. The most prominent single cause of death in each area is pneumoconiosis, with other chest diseases also significant. When S.M.R.s in mining in different areas in England and Wales[2] are compared, we see that the Welsh counties, and the adjacent counties of Gloucester and Somerset, had very high death-rates. To some extent this is because these counties were also those which suffered the

TABLE 86

(a) Wales, and England and Wales: Infant mortality rates (per 1,000 live births of legitimate infants) by social class, 1949–53

	Social class					All classes
	I	*II*	*III*	*IV*	*V*	
Welsh rate in each class as % of rate in England and Wales . . .	115	123	122	115	115	120
Welsh urban area rates as % of rates in England and Wales . . .	106	109	121	117	119	121
Welsh rural area rates as % of rates in England and Wales . . .	135	139	122	110	109	119
Welsh urban area rates as % of total Welsh urban area rate . . .	55	66	97	110	136	100
Welsh rural area rates as % of total Welsh rural area rate . . .	72	85	99	106	127	100
Welsh all-area rates as % of total Welsh all-area rate	60	75	98	109	132	100
England and Wales all-area rates as % of total England and Wales all-area rate . . .	63	73	97	115	138	100

[1] See Registrar-General's *Decennial Supplement, 1951, Occupational Mortality* Part II, vol. ii, Table 10.
[2] Ibid., Table 3A.

(b) *Wales, and England and Wales: Still-birth rates (per 1,000 total births) by social class, 1949–53*

	Social class					All classes
	I	*II*	*III*	*IV*	*V*	
Welsh urban area rates as % of total Welsh urban area rate . . .	73	83	97	111	120	27·5 = 100%
Welsh rural area rates as % of total Welsh rural area rate . . .	60	90	101	107	115	27·0 = 100%
Welsh all-area rates as % of total Welsh rate .	69	85	98	109	119	27·4 = 100%
England and Wales all-area rates as % of total England and Wales rate	71	87	99	107	120	22·8 = 100%

SOURCE: Registrar-General's *Decennial Supplement, 1951, Occupational Mortality*, Part II, vol. i, pp. 157–62.

heavier emigration of miners during the thirties, and those remaining behind were often the least fit. Table 86 brings out the depressing fact that infant mortality is higher in Wales than in England in every social class, both in the urban and in the rural areas.

X

CONCLUSION

By BRINLEY THOMAS

IN the Victorian period Wales went through a unique phase of vigorous growth, the character of which was determined by her inter-relation with England. Her industries were dominated by the inter-national market; Welsh coal and steel were a part of the British export sector. Our analysis in Chapter I showed that upswings in the British export sector were times of rapid development in the South Wales coalfield with a considerable influx from the Welsh rural areas; downswings in the British export sector were accompanied by booms in capital construction in England, and at such times English coal-fields grew rapidly and surplus labour from the Welsh country-side was absorbed easily in England. The inverse relation between phases of growth in Welsh and English coalfields between 1850 and 1913 is a key to the understanding of the evolution of the Welsh economy in that period. It explains why Wales lost only a trifling percentage of its natural increase through net migration and why the movement to oversea countries was insignificant.

Between 1881 and 1921 there was an average annual loss of popu-lation through migration of 44 per 10,000 in Scotland and 65 per 10,000 in Northern Ireland, but Wales had an average annual *gain* of 8 per 10,000. The collapse in Wales in the depression between the wars was all the more shattering—an average annual loss of 102 per 10,000 in 1921–31 as against 80 in Scotland and 82 in Northern Ireland. After the spring tide of the Edwardian era the ebb was low indeed, leaving its most cruel mark on the centre of the steam-coal trade, the Rhondda valleys, where population fell by 13 per cent., from 162,700 in 1921 to 141,300 in 1931. About 33,500, or one-fifth of the 1921 population, left the Rhondda in that decade; 52 per cent. of them were aged 15–29 and 19 per cent. aged 30–44. No less than a quarter of a million people were lost through migration from South Wales in 1921–31, and 54 per cent. of them were between the ages of 15 and 29. It looked as if Wales would have to face a period of prolonged impoverishment as the penalty of over-specialization. However, all such fears were belied by events after the war.

What a striking contrast there is between the recovery in 1945–60 and the expansion in 1900–14. In the first fifteen years of this century the rate of growth was based on intensive specialization in the coal export trade involving a huge increase in the demand for manpower which could be satisfied only by drawing in large numbers of migrants. In the corresponding period since 1945 there has been a marked trend towards diversity, and new labour has been recruited internally from the hitherto untapped supply of female workers.

Manufacturing now accounts for 23 per cent. of employment in Wales as against only 11 per cent. before the war; in the ten years, 1948–58, this sector expanded twice as fast as it did in Great Britain, the outstanding rates of growth being miscellaneous manufacturing (91 per cent.), precision instruments (60 per cent.), engineering (50 per cent.), paper and printing (46 per cent.), and nylon (33 per cent.). A notable part has been played by the Industrial Estates. By the middle of 1960 about 51 million square feet of industrial building had been approved in Wales, and three-quarters of the total was privately financed. That these locations have been conducive to rapid growth is proved by a number of spectacular successes. The value of gross output in electrical engineering in Wales rose from £2,927,000 in 1948 to £12,403,000 in 1954, and Welsh productivity in this industry in relation to Great Britain went up from 63 per cent. to 110 per cent. One of the leading firms, the South Wales Switchgear Ltd., with its main factory at Blackwood, Monmouthshire, has flourishing export markets in countries such as the United States, Canada, Mexico, India, and Pakistan. British Nylon Spinners at Pontypool is the centre of one of the most buoyant of the 'growth' industries, whereas in North Wales the production of plastic-coated steel sheet by John Summers Ltd. at Shotton is a striking new departure. Forty per cent. of the British output of aluminium sheet, strip, extrusions, wire, and cable is produced in Wales. The new factory of the Pressed Steel Co. near Swansea, which will have one of the most up-to-date machine shops in Europe, will employ 3,000–4,000 people and will have an output of 10,000 domestic refrigerators a week, much of which will be for export. There is no substance in the notion that manufacturing has taken on in Wales because of the attraction of relatively cheap female labour. We saw in Chapter II that the big increase in scale has been achieved without any general substitution in favour of women workers; indeed, in some of the more rapidly expanding industries the tendency is to employ relatively fewer women. The analysis in Chapter II indicated the broad range of the Welsh economy in which productivity is increasing faster than in Britain as a whole.

The underlying strength of the economy since the war is shown by the fact that the average annual net loss of population through migration between 1946 and 1957 was as low as 17 per 10,000 in Wales, as against 67 per 10,000 in Northern Ireland, 70 in Scotland, and 100 in Eire. And it should be noted that Scotland was losing at that rate at a time when she was attracting a lion's share of the foreign investment made in the United Kingdom. It has been estimated that two-thirds of the increase in labour employed by American-financed firms in development areas between 1940 and 1953 was located in an area within a 15-mile radius of Glasgow and Dundee. Dr. J. H. Dunning has pointed out that

. . . first, a high proportion (nearly 75 per cent.) of the post-war employment expansion in United States firms has been confined to the engineering industries, and the facilities offered by the Scottish Development Area—with its solid background of well-reputed skill in general engineering and ship-building—have been equal to, and generally more attractive than, those available in other Development Areas. Secondly, the publicity afforded by the Scottish Council as to these facilities has been in a class of its own and the concentrated effort made to attract U.S. investment has far exceeded in quality and enthusiasm anything attempted by the other Development Areas or the United Kingdom as a whole.[1]

The new Development Corporation for Wales set up in 1958 hopes to have an important influence on the future pattern of capital inflow. Direct investment by American firms has tended to follow the locations evolved by British industries, and the relatively rapid growth of the manufacturing sector in Wales is a significant pointer.

A recent study of the experience of the north-east of England argued that

. . . Development Area policy by itself can play little part in protecting a region against the rigours of the trade cycle. . . . It is worthy of note that in the generally prosperous period since 1945 the main short-term recessions in this country have been in such durable consumer-good industries as textiles, clothing and sections of the electrical goods trade, which have been predominant among the industries guided to the Development Areas. Perhaps even more significant is the fact that the recessions suffered by

[1] John H. Dunning, *American Investment in British Manufacturing Industry*, Allen & Unwin, London, 1958, p. 88.

these industries were caused only partly by a decline in export demand and that an important factor was a falling off in sales at home. This underlines our earlier comments that even home market durable consumer-good industries are liable to short-term fluctuations in trade and in a cyclical depression would tend to share in a general decline.[1]

This line of argument is somewhat ambiguous; it seems to ignore the real differences between post-war and pre-war fluctuations. The short-term downswings experienced by the British economy since 1945 have been the result of measures which had to be applied to curb extreme inflationary pressure and deflect resources from the swollen home market into the export trades. These oscillations of a brimful economy are not 'the rigours of the trade cycle'. In the Midlands and London–South-east these oscillations have for the most part been variations in the intensity of excess demand, but in Wales one could discern something reminiscent of the old-fashioned trade cycle. We saw in Chapter III that Wales stood up very well to the 'rigours' of this cycle. In the upswing phase, 1948–55, unused resources were absorbed and a considerable amount of capacity was built up with the aid of Development Area investment, and the ceiling was reached in 1955. The relative incidence of the recession in 1957–8 was remarkably mild. When unemployment in the British economy was almost at its post-war maximum—in December 1958—the rate in Wales was only twice as high as in the Midlands, whereas in 1948 it had been nine times as high. If we mean by 'sensitivity to cyclical fluctuations' what the authors of the Distribution of Industry Act had in mind, we must conclude that the economy of Wales has developed fairly strong powers of resistance.

The problems of agriculture and the depopulation of the countryside are frequently misunderstood. This book has tried to interpret them in terms of the process of economic growth. An individual does not bemoan the fact that as he gets richer he spends a smaller fraction of his family budget on bread and potatoes: as the standard of living of a community rises, we must expect the proportion who earn their living on the land to decline. Welsh farmers have not been backward in applying mechanized methods; they have one tractor for every 20 acres of arable area, as against one for every 33 in England. They have also found that agricultural co-operation pays; Wales has one-fifth of the membership of Agricultural Co-operative Societies in

[1] E. Allen, A. J. Odber, and P. J. Bowden, *Development Area Policy in the North East of England*, North East Industrial and Development Association, Newcastle upon Tyne, 1957, pp. 30–31.

the United Kingdom. The rise in farming productivity per head and the progress of the industrial sector entail an exodus from the land, the more so in Wales where a high proportion of farmers cannot achieve the net real income of an agricultural employee. Chapter IV pointed out that, as government policy has for the past twenty years been encouraging these 'problem' farmers to stay on the land, social justice requires that their fate should now be recognized as a national responsibility.

If due regard is paid to amenity and design, the growth of small rural industries can be an unmixed blessing to the country-side. Another factor which has already had a profound influence is the tourist traffic. It is estimated that in 1958 2½ million British people and 150,000 overseas visitors took holidays in Wales, and they spent about £35 million.[1] One cannot but deplore, however, the unsightly consequences in some of the more frequented coastal areas. Even on the most material plane it should surely be recognized that the preservation of the country-side is a social necessity. When new economic strength is infused through afforestation, there are unique opportunities to add beauty as well as material well-being. And this sometimes means departing from tradition, as shown by the following example.

The Forestry Commission is building a series of eight new villages in its great new forests in the remote valleys of Northumberland just south of the Scottish border. The hills there, above the winding valley bottoms, have hitherto been clothed in soft gradations of greens and fawns and rust browns of bent grass and bracken and heather. The scattered farmsteads and shepherds' cottages have traditionally been built of a grey brown stone, stone-roofed. But the new forests are taking all the soft flowing colours out of the landscape and are clothing it, for distances as far as the eye can see, in an unchanging monotone of blue-green. The old stone buildings would be lost in this; so the Commission is having the new villages (except the main buildings, the churches, the village halls and others) finished in white and cream wash, which though it is familiar in the County Durham landscape sixty miles or so to the south, is quite untraditional in this particular countryside. In this way the new villages will not only be lively in themselves, they will enliven many a forest panorama. Here will be a wholly untraditional development. But then the new landscape itself will be wholly untraditional too.[2]

[1] We are indebted to the Welsh Tourist and Holidays Board, Cardiff, for this information.
[2] Thomas Sharp, in *Design in Town and Village*, Ministry of Housing and Local Government, H.M.S.O., 1953, pp. 11–12.

Whether there is scope for such imaginative projects in rural Wales may be open to debate; but few will deny that a wholly untraditional approach to planning and architectural design would be a refreshing change in the urban areas, most of which are a depressing monument to their Victorian begetters and their modern imitators.

The change in the balance of Welsh economic life is a challenge to conventional ideas and ancient prejudices. It is of the essence of innovations that they enrich society by extinguishing outmoded methods of production, but those who have invested their capital or skill in the latter have a vested interest in putting a brake on progress. We have seen how transport facilities have lagged behind the requirements of the post-war Welsh economy. Those who demand that traffic should be diverted to the South Wales ports will not face up to the fact that this capital equipment was built for an export trade which has gone for ever. There is no sense in giving artificial respiration to economic dinosaurs. What the public interest urgently requires is action to eliminate the worst transport bottlenecks and a concentration on the types of transport which best suit the growing industries.

The earlier expectations about the long-run trend in the demand for coal have not been fulfilled; in 1958 and 1959 unemployment remained low simply because coal that could not be sold was being stocked. One certainly sympathizes with miners who were recruited into the industry in the belief that prospects were secure and who now find that the outlook is precarious. Nevertheless, there would be no justification for handicapping the oil industry in the interests of mining.

Before the war coal-mining, the mainstay of the Welsh economy, was a sick industry, plagued by over-production, low wages, and heavy losses, and frustrated by bitter relations between owners and workers. It took years under nationalization to induce convalescence and a new spirit. There has been a marked contraction in scale. Whereas before the war one-quarter of the working population of Wales was in coal-mining, today only one-eighth are in it. Production has been concentrated in the most efficient pits, mechanization has proceeded rapidly, and there has been a remarkable improvement in industrial relations. In recent years the number of pits has fallen from 203 to 118; average output per man-shift rose from 15·9 cwt. in 1947 to 20·3 cwt. in 1959—an overall increase in physical productivity of nearly 28 per cent.

The coal export trade has become negligible; in the life-span of one man it went full circle from 1·7 million tons in 1860 to a peak of 35 million in 1913 and then down again to 1·6 million by 1944. In the early post-war years the big problem was to attract enough manpower, particularly in view of the competition of the new industries and the incidence of pneumoconiosis in mining. Special efforts were made to recruit young men by organizing training schemes and improving the chances for promotion; but the most potent factor was the 94 per cent. increase in the earnings of face-workers between 1948 and 1957 until they reached an average of £15. 6s. 0d. a week.

For the first time since the war the problem of excess supply began to trouble the coal industries of all countries in the recession years 1957–8. Long-run forecasts about the demand for fuel, on which planning had been based a decade ago, have proved to have been excessive. Supplies of oil have been more plentiful and the price lower than had been expected. To avoid unemployment much of current output of coal had to go into the accumulation of very large stocks. The investment plans of the National Coal Board have been revised; the closing of inefficient pits is being expedited, and the labour force is expected to decline more rapidly than was originally intended.

The remarkable thing about the South Wales coalfield is that its long-term prospects are better now than they have ever been, notwithstanding the temporary difficulties.

First, the expansion of the steel industry is a potent factor. The new plant at Llanwern is going to mean an enormous increase in the demand for coke; moreover, the demand for high-grade metallurgical coke for foundries is rising rapidly. To meet these new requirements South Wales has huge resources of the highest quality. This prospect is the main reason why South Wales has been given the second highest allocation of new investment among all the Divisions of the National Coal Board.

Secondly, technical innovations in industry generally are putting a premium on some of the particular varieties of coal for which South Wales is the main source of supply; the increasing emphasis on smokeless fuels, metallurgical fuels, and chemical syntheses entails an expanding demand for the anthracite, steam and coking coals in which South Wales is rich. While mounting stocks continued to be a general problem, it was significant that in the latter half of 1959 the stocks of high-grade metallurgical coke produced at the new Cwm coke ovens showed a substantial decline.

Thirdly, at the very time when a new impetus is needed, the heavy capital investment since 1950 is now beginning to yield substantial returns in increased productivity. Economies of scale are being reaped; mechanical haulage has been displacing rope haulage; 'horizon mining' is making progress; and already as much as 20 per cent. of the output is power-loaded—a remarkable achievement considering the genuine conviction of many miners that it ought not to be introduced in the conditions usually prevalent in South Wales. The average output per man-shift in the coalfield in 1959 was 20·3 cwt. as compared with 15·9 cwt. in 1947; the increase in productivity is now gaining momentum, and by 1965 output per man-shift is expected to reach 25 cwt., which would be an advance of 23 per cent. in five years.

Finally, perhaps most important in the long run is the new feeling of confidence in the future and the improvement in the quality of management. The increase in productivity is not just the consequence of mechanization. On the contrary, in some pits where mining technique has not been changed, a striking increase in output per man-shift has been achieved as a result of better industrial relations and skilful management. The bonus of rising productivity that can come from this source is considerable. It has been roughly calculated that for every 1 per cent. rise in output per man-shift costs of production fall by 3s. a ton, assuming wages and prices remain the same. The end of 1959 saw recruitment of new miners beginning to rise again. Significantly, also, the feeling that a new phase of prosperity may be round the corner is adding strength to the view that the interests of the South Wales miner may not be served in future by rigid agreements binding on all Divisions. There is every prospect that the 1960's will be a prosperous phase in the history of the South Wales coalfield, based on high capitalization, high wages, and low costs.

Where unemployment, judging by post-war standards, has been serious, it has been mainly due to technical progress. In Anglesey and Caernarvonshire, where the situation is made more difficult by the secular decline of slate quarrying, a partial remedy lies in increased public investment, such as, for example, the new atomic power station at Trawsfynydd, and a more active promotion of rural industries.

The western part of South Wales has also been through a painful transition. In January 1953 the Government set up a committee under the chairmanship of Lord Lloyd to make plans to cope with the unemployment which would be created as soon as the new strip mills built by the Steel Company of Wales were in full production. Its reports have never been published. According to the 1954 *Report on Government Action in Wales*, the Lloyd Committee '. . . made a very thorough survey of the problems which were referred to it arising out of the modernization of the tinplate industry in west South Wales'. It submitted to the Minister for Welsh Affairs three reports—on road communications, rail services, and the attraction of new industry. In June 1954 the Government announced that they were still considering the recommendations contained in the second and third reports which were based on confidential information obtained by the committee from industrial and other sources. Meanwhile, under the influence of the boom of 1954–5, the tinplate trade suddenly revived again and the companies did all they could to increase output in the hand-operated mills. Instead of an orderly transfer of labour to industries with long-term prospects, there was actually a planned immigration of 900 Italian workers into these obsolete mills with a sentence of death hanging over them. The companies must have known that this was a precarious prosperity but they could not resist the temptation to exploit it to the utmost; the day of reckoning was postponed and it was bound to be more painful when it came. In 1957, four years after the Lloyd Committee was set up, the Swansea and Llanelly tinplate areas began to feel the full force of the dreaded event—unemployment on a scale unknown since the thirties. The Italians were placed in jobs in England or were sent home, and the redundant Welsh tinplate men had to make the best of it at a time when a general recession had set in. The problem had been made far worse than it need have been. If action had been taken in 1954 the reabsorption of the surplus labour would have been much easier.

Society is no longer subject to the creeping paralysis of mass unemployment caused by lack of effective demand: the trouble now is something quite different—the growing pains associated with technical progress. The crux of the matter was put by Philip Wicksteed fifty years ago in a passage which is as relevant today as when he wrote it.

When we understand that local distress is incidental to general progress, we shall not indeed try to stay general progress in order to escape the local distress, but we shall try to mitigate the local distress by diverting to its relief some portion of the general access of wealth to which it is incidental. To mitigate the penalties of failure, without weakening the incitements to success, and to effect an insurance against the disasters incident to advance, without weakening the forces of advance themselves, is the problem which civilization has not yet solved. No wonder, for it is only just beginning to understand what the problem is, and to recognize the 'deeply inherent limits' within which it must be solved.[1]

Sustained industrial expansion has entailed a striking rate of growth of private expenditure, particularly on durable consumer goods. Here the contrast with pre-war years is remarkable. Between 1948 and 1959 the number of motor-cars licensed in Wales rose from 90,200 to 240,200, an increase of 166 per cent. as against 153 per cent. in Great Britain. The sales of gas appliances in Wales between 1950–1 and 1958–9 went up from £749,000 to £1,689,000, an increase of 126 per cent. as against 71 per cent. in Great Britain; the rate of increase in sales of these appliances on hire purchase in Wales was 167 per cent. as compared with 71 per cent. in Great Britain. This growing affluence reflects the relatively high level of earnings in the steel and coal industries, the expansion of manufacturing, and the increased employment of women. Furthermore, the proportion of the insured population engaged in professional services (11 per cent.) is now as high as in Great Britain as a whole.

Together with a flourishing consumer market there is a high propensity to invest. The amount of electricity generated has gone up ninefold since 1938. In the last decade the output of pig-iron in Wales has trebled and that of steel has doubled. In 1960 the total value of planned construction in Wales (i.e. works costing over £10,000) was about £250 million, twenty-three of the projects costing over £1 million each. They include the Spencer steelworks near Newport, Monmouthshire (over £100 million), the nuclear power station at Trawsfynydd in North Wales (£55 million), and the Tryweryn valley water-supply scheme (£20 million). A significant proportion of the total is public investment.

A long upswing in investment coming after a long period of stagnation creates serious disproportions. A glaring example is the lag in the provision of transport facilities described in Chapter VII. There has been an immense amount of government-sponsored investment in new steel capacity, but the road transport implications

---

[1] Philip H. Wicksteed, *The Common Sense of Political Economy*, vol. i (1910), edited with an Introduction by Lionel Robbins, Routledge, London, 1933, p. 357.

have been virtually ignored; the result has been two of the worst bottlenecks in the country—at Newport and Port Talbot. The peak traffic over Newport Bridge in 1953 was 2,177 vehicles an hour; in 1960 it had grown to 3,371. At this rate of increase it would be 7,000 vehicles an hour by 1970, or double the amount which could be safely permitted. As long ago as 1950–1 the Development Plan of the County Borough of Newport envisaged a second bridge across the river, but this did not commend itself to the Ministry of Transport. A sterile controversy about the relative merits of a new bridge and a by-pass road has gone on for several years; meanwhile the nemesis has arrived. Even when Parliament accepts Newport's proposed legislation to authorize a new bridge, it cannot be built in under three years. The rapid growth of ordinary traffic will be much accentuated in 1962 when production starts at the Spencer steelworks. Thirteen years will have elapsed without any effective alleviation of this appalling bottleneck and the situation at Port Talbot is quite as bad. This is the negation of intelligent planning. It is reassuring, however, that at the western end of the South Wales basin the needs of the future have been well anticipated at Milford Haven, for example, through the opening of the new tanker terminal at Angle Bay by British Petroleum Ltd. This is one of the very few ports in Europe which will be able to accommodate the modern tankers of 65,000 tons which, when fully laden, draw more than 45 feet of water. A 60-mile pipeline has been laid to carry 5 million tons a year of crude oil to Llandarcy refinery near Swansea.

Hitherto the supply of water has not been regarded as a limiting factor in Great Britain. Industrial demands are met mainly from private sources rather than by public water undertakings, and as a proportion of the value of output the cost of water is usually negligible. There are signs, however, that demands are likely to increase appreciably in the next two or three decades and that government action will be needed to promote conservation.[1] The water resources of Wales in relation to the probable course of demand have been analysed by the Welsh Advisory Water Committee.[2] The following passage is highly relevant to the future of the Welsh economy.

In an era when water will become relatively more scarce in relation to demand, a country of heavy rainfall will have an increasing comparative

[1] See Central Advisory Water Committee, *Sub-Committee on the Growing Demand for Water*, First Report, H.M.S.O., 1959.
[2] Welsh Advisory Water Committee, *Report on the Water Resources of Wales*, Cmnd. 1331, 1961.

advantage; public opinion in Wales will not take kindly to the idea that
her duty in these circumstances is to export as much water as possible
irrespective of her own long-run requirements. The very fact that Wales
will have an increasing comparative advantage will make it a more
favourable location for water-seeking firms and for agricultural irrigation;
and this will in turn increase the rate of growth.[1]

On the basis of projections of maximum effective water resources
in relation to demand over the next thirty years, the report finds
that the rapidly developing south-eastern area will have a deficit
which should be given first priority; in Wales as a whole, and particularly in the central area, there will be an ample surplus.

There are grounds for optimism not only about the adequacy of
natural resources but also about the future supply of capital both
from the undistributed profits of existing firms and from new sources
outside. Moreover, the old image of South Wales as an area prone
to industrial disputes is now a travesty of the facts: disputes in 1957
caused a loss per man employed of 0·3 days in Wales as against 0·4
days in the rest of Great Britain, and in 1958 0·1 as against 0·16. In
industries other than coal-mining the number of working days lost
through disputes in Wales in 1958 (as a proportion of the number
employed) was only one-third of the rate of loss in the rest of Great
Britain. Unlike their predecessors, the present generation of Welsh
trade unionists are less belligerent than their counterparts across
the border.

Industrial expansion has been accompanied by an influx of
business managers and highly qualified technologists. This welcome
trend is offset, however, by serious deficiencies in the system of
technical education. Here we find too many reminders of out-dated
attitudes stemming from pre-war years. The verdict of the Report of
the Central Advisory Council for Education (Wales) leaves little
room for complacency.

Recruitment to craft apprenticeships tends to be haphazard and to be
related to current needs rather than long-term requirements of industry·
. . . There is need to relax the restriction imposed by the Trade Unions on
the maximum number of craft apprentices recruited to a given trade. . . .
Pupils who remain at school beyond the age of 16 should not be denied
the opportunity of obtaining a craft apprenticeship. . . . Advanced sandwich diploma and university degree courses should become the accepted
routes to the status of technologist. . . . The lack of support for sandwich
courses in chemistry or industrial chemistry in South Wales, where there

[1] Welsh Advisory Water Committee, *Report on the Water Resources of Wales*,
Cmnd. 1331, 1961, p. 16.

is a concentration of a variety of chemical industries, is a matter for serious concern. In particular, if the chemical industry did more to encourage the education and training of National Certificate students who show promise they would need to recruit fewer graduates from universities, and thus indirectly relieve the shortage of graduate science teachers in schools. . . . The lack of support for advanced sandwich courses in science and technology at the College of Advanced Technology in Cardiff to date creates doubts as to whether the existence of a college of this status in Wales can be justified. . . . The overall provision in Wales for advanced courses greatly outruns the present demand.[1]

There can be no doubt that drastic reforms are essential if Wales is to have an adequate supply of qualified manpower. The policy of the Government, based on the principle that apprenticeship should be exclusively a matter for industry, needs critical review. There is a strong case for introducing a national craft apprenticeship system to be administered by the State through the Ministry of Education on the lines outlined by the Central Advisory Council's Report.[2] An unconventional approach to technical education is particularly necessary in Wales if the post-war rate of industrial advance is to continue.

Finally, we must consider how Wales would be affected if Britain joined the European Common Market. The outcome hangs on a number of factors which are difficult to assess, and much will depend on the conditions of entry. How would the gains and losses be distributed among various British industries? We can say with some confidence that the industries likely to gain most would be chemicals, electrical engineering, general engineering, steel, motor vehicles, wool, rubber manufactures, hosiery, and clothing. Some advantage would also be reaped by aircraft, metal manufactures, oil-refining, non-ferrous metals, glass, scientific instruments, and sports goods.

From the Welsh point of view this list is of particular interest. The majority of these industries have already been expanding relatively fast in Wales, and the rate of increase of productivity has tended to exceed the British average. This has been the case in chemicals, iron and steel (melting and rolling), iron foundries, steel sheets, mechanical engineering, electrical engineering, radio and telecommunications. It is also probable that the coal industry will benefit. On the losing side would be those industries which are now most heavily protected,

[1] *Technical Education in Wales*, Report of the Central Advisory Council for Education (Wales), H.M.S.O., 1961, pp. 58-60.
[2] Ibid., pp. 51-53.

i.e. watches (33⅓ per cent.), optical instruments (33⅓ to 50 per cent.), and toys (25 per cent.). Moreover, there would be handicaps for cotton, paper, and leather, and possibly for china and footwear. Some of these are represented in Wales, but they are a small minority compared with the lines of output likely to prosper.

The impact on agriculture might be considerable, since Britain would have to conform to the common agricultural policy laid down by the European Economic Community. It was shown in Chapter IV that Welsh farmers are receiving over £14 million a year in direct subsidies and production grants. Many farmers in Wales are unable, without assistance, to obtain a net income higher than that of an agricultural employee, and a curtailment of 'deficiency payments' would have a serious effect on them.

Moreover, the incidence on horticulture would be unfavourable. Substantial protection in the form of specific duties is given to the production of fruit, vegetables, and cut flowers; at certain seasons these duties are quite high—the duty on tomatoes being sometimes equal to more than half the value of the product. Imports of apples, pears, and main-crop potatoes from Europe are subject to quantitative restrictions. The gross output of potatoes in the United Kingdom in 1958–9 amounted to £101 million, and the imports from Europe came to £15 million. Potatoes and tomatoes from the Channel Islands get the same degree of protection as British produce generally. We must face the fact that, if Britain were inside the European Community, horticultural produce from the Netherlands and Italy would have an appreciable advantage in our markets, particularly London. Pembrokeshire might be dealt a hard blow. The hope here is that, since all countries have a common interest in maintaining stability in horticultural prices, it might be possible for Britain to reach a reasonable compromise with the Six on this matter. Given a fundamental change in policy, some sections of agriculture are bound to suffer while the more efficient ones will flourish and expand. There might be a transitional period of six to ten years during which measures could be taken to ease the burden.

In some respects Wales has shared the experience of continental countries since the war; her economy has been reconstructed on new foundations and she is now liberally equipped with industries which have a high potential rate of growth. The fact that her production is much more geared to the demand for durable consumer goods is not a disadvantage: on the contrary, the scope in this direction in

Europe as a whole is enormous. In the European Economic Community there has been a spectacular increase in the number of motorcars in use; in 1960 there was one car for every 14 persons as compared with one for every 40 in 1950. In the United Kingdom it was one for every 10 persons. Europe has a long way to go before reaching the United States ratio of one car for every 3 persons.

The impact of the Common Market will not be merely from a lowering of tariff barriers: it will constitute a vigorous competitive challenge both to workers and employers. A European Economic Community with a population of 250 million would open up tremendous possibilities, and there is no reason why the Welsh economy should not give a good account of itself.

INDEX OF SUBJECTS

INDEX OF NAMES

PRINTED IN GREAT BRITAIN
AT THE UNIVERSITY PRESS, OXFORD
BY VIVIAN RIDLER
PRINTER TO THE UNIVERSITY